JOHN STUART MILL
AND
HARRIET TAYLOR

JOHN STUART MILL
AND
HARRIET TAYLOR

*Their Correspondence
and Subsequent Marriage*

BY

F. A. HAYEK

THE UNIVERSITY OF CHICAGO PRESS

CHICAGO ILLINOIS

THE UNIVERSITY OF CHICAGO PRESS, CHICAGO 37

Routledge & Kegan Paul Ltd., London E.C.4, England

British Book Services (Canada) Ltd., Toronto, Canada

Copyright in the International Copyright Union

All rights reserved. Published 1951. Printed in

Great Britain

Contents

Illustrations

7

Acknowledgements

THE originals of most of the letters and other documents reproduced in this volume are preserved in the Yale University Library and in the British Library of Political and Economic Science and my greatest obligation is to the Library Committees of these two institutions for their permission to reproduce these documents which has made this volume possible. I am similarly indebted to the Provost and Fellows of King's College, Cambridge, who have not only allowed me to use some letters bequeathed to them by the late Lord Keynes but have also presented to the British Library of Political and Economic Science a set of letters by Mrs. Mill when it was noticed that at some earlier stage these had become accidentally detached from a larger collection of similar documents now in the latter Library; to the National Library of Scotland and to the Huntington Library in Pasadena, California. The National Provincial Bank, Ltd. (as representatives of the late Miss Mary Taylor), and Mr. Stuart Mill Colman of Galmpton, Devonshire, have made substantial contributions to this volume by presenting documents in their possession to the British Library of Political and Economic Science; and Mrs. Hugh Gemmel of East London, S.A., and Mrs. Vera Eichelbaum of Wellington, New Zealand, have similarly assisted by their permission to reproduce or use documents in their possession.

Of those who have helped in other ways I must in the first place mention Professor Jacob Viner of Princeton University, who originally drew my attention to the collection at Yale University Library. To Professor Arthur H. Cole, Librarian of Harvard University, I am under a special obligation for his help in procuring in war-time from British Columbia, where it had strayed, the portrait of Harriet Taylor reproduced facing page 128 of this volume. Mrs. Z. J. Powers, Librarian of Historical Manuscripts of Yale University Library, and Mr. W. Park and Mr. J. S. Ritchie of the Department of Manuscripts of the National Library of Scotland have been good enough more than once to supply copies or to check transcriptions when I was not able myself to inspect documents in their care.

Finally I must mention Dr. Ruth Borchardt and Mrs. Dorothy Hahn, who in different stages of the work on the collection of John Stuart Mill's general correspondence have assisted me for long periods and on the result of whose work I have been able to draw to a large extent in preparing this volume. To all these as well as to the many others who have more indirectly helped in its production I wish to express my most sincere thanks.

Abbreviations and Symbols Used

J.S.M.: John Stuart Mill.

H.T.: Harriet Taylor (Mrs. John Taylor—until 1851).

H.M.: Harriet Mill (Mrs. John Stuart Mill—from 1851).

MTColl.: Mill-Taylor Collection in the British Library of Political and Economic Science (London School of Economics). The references (e.g. XXVII/233) are to the volume and the number of the item (*not* the folio), unless they refer expressly to one of the boxes separately numbered in Roman numerals.

Letters (ed. Elliot): *The Letters of John Stuart Mill*, edited with an Introduction by Hugh S. R. Elliot, Two volumes, London, 1910.

Letter of T.C. to J.S.M.: Letters of Thomas Carlyle to John Stuart Mill, John Sterling and Robert Browning, edited by Alexander Carlyle, London, 1910.

MacMinn, *et al., Bibliography : Bibliography of the Published Writings of John Stuart Mill*. Edited from his Manuscript with Corrections and Notes by Ney MacMinn, J. R. Hainds and James McNab McCrimmon. North-Western University, Evanston, Illinois, 1945.

Autobiography: J. S. Mill, *Autobiography*. The page references are to the 'World's Classics' edition (Oxford University Press), except where they are expressly to the complete edition published in 1924 by Columbia University Press.

D.D.: J. S. Mill, *Dissertations and Discussions*, London, 1858, and later.

[ ] Square brackets are used to indicate editorial insertions in the text of documents.

[?] and [??] indicates a gap of one or more words.

(?) and (??) indicates that the reading of the preceding word or words is doubtful.

. . . indicates omissions or parts missing from the manuscript.

Introduction

I

T HE literary portrait which in the *Autobiography* John Stuart Mill has drawn for us of the woman who ultimately became his wife creates a strong wish to know more about her. If Harriet Taylor, to give her the name which she bore during the greater part of her life, was anything like what Mill wished us to believe, we should have to regard her as one of the most remarkable women who ever lived. Even if merely her influence on Mill was as great as he asserts, we should have to think of her as one of the major figures who shaped opinion during the later Victorian era. Yet until now it has been solely Mill's account on which we have had to rely in forming an estimate; and the very extravagance of the language he employed in her praise has generally produced more disbelief than conviction. It is natural to dismiss as the product of an extraordinary if not singular delusion a description which represents her as more a poet than Carlyle, more a thinker than Mill himself and as the only equal to his father in 'the power of influencing by mere force of mind and character the convictions and purposes of others and in the strenuous exertion of that power to promote freedom and progress'.[1] The best known version of Mill's estimate of his wife's genius in the *Autobiography* is too long to be quoted in full, and it would probably be unnecessary to do so. A few sentences will recall the general tone of a description which extends over many pages:[2]

'In general spiritual characteristics, as well as in temperament and organization, I have often compared her, as she was at this time, to Shelley: but in thought and intellect, Shelley, so far as his powers were developed in his short life, was but a child compared with what she ultimately became. Alike in the highest regions of speculation and in the smaller practical concerns of daily life, her mind was the same perfect instrument, piercing to the very heart and marrow of the matter;

13

always seizing the essential idea or principle. The same exactness and rapidity of operation, pervading as it did her sensitive as her mental faculties, would, with her gifts of feeling and imagination, have fitted her to be a consummate artist, as her fiery and tender soul and her vigorous eloquence would certainly have made her a great orator, and her profound knowledge of human nature and discernment and sagacity in practical life, would, in times when such a *carrière* was open to women, have made her eminent among the rulers of mankind. Her intellectual gifts did but minister to a moral character at once the noblest and the best balanced which I have ever met with in life. Her unselfishness was not that of a taught system of duties, but of a heart which thoroughly identified itself with the feelings of others, and often went to excess in consideration for them by imaginatively investing their feelings with the intensity of its own.'

Though this fullest expression of his feelings did not appear until the posthumous *Autobiography*, Mill had not hesitated to announce them earlier in similar tones. The prefaces to *On Liberty* and to the reprint of the article on 'The Enfranchisement of Women' in *Dissertations and Discussions*, both published shortly after her death, are in a similar strain. A few sentences from the latter may also be quoted:[3]

'All that excites admiration when found separately in others, seemed brought together in her: a conscience at once healthy and tender; a generosity, bounded only by a sense of justice which often forgot its own claims, but never those of others; a heart so large and loving, that whoever was capable of making the smallest return of sympathy, always received tenfold; and in the intellectual department, a vigour and truth of imagination, a delicacy of perception, an accuracy and nicety of observation, only equalled by her profundity of speculative thought, and by a practical judgment and discernment next to infallible.'

But it was not only in the anguish and grief over her loss that Mill expressed himself in such terms. He used similar language to others and, as we shall see, to her before they were married, and in the Dedication of his *Principles of Political Economy* had expressed his admiration in print, though confined to a limited number of copies, while her first husband was still alive.

Was all this sheer delusion? Some of Mill's friends evidently thought so and their views, especially Carlyle's, have largely determined the opinions of later generations. Yet even if it had been nothing more it would not only present us with a curious psychological puzzle, but also leave open the question how far Mill's ideas, and especially his changes of opinion at a critical juncture of European thought, may have been due to this delusion. Yet it is not altogether easy to accept the view that so eminently sober, balanced and disciplined a mind, and a man who chose his words as deliberately and carefully as Mill, should have had no foundation for what he must have known to be unique claims on behalf of any human being. Before one accepts that view and all that it implies for our judgment of the man and of the *Autobiography*, one would like some independent evidence. Apart from Mill none of those who expressed views about Harriet Taylor's qualities have really had much grounds on which to base them, except W. J. Fox, whose is also the only other voice that joins in her praise.[4]

Mill himself, however, on one occasion, has emphatically denied that a proper memoir of his wife could be written. In a letter sent in 1870 to Paulina Wright Davies, the American champion of women's rights, he wrote:

'Were it possible in a memoir to have the formation and growth of a mind like hers portrayed, to do so would be as valuable a benefit to mankind as was ever conferred by a biography. But such a psychological history is seldom possible, and in her case the materials for it do not exist. All that could be furnished is her birth-place, parentage, and a few dates, and it seems to me that her memory is more honoured by the absence of any attempt at a biographical notice than by the presence of a most meagre one. What she was, I have attempted, though most inadequately, to delineate in the remarks prefaced to her essay, as reprinted with my "Dissertations and Discussions".'[5]

We have of course even less information about Mrs. Taylor now than was in Mill's possession, and if our main aim were to reconstruct a full-scale picture of her person that task would indeed be impossible. It is little that we can do to give life to the improbable picture of a paragon of all excellencies which he has drawn for us. But though we may not be able to do justice to her, and though we may not be able to learn much about her person, we must welcome all independent evidence on the character of their relation and the nature of her influence on his work. Mill has given us his picture of this connexion as it appeared to him and he was perhaps entitled to feel that he had nothing to add to it. This does not mean that there may not be material which is of interest to us because of the light it throws on that picture.

II

Whether the existence of an autobiography always means that we know its author better than we would without it is a question on which different opinions are possible. No doubt almost any autobiography tells us much that without it we should never know. A self-portrait as candid and patently truthful as Mill's enables us to see some aspects of his person as is possible with few other figures of the past. Yet in some respects the existence of an autobiography may be the cause of our knowing less about its subject. The more successful it is the more it is apt to discourage biographical studies by others. It certainly makes us see the author more as he saw himself, often looking back from old age, than as he appeared to his contemporaries. Even where there was no intention to mislead, as there certainly was not in the case of Mill, the impression conveyed may be very one-sided. What seems most important to the man himself need not appear so to others, and what he has left out may be as characteristic of him as what he has included.

All this is in a high degree true of John Stuart Mill's *Autobiography*. It is probably the one among his works which will live longest, through which he has already exercised the greatest influence, and which is likely to determine his permanent place in the history of ideas. It may well prove that his purely scientific achievements, his *Logic* and his *Political Economy*, will occupy more modest places in that history than seemed probable to his contemporaries, and that even *On Liberty* and his other contributions to political philosophy will represent a more rapidly passing phase of thought than they would have thought possible. But even if in the final estimate Mill should not be ranked as an original thinker of the first order, I believe that his reputation will emerge from its present eclipse; he will again be recognized as one of the really great figures of his period, a great moral figure perhaps more than a great thinker, and one in whom even his purely intellectual achievements are mainly due to his profound conviction of the supreme moral value of unrelenting intellectual effort. Not by temperament but out of a deeply ingrained sense that this was his duty did Mill grow to be the 'Saint of Rationalism', as Gladstone once so justly described him.

There is thus perhaps no other instance where an autobiography had so much to tell us and where at the same time such a purely intellectual account of a man's development is so misleading. The *Autobiography* is as remarkable for what it leaves out as for what it discusses—what it leaves out not in any desire to suppress but because Mill thought it genuinely irrelevant. It is one of the most impersonal accounts of a mental development ever attempted, an account in which only the factors found a place that in Mill's view ought to have influenced it. Of what in the ordinary sense of the word we should call his life, of his human interests and personal relations, we learn practically nothing. Even the account of 'the most valuable friendship of his life' is scarcely an exception to this; the feeling of incongruity which this account of Mill's greatest experience conveys is not least due to its being represented as a purely intellectual experience. It would certainly be a mistake to believe that Mill really was like that, that what he regarded as deserving of a public record gives us a picture of the whole man. It is even doubtful whether we can fully appreciate the significance or the lesson of the *Autobiography* until we know much more of the very human being whose strongest beliefs have led him thus to depict himself.

If, however, the existence of the *Autobiography* increases rather than lessens the need for an adequate biography, it is no accident that three-quarters of a century after Mill's death no such work exists. Without additional knowledge on what, according to his own account, was the decisive factor in his life, such a biography could not be written. It is not the only but the most important point on which the essential material for such a biography was wanting.

The present volume is no more than an attempt to fill this particular gap—material for a future biography rather than an attempt at an appreciation. But since, for reasons immediately to be explained, I have in the book itself refrained from any interpretation or estimate of this new material, I may perhaps here express the conclusions I have formed on the significance of Harriet Taylor in Mill's life. They are, that her influence on his thought and outlook, whatever her capacities may have been, were quite as great as Mill asserts, but that they acted in a way somewhat different from what is commonly believed. Far from it having been the sentimental it was the rationalist element in Mill's thought which was mainly strengthened by her influence. I know of only one study, a little known essay by the Swedish writer

Knut Hagberg, which has correctly seen the nature of this influence as it now reveals itself.

'It is obvious', writes Hagberg, 'that it was this woman who made him into a Radical rationalist. She has given the impress of her personality to all his greater works; to all her opinions Mill has given the form of philosophic maxims. But even in his most arid reflexions on woman's similarity with man and on the nature of Logic, Mill is in reality a romantic.'[6]

III

The present book is the outcome of work originally undertaken without any such design. It grew unexpectedly out of an effort to bring together Mill's correspondence during the earlier part of his life, which had never been systematically collected. A considerable number of these letters have been assembled and are waiting to be edited and published. In the course of this work the material now presented has come to light and it soon became clear that it would not fit into the contemplated edition of Mill's professional correspondence. These private letters clearly demanded a treatment different from the simple chronological presentation with a few explanatory footnotes which would suffice for his more formal letters. To be intelligible most of them require much more knowledge of the circumstances in which they were written. Those letters of Harriet Taylor to Mill which have been preserved, and certain other pieces of family correspondence, were clearly of as much interest in this connexion as Mill's own. On the other hand, a considerable part of their correspondence, belonging to the period following their marriage and dealing with purely domestic matters, is hardly of sufficient interest to justify publication. Neither their maids' meat consumption, nor their neighbour's rats, nor all the voluminous reports about the momentary state of their health are suitable for printing. Some selection thus became imperative. Finally, much of this correspondence belongs to the period after 1848, which is so fully represented in H. S. R. Elliot's edition of *The Letters of John Stuart Mill* (1910) that a new collection of Mill's general correspondence for this period is not called for.

It soon appeared that the most satisfactory solution of these problems would be to take the private letters out from the general correspondence and to combine them with certain other material in a volume of a somewhat different character. There was some temptation to go beyond such a mere presentation of the documents, and to use them instead as the foundation for a book about Mill and Harriet Taylor. I have deliberately refrained from attempting this. To some readers this volume will therefore appear as the material for a book rather than the finished product. The justification for presenting the documents in this fashion is that they could provide the material for several different books which might be written around them; thus any attempt at interpretation would almost inevitably have interfered with the impartial presentation of the documents. Not all the fragments which accident has preserved can be made to fit into one coherent story which at the same time they are sufficient to justify. Yet any selection guided by an interpretation would have been likely to omit documents which from a different point of view might prove significant.

I have therefore endeavoured to reproduce for the first eighteen years of Mill's friendship with Harriet Taylor, for which the material is scanty, practically every available scrap of correspondence which I have been able to date with any degree of confidence. To this I have added whatever other contemporary material throws light on these letters, including a collection of the comments of their friends and acquaintances. Most of the latter have already appeared in print and the picture of the relationship now generally held is mainly derived from them.

For the period from 1849 onwards we possess one continuous set of notes of Harriet Taylor to Mill and two long and several shorter series of letters by Mill written to his wife after their marriage in 1851. Of these only selected passages are reproduced. Any selection of this sort is bound to be arbitrary in some measure and at least Mill's accounts of his journeys might deserve to be printed at greater length in a different context. If that part of the volume was not to grow to disproportionate size, however, only a few samples of his descriptions of his travels could be included, to secure space for passages which bear more directly on the interests which he shared with his wife.

A few words should be said here about the method of transcription and the principles of editing which have been followed. Full observation of the strictest canons of literary editorship would in this case have unduly impaired readability. The character of the manuscripts, many of them hastily written informal notes, and certain habits of both Mill and Mrs. Taylor, made some editorial emendations indispensable if the printed text was to be read with ease. If every possible doubt about the correct reading of a word, or every punctuation sign which had to be inserted, had been indicated, the text would have been intolerably encumbered. Where, as is true of most of their letters, the same kind of mark, which might be a full stop, a comma, or a hyphen, is made to serve for all three, where punctuation is often altogether absent (Mill practically always omitted punctuation signs at the end of a line), or its need indicated only by the spacing of the words, and where capital letters are employed in the most haphazard manner, it would have been merely irritating if every full stop inserted had been enclosed in square brackets or every other sign of punctuation queried as possibly intended for something else. A reasonable compromise between faithfully reproducing the general character of the manuscripts and achieving easy readability was necessary. Where there could be no real doubt about the meaning I have not hesitated to make the needed corrections without at the same time eliminating those peculiarities and idiosyncrasies which did not affect the readability. Where the spelling, grammar, or punctuation is unusual the reader may therefore assume that it follows the manuscript, even though no '*sic*' or exclamation mark draws special attention to these peculiarities and though in other places similar defects have been tacitly corrected.

IV

It remains to give a brief account of the sources of the material which is here presented. Most of it derives from Mill's own papers, which were left by him to his stepdaughter Helen Taylor, who jealously guarded them during her life. A full account of the later fate and ultimate dispersal of these documents will have to be given in the edition of Mill's general correspondence, and for the present a brief sketch may suffice. Some of the papers were probably destroyed and others dispersed when in 1905 Helen Taylor gave up the cottage at Avignon where Mill had spent the greater part of the last fifteen years of his life, and, after he had left the house at Blackheath Park, presumably kept most of his documents. Parts of the contents of the cottage were then hurriedly disposed of by some friends.[7] Most of Mill's papers were however preserved and shipped to England and on Helen Taylor's death in 1907 passed to her niece Mary Taylor. It was while the papers were in the latter's possession that Mr. H. S. R. Elliot was given an opportunity to prepare, mainly from the drafts of his letters which Mill kept from about 1848 onwards, the two-volume edition of the *Letters of John Stuart Mill* published in 1910. But although Elliot was allowed to see, he was not permitted to print any of Mill's intimate letters, which Mary Taylor reserved for publication by herself at a later date.[8] This intention, to which she repeatedly referred, was never carried out. Shortly before her death in November 1918 she was corresponding with a literary agent about a volume of such letters[9] which seems to have existed in typescript and which probably contained most of the material in the present volume and perhaps also other documents which have since been lost. It has not been possible to trace this typescript and since the offices of the literary agency as well as those of the publisher who had been approached, of Mary Taylor's solicitors, and the depository where her executors kept some of the papers concerning her, were destroyed by fire during the London 'Blitz' in December 1940, there is little likelihood that it has survived.

Excepting only some, the more intimate family letters, the whole of the Mill documents which had been in Mary Taylor's possession were sold, at the instruction of her executors, at two auctions at Messrs. Sotheby's of London, on 29 March 1922 and 27 July 1927. Almost all the items were bought in the first instance by various booksellers but, excepting only a few pieces which probably went to private collectors, seem sooner or later to have found a permanent resting-place in one or another of a number of University Libraries in Great Britain and the United States. Major parts of the collection are now at the Libraries of the London School of Economics, Leeds University, Johns Hopkins University, Yale University, and North-Western University. Of these the 'Mill-Taylor Collection' of the British Library of Political and Economic Science (as the Library of the London School of Economics is correctly described) is much the largest, and in the course of the work on Mill's correspondence it has been possible to acquire for it a good deal of additional material, deriving from the same and from other sources, including the family letters retained by Mary Taylor's executors at the time of the sales, and a number of letters preserved by the descendants of some of Mill's relatives and of some of his other correspondents. But, although the London collection is probably the richest so far as Mill's general correspondence is concerned, the smaller collection at Yale University Library has made the greatest contribution to the present volume. Almost all of Mill's letters to his wife which have been preserved and the most important of his letters to W. J. Fox are in that collection. Other Libraries have of course also contributed and a full list of these will be found above under *Acknowledgements* and in the notes giving the whereabouts of the individual letters.

Chapter One

HARRIET TAYLOR AND HER CIRCLE
1830

JOHN STUART MILL probably met Harriet Taylor for the first time in the summer or early autumn of 1830 when she was still in her twenty-third year but already married for more than four years and the mother of two sons.[1] The special register, kept at the time for the voluntary use of Dissenters at Dr. Williams' Library, records on 10 October 1807, the birth at No. 18, Beckford Row, Walworth, in the South of London, of Harriet, daughter of Thomas Hardy, 'surgeon and man-midwife'. Her granddaughter Mary Taylor states[2] that the Hardys had for some centuries been lords of the manor of Birksgate, near Kirkburton, where Thomas Hardy lived in retirement for the last ten years or so of his life before he died in 1849. If this is more than an unfounded affectation of gentility he was probably a younger son who early went to London to take up a profession. He appears at any rate to have practised at Walworth for many years since at least 1803, and even earlier to have married the daughter of a citizen of Walworth; other members of the Hardy family also seem to have lived in London. Thomas Hardy's practice apparently was sufficiently lucrative to enable him to give his numerous children a fairly good education. Occasional glimpses of him which we get in the family letters do not show him as an altogether amiable character. The impression they leave is of a somewhat domineering and difficult person, and since at least in later life Harriet Taylor's relations to her parents were not too cordial, the tradition that it was an unhappy home which drove her into an early marriage is at least credible.

23

John Taylor, to whom she was married on 14 March 1826, only five months after her eighteenth birthday, was eleven years her senior. He was a junior partner of David Taylor & Sons, a firm of wholesale druggists or 'drysalters' that had been carrying on a prosperous business in the City for at least fifty years. The firm had long been established in Finsbury Square and the adjoining Cross Street, and had already been conducted there by John Taylor's grandfather, that 'fine specimen of the old Scotch Puritan; stern, severe, and powerful, but very kind to children, on whom such men make a lasting impression',[3] who, as Mill tells us, had lived in his childhood in the next house to James Mill's at Newington Green and had sometimes invited young John to play in his garden. At least three of the sons of this old man, David, George and John Taylor, succeeded him in the firm, and by the time his grandson, John the younger, married, 'uncle David' appears to have been the senior partner and to have remained in that position during his nephew's life.

What we know about John Taylor on the whole tends to support the description of him given in the *Autobiography*: 'a most upright, brave, honourable man, but without the intellectual or artistic tastes which would have made him a companion' for his wife. Carlyle's characterization of him as 'an innocent dull good man',[4] though perhaps less fair, is probably also not quite wrong. But if John Taylor was above all a prosperous business man who enjoyed the good things of life, his interests extended beyond this limited sphere. He devoted a good deal of time to the management of the finances of the Unitarian congregation to which the Taylors as well as the Hardys belonged, and conducted the occasionally difficult negotiation with its strong-willed minister, William Johnson Fox. As a convinced radical he took an active interest in politics; there is also some evidence that on behalf of the Unitarians he concerned himself with the affairs of the new University of London.[5] In 1836 we find him among the original members of the Reform Club, which suggests that he was regarded as one of the more important radical business men. He also seems to have made a special point of looking after the interests of the numerous political exiles from France and Italy who had arrived in London.

For the first five years after their marriage John Taylor and his wife lived in the City in a house at 4, Christopher Street, Finsbury Circus, in close vicinity both to the firm and W. J. Fox's new chapel at South Place. Their first son, Herbert, was born there on

24 September 1827, and a second son, Algernon, invariably called Haji, followed on 2 February 1830. The third and last child, Helen (usually called Lily), was born on 27 July 1831. One or two surviving letters exchanged between husband and wife during the first few years of their married life show Mrs. Taylor as a devoted young wife and happy mother.[6] But there is no reason to doubt that a certain disparity of tastes made itself felt long before her friendship with Mill began.

The only description of Harriet Taylor's appearance at that time comes from W. J. Fox's daughter, who, if she really refers as she says to about 1831, would then have been a small girl of about seven. As it mentions Mrs. Taylor's age as about twenty-five, it probably dates from two or perhaps even more years later and is practically contemptoraneous with the portrait given as a frontispiece to this volume which it singularly well confirms:

'Mrs. Taylor at this date, when she was, perhaps about five and twenty years of age, was possessed of a beauty and grace quite unique of their kind. Tall and slight, with a slightly drooping figure, the movements of undulating grace. A small head, a swan-like throat, and a complexion like a pearl. Large dark eyes, not soft or sleepy, but with a look of quiet command in them. A low sweet voice with very distinct utterance emphasized the effect of her engrossing personality. Her children idolized her.'[7]

This delicate frame evidently harboured very strong convictions and emotions which during these early years however were still seeking an outlet and adequate means of expression. It is probable that from an early stage her character and outlook had been shaped by a violent revolt against the social conventions which not only, at the time of life when she did not comprehend what it meant, had placed her in permanent dependence on a man whom she regarded as her inferior in intellect and general culture, but which also excluded her from almost all those activities for which she regarded herself fit. There is almost certainly an autobiographical element in a passage of one of her early literary efforts in which she complains that 'in the present system of habits and opinions, girls enter into what is called a contract perfectly ignorant of the conditions of it, and that they should be so is considered absolutely essential to their fitness for it!'[8] But if the conditions of women, their education and their position in marriage were at the time

25

Mrs. Taylor's main concern and probably the starting point of her other reflections, they were by no means the limit of her rationalist revolt against the tyranny of public opinion.

What we know about her views and interests during these early years must be derived from a sheaf of notes and drafts which seem to belong mostly to the time just before or soon after she met Mill, but none of which can be dated with any certainty. There is no clear evidence that she attempted any prose composition before she met Mill or before, soon afterwards, she began to contribute to Fox's *Monthly Repository*. But the variety of drafts and scraps on the position of women, on education and various social usages and conventions, which date from about the same period, suggest that these problems must have been occupying her for some time. The most interesting of these essays, which in parts curiously anticipates some of the arguments of *On Liberty*, is reprinted as Appendix II to the present volume.

Mrs. Taylor had however tried her hand at poetry for some time before 1830. The six poems of hers that have been preserved, three of them printed in the *Monthly Repository*, are of unequal quality. They suggest the inspiration of Shelley and the best show some real poetic gift, though in execution they are probably not much superior to the production of many young women of her time. Two of her published and one of her unpublished poems are also printed in Appendix I.

The only members of Mrs. Taylor's circle of whom we can form a distinct picture, and probably the only ones who mattered in con-nexion with Mill, were William Johnson Fox and the two remarkable young women with whom he had become closely associated only a short time before : Eliza and Sarah Flower. In 1830 Fox was a man of forty-four and at the height of his fame as a Unitarian preacher but, as editor of the *Monthly Repository* since 1827, already at the beginning of a transition to an even more influential position as a radical journalist and politician. He had risen from a small farmer's son, and later a weaver's boy and bank clerk in Norwich, to be a considerable public figure mainly through that eloquence which in later years made him famous as one of the most powerful orators of the Anti-Corn-Law League. At the time he was however still one of the leading figures of the Unitarian Association, but this connexion soon became looser, and in later years, though he continued to preach at South Place Chapel, it was more as a precursor of the Ethical Movement of his successor Moncure Conway than as the representative of any Christian denomination. The alienation from the more strict body of Unitarians was partly the result of his connexion with Eliza Flower.

Fox was unhappily married and had been brought in close contact with the two beautiful and highly gifted sisters when on the death of their father in 1829 he had become their trustee. Aged twenty-seven and twenty-five respectively in 1830, and thus only slightly older than Mill and Harriet Taylor, Eliza and Sarah Flower must have been fascinating persons. Eliza was a composer of some distinction and Sarah wrote poetry of merit and is to-day remembered as the author of the hymn 'Nearer, my God, to Thee'. After the early death of their mother they had been educated solely by their father and had developed their natural gifts without systematic training or much discipline of any sort. There can be little doubt that it was Eliza Flower to whom Mill refers in the *Autobiography* when he speaks of Mrs. Taylor's 'life of inward meditation, varied by familiar intercourse with a small circle of friends of whom one only (long since deceased) was a person of genius or of capacities of feeling or intellect kindred with her own.'[9] A series of informal notes by Eliza Flower to Mrs. Taylor which have survived[10] show that for some years in the early 'thirties the two women were fairly intimate and that the fragile and somewhat unstable Eliza Flower was rather looking up to the younger but more self-possessed and more happily circumstanced married woman. Known as 'Ariel' in her intimate circle, Eliza Flower seems indeed to have had in her something of that ethereal spirit. Fox's biographer describes her as

'Emphatically a child of nature, open and transparent as the day. She worshipped Mozart, Shakespeare, Milton, Burns, Byron, but if these had never existed, Eliza Flower would still have been Eliza Flower. While this independence and spontaneity gave an indescribable charm to her character, they were not wholly favourable to her in the world of Art. Music came so naturally to her that she never realized the importance of strenuous study, and such a professional training as, indeed, it would probably have been beyond her means to procure.'[11]

Eliza Flower became Fox's closest friend, devoting all her energies to assist him in his literary work, and after his separation from his wife in 1835 came to superintend his household, inevitably causing scandalous talk which for a time made Fox's position in the congregation difficult. This may also have been one of the reasons which made it appear inadvisable for Mrs. Taylor to maintain the connexion when her own position came under similar criticism, although Eliza Flower's increasing eccentricity probably also made the two women gradually drift apart.

In her way the younger sister, Sarah Flower, seems to have been no less remarkable a person and by her marriage in 1834 to William Bridges Adams brought another strong personality into the closer circle of friends in which Mrs. Taylor and Mill moved. W. B. Adams, who had been married before to a daughter of Francis Place, was then mainly active as a radical writer and for several years was one of the most frequent contributors to the *Monthly Repository*. He later became a successful carriage manufacturer and eminent railway engineer. For some time he seems to have been on cordial terms with Mill, who took great trouble to draw attention to a book, *The Producing Man's Companion*, which Adams had published under the pseudonym of 'Junius Redivivus'.[12]

Around this inner group there gathered in the early eighteen-thirties a number of minor literary and artistic figures, mostly contributors to the *Monthly Repository* and including a considerable number of women. For some time Harriet Martineau, then at the very beginning of her literary career, was among Fox's most regular contributors. Two other gifted sisters, Margaret Gillies, the miniature painter, and Mary Gillies, the novelist, also appear to have belonged to the somewhat unconventional and strongly feminist group of whose members Leigh Hunt has drawn a picture in his *Bluestocking Revels*.[13]

The *Monthly Repository* itself during Fox's editorship, especially after he had purchased it in 1831 and largely divorced it from its predominantly Unitarian character, was an organ of very considerable distinction and influence both in its political and literary department.[14] Some of the articles, especially Crabb Robinson's series on Goethe, are landmarks of the literary history of the period. But the feature which distinguished it from the other radical periodicals of the time and which, while it alienated its Unitarian supporters, must have made it particularly congenial to Harriet Taylor, was its strong feminist bias. Both W. J. Fox, whose views on divorce show a Miltonian strain, and W. B. Adams wrote in it extensively on the subject, and their arguments often so closely resemble some of Mrs. Taylor's manuscript drafts of the period that one wonders whether it was merely that she imbibed her ideas from them or whether her somewhat unpolished drafts did not perhaps serve as the basis for the articles of the more skilled writers.

It is probable that John Stuart Mill was in close contact with Fox's circle for some time before he met Mrs. Taylor. It has even been said that he was supposed at one time an aspirant for Eliza Flower's hand.[15] There existed many connexions between the group of the Utilitarians and Fox's Unitarian congregation, which included such immediate disciples of Jeremy Bentham as Dr. John Bowring and Dr. Southwood Smith; Fox himself in 1826 had contributed to the first number of the *Westminster Review*.

The impressions we derive from the *Autobiography* are rather misleading when we try to form a picture of John Stuart Mill at the age of twenty-four when he was introduced to Mrs. Taylor. That work conveys to us mainly, on the one hand, an image of the object of that extraordinary educational experiment which is its main theme, and on the other, of the author when he wrote it in late middle age. But the Mill of the intermediate period who concerns us here was in many ways a very different person from either. He was no longer simply the creation of his father, the perfectly constructed intellectual instrument zealously serving the cause for which his father had designed him. That period had ended with the 'crisis in his mental development' which occurred in his twentieth year. Nor was he yet the austere, secluded and severe philosopher he became soon after the age of thirty. Even in appearance we must imagine him very different from the familiar picture which we derive mainly from Watt's portrait painted in the last year of his life or from the photographs of not much earlier date. Long before then ill health, overwork and constant nervous strain had prematurely made him look old. No early portrait of Mill as a young man exists and we must try to reconstruct his appearance from the few descriptions by contemporaries.

Carlyle, first meeting him in 1831, described him as 'a slender, rather tall and elegant youth, with a small clear Roman-nosed face, two small earnestly-smiling eyes; modest, remarkably gifted with precision of utterance, enthusiastic, yet lucid, calm; not a great, yet a distinctly gifted and amiable youth'.[16] Much later he remembered him as 'an innocent young creature, with rich auburn hair and gentle pathetic expression, beautiful to contemplate'.[17] The earliest portrait which has been preserved, the medallion reproduced here, is also of a later date. It would appear to represent him in his late thirties and is probably identical with the portrait done by a certain Cunningham in Falmouth in 1840 which Caroline Fox describes as 'quite an ideal head, so expanded with patient thought, and a face of such exquisite refinement'.[18] But by then Mill had already passed through his first bout of severe illness, lost most of his hair and acquired that nervous twitch over his eyes which he retained during the remainder of his life. If, however, after his thirtieth year Mill was permanently handicapped by ill health, and though he may even never have fully recovered from the nervous breakdown of ten years before, he appears to have been naturally endowed with a splendid constitution, which enabled him not only to overcome these handicaps but to continue to perform an amount of work and to remain even during acute illness capable of an amount of physical exertion which sometimes seem scarcely credible.

The story of his education is too well known to need retelling even in outline. On the basis of the full account of this education which we possess, he has, in a recent study of child geniuses,[19] been awarded the highest intelligence quotient of all recorded instances of specially precocious children; but, as the author of that study rightly suggests, this may well be merely the result of our knowing so much more about Mill's childhood performances than about those of most others. Indeed, astounding as the speed is with which he passed as a child through a course of education which normally lasts into early manhood, and amazing as are his powers of retention and the discipline of orderly thought and exposition which he acquired, there is little sign of originality or creative powers in his early years. His own modest estimate of his innate capacities indeed may be nearer the truth. In the *Autobiography* he represents his father's educational experiment as conclusive precisely because in

'natural gifts I am rather below than above par; what I could do, could assuredly be done by any boy or girl of average capacity and healthy physical constitution: and if I have accomplished anything, I owe it, among other fortunate circumstances, to the fact that through the early training bestowed upon me by my father, I started, I may fairly say, with an advantage of a quarter of a century over my contemporaries.'[20]

That when this education ended John Mill was for some years little more than the 'reasoning machine' depicted in the *Autobiography* we need not doubt. The description given of him at the age of eighteen

or nineteen by his friend John Roebuck is probably very just; he writes
that when he first met Mill he found that:

'although possessed of much learning, and thoroughly acquainted with
the state of the political world, [he] was, as might have been expected,
the mere exponent of other men's ideas, these men being his father
and Bentham; and that he was utterly ignorant of what is called
society; that of the world, as it worked around him, he knew nothing;
and above all, of *woman* he was as a child. He had never played with
boys; in his life he had never known any, and we, in fact, who were
now his associates, were the first companions he had ever mixed
with.' 21

When one reads the chapters of the *Autobiography* devoted to these
years and the prodigious amount of work accomplished, it is only too
easy to forget that Mill was still only twenty years of age when the
period terminated in a severe and prolonged attack of melancholia.
That one of the main causes of the acute dejection, from which he
emerged only gradually over a period of years, was, in addition to overwork, the struggle to emancipate himself from the complete intellectual
sway which his father had held over him, one may readily believe
without subscribing to the full to the psycho-analytical interpretation
given of it recently in an interesting study.22 To that essay we are
indebted also for an important passage omitted from the published
version of the *Autobiography*. It is taken from the manuscript of an
early draft, quite possibly the same which we shall later find Mill
discussing with his wife in 1854, which was in the possession of the
late Professor Jacob H. Hollander and is presumably still among his
library:

'But in respect to what I am here concerned with—the moral
agencies which acted on myself—it must be mentioned as a most
shameful one that my father's older children neither loved him nor
with any warmth of affection anyone else.

'That rarity in England, a really warm hearted mother would in
the first place have made my father a totally different being and in the
second would have made the children grow up loving and being loved.
But my mother with the very best intentions only knew how to pass
her life in drudging for them. Whatever she could do for them she did
and they liked her because she was kind to them but to make herself
loved, looked up to, or even obeyed, required qualities which she

31

unfortunately did not possess. I thus grew up in the absence of love and in the presence of fear; and many and indelible are the effects of this bringing up in the stunting of my moral growth.

'I grew up with an instinct of closeness. I had no one to whom I desired to express everything which I felt and the only person I was in communication with to whom I looked up, I had too much fear of to make the communication to him of any act or feeling ever a matter of frank impulse or spontaneous inclination.

'Another evil I shared with many of the sons of energetic fathers. To have been through childhood under the constant rule of a strong will certainly is not favourable to strength of will. I was so much accustomed to be told what to do either in the form of direct command or of rebuke for not doing it that I acquired the habit of leaving my responsibility as a moral agent to rest on my father and my conscience never speaking to me except by his voice.'[23]

This passage is significant not only because of the candid description of Mill's attitude towards his father but no less because of the reference to his mother, whose complete absence from the *Autobiography* has so often been commented upon. Yet it is doubtful whether the harsh judgment expressed in it, very probably written during the period of his estrangement from his mother following his marriage, truly represents his feelings as a young man. There is some testimony to the contrary by contemporaries, and even though the unfavourable comments evoked by the *Autobiography* may have led them to overemphasize this point, they agree too well to be dismissed.

H. Solly, who had been a classmate of John's younger brother James at University College and in the summer of 1830 had spent a week with the Mills at their cottage at Mickleham, near Dorking in Surrey, says that

'John Mill always seemed to me a great favourite with his family. He was evidently very fond of his mother and sisters, and they of him; and he frequently manifested a sunny brightness and gaiety of heart and behaviour which were singularly fascinating.'[24]

Elsewhere Solly remembers

'the impression he made on us by his domestic qualities, the affectionate playfulness of his character as a brother in the company of his sisters, and of the numerous younger branches of the family.'[25]

J. Crompton, another member of the same class at University College, records his impressions from similar visits in almost the same words:

'In these days John was devotedly attached to his mother and exuberant in his playful tokens of affection. Towards his father he was deferential, never venturing to controvert him in argument nor taking a prominent part in the conversation in his presence.'[26]

John Mill was then, of course, living at his parents' home and continued to do so after James Mill's death in 1836 until his marriage fifteen years later. At the time of which we are speaking he shared that home with eight younger brothers and sisters, ranging down to George who must have been nearly twenty years his junior.[27] John had then taken over from his father most of the task of instructing the younger members of the family, a duty which must have made considerable inroads on his time but of which he makes practically no mention in the *Autobiography*.[28] But though Mill continued these duties, the home must have become increasingly uncongenial to him as he slowly detached himself from the beliefs of the father whose strong personality dominated it. His position was not made easier by the fact that since 1823, when he had entered the offices of the East India Company, his father had become also his official superior with whom he must have been in constant close contact after, in 1828 and at the age of twenty-two, he had himself been promoted to a senior position. He could expect no sympathy from the older man for the many new impressions and ideas which he readily absorbed in those years and which led him more and more away from the utilitarian faith. It was particularly in these years following the 'crisis in his mental history' that he proved that exceptional capacity of which he justly prides himself in the *Autobiography*, his 'willingness and ability to learn from everybody'.[29] But few systems of thought can have been more antipathetic to James Mill than those by which in these years his son was most attracted, those of Coleridge and his German inspirers, of the French Saint-Simonians, and soon of Carlyle. For a time we feel in his correspondence with some of his contemporaries, particularly in his letters to John Sterling and Adolphe d'Eichthal, how he suffered from the intellectual isolation in which he has been led and how he longed for a real companion with whom he could fully share his new interests. But, although this is the one period in his life when he went out of his way to seek friendships with other men and when he freely mixed in various kinds of society, he remained essentially lonely. There is a significant letter to John Sterling which bears quoting at some length since it better than any other document describes his emotional state not long before he met Harriet Taylor.

J. S. M. to John Sterling, 15 April 1829:[30] I am now chiefly anxious to explain to you, more clearly than I fear I did, what I meant when I spoke to you of the comparative loneliness of my probable future lot. Do not suppose me to mean that I am conscious at present of any tendency to misanthropy—although among the various states of mind, some of them extremely painful ones, through which I have passed through the last three years, something distantly approaching misanthropy was one. At present I believe that my sympathies with society, which were never strong, are, on the whole, stronger than they ever were. By loneliness I mean the absence of that feeling which has accompanied me through the greater part of my life, that which one fellow traveller, or one fellow-soldier, has towards another—the feeling of being engaged in the pursuit of a common object, and of mutually cheering one another on, and helping one another in an arduous undertaking. This, which after all is one of the strongest ties of individual sympathy, is at present, so far as I am concerned, suspended at least, if not entirely broken off. There is now no human being (with whom I can associate on terms of equality) who acknowledges a common object with me, or with whom I can co-operate even in any practical undertaking, without the feeling that I am only using a man, whose purposes are different, as an instrument for the furtherance of my own. *Idem sentire de republica*, was thought, by one of the best men who ever lived, to be the strongest bond of friendship: for *republica* I would read 'all the great objects of life', where all the parties concerned have at hearts any great objects at all. I do not see how there can be otherwise that *idem velle, idem nolle*, which is necessary to perfect friendship. Being excluded, therefore, from this, I am resolved hereafter to avoid all occasion for debate, since they cannot now strengthen my sympathies with those who agree with me, and are sure to weaken them with those who differ.

Unsettled though Mill's mind was in these years, they were nevertheless one of the periods of his greatest productivity and perhaps that of his most original thought. Indeed it seems that most of the ideas which he later developed in his major works were first conceived during the few years following his recovery form the period of dejection. It was in 1829 that Macaulay's famous attack on James Mill's *Essay on Government*, perhaps together with some of the early works of Auguste Comte which John Mill read at the same time, started the train of thought which led to his characteristic ideas on Logic on which he began to work at the beginning of the following year. About the same time he wrote his first and most original work on economic theory, the *Essays on Some Unsettled Questions of Political Economy.* He also continued to steep himself in the history of the French Revolution on which he had started to work when, early in 1828, he had reviewed Walter Scott's Life of Napoleon and which a few years later still seemed his favourite topic of conversation.[31] His interest in French politics had then been rekindled by a visit to Paris immediately after the Revolution of July 1830, and therefore either just before or just after he first met Mrs. Taylor; and for some time thereafter French affairs greatly occupied his attention until they were partly superseded by the even more direct concern with the Reform Bill agitation at home into which he threw much of his energy.

Chapter Two

ACQUAINTANCE AND EARLY CRISES
1830–1833

EVEN if we do not accept all of Thomas Carlyle's later adornments of the story,[1] there is no reason to doubt the tradition that it was W. J. Fox who brought Mill to Mrs. Taylor. To the dinner-party at the home of the Taylors at which the introduction was effected not only Mill but the whole 'Trijackia' was invited, that is, he and his closest friends of the preceding years, John Roebuck and George John Graham.[2] Harriet Martineau was also of the party and later appears to have been fond of telling the circumstances, but Bain's discretion has refrained from passing her story on to us.[3] Apparently a strong mutual attraction was at once felt. In the *Autobiography* Mill says that 'it was years after my introduction to Mrs. Taylor before my acquaintance with her became at all intimate or confidential'.[4] But though we know little about the first two years after the meeting, the connexion seems even then to have been closer than these words suggest. There are no dated documents before the birth of Mrs. Taylor's last child, Helen, on 27 July 1831, and if it were not for one curious fact one would be inclined to assign the few undated early letters referring to Mill to a date after this. There exists, however, a note by Eliza Flower to Mrs. Taylor in which, with reference to an article on Lord Byron in the *Edinburgh Review*, she asks 'Did you or Mill do it?'[5] This must refer to the review of Thomas Moore's *Letters and Journals of Lord Byron* which appeared in the *Edinburgh Review* for June 1831, and since the date of the letter seems to be 30 June

1831, it would appear as if at this early date Mrs. Taylor's closest friend was already so familiar with the similarity of her and Mill's views as to believe (without justification) that the article must be by either of them.[6]

This circumstance gives one more confidence than one might feel otherwise for assigning the earliest letters relating to their connexion to the preceding winter, when the Saint Simonian Bontemps who is mentioned in one of them is known to have been in London. These early letters are all connected with a certain Monsieur Desainteville, a Frenchman living in London and occasionally contributing to the *Monthly Repository*.[7] The earliest extant letter by Mrs. Taylor to Mill refers to him.

H. T. to J. S. M., Winter 1830/31 (?).[8] Friday Morning/ My dear Sir/You may imagine how much we were afflicted by this sad story of our poor friend M. Desainteville the *first* intelligence of which I got from your two notes which I received together yesterday: how unkind and neglectful we must have appeared? Pray express to him my sympathy and best wishes. Mr. Taylor has seen him and found him better than he expected: what a terrible state of emotion he must have suffered so to have reduced him.

In haste yours very truly
H. Taylor

B. E. Desainteville to John Taylor, early 1831 (?).[9] Desainteville en acceptant avec plaisir l'invitation de Monsieur Taylor croit devoir l'informer que M. Bontemps connait parfaitement Mill et que ce dernier ne serait pas à la table de M. Taylor l'un des convives les moins intéressants pour M. Bontemps. Si Monsieur Taylor n'y voit aucun inconvénient, Desainteville le prier d'inviter Mill à diner avec nous, ce serait en outre le vrai moyen de sceller *joliment* la réconciliation qui s'est opéré entre Monsieurs Taylor et Mill.

We have no knowledge why a reconciliation between John Taylor and Mill should have been necessary at so early a date.[10]

Whether these documents belong to the first or to the second year of the acquaintance, they at least agree with the strong probability that at the end of two years it had become fairly intimate. If we correctly interpret the reference to the 'Nouvelle Forêt' in the following undated note by Mill, it would appear that at the beginning of August 1832, when he returned from a walking tour in Hampshire, West Sussex, and the Isle of Wight, ending up in the New Forest,[11] he found a letter from Mrs. Taylor telling him that they must not meet again.

J. S. M. to H. T., late July 1832 (?):[12] Benie soit la main qui a tracé ces charactères! Elle m'a écrit—il suffit: bien que je ne dissimul pas c'est pour me dire un éternel adieu.

Cette adieu, qu'elle ne croie pas que je l'accepte jamais. Sa route et la mienne sont séparé, elle l'a dit: mais elles peuvent, elles doivent, se recontrer. A quelque' époque, dans quelque' endroit, que ce puisse être, elle me trouvera toujours ce que j'ai été, ce que je suis encore.

Elle sera obéie: mes lettres n'iront plus troubler sa tranquillité, ou verser une goutte de plus dans sa coupe des chagrins. Elle sera obéie, par les motifs qu'elle donne—elle le serait quand même elle se serait bornée à me communiquer ses volontés. Lui obéir est pour moi une nécessité.

Elle ne refusera pas, j'espère, l'offrande de ces petites fleurs, que j'apportee pour elle du fond de la Nouvelle-Forêt. Donnez-les lui s'il le faut, de votre part.

A few weeks later, however, normal relations between them seem to have been re-established. At least on 1 September Mill wrote to John Taylor the only letter exchanged between the two men which has been preserved.

J. S. M. to John Taylor, 1 September 1832:[13] Saturday/ I.H./ My dear Sir/Two acquaintances of mine, MM. Jules Bastide and Hippolyte Dussard,[14] distinguished members of the republican party in France, have been compelled to fly their country for a time in consequence of the affair of the fifth and sixth of June. They were not conspirators, for there was no conspiracy, but when they found the troops and the people at blows, they took the side of the people.   Now I am extremely desirous to render their stay here as little disagreeable as possible, and to enable them to profit by it, and to return with a knowledge of England and with those favourable sentiments towards our English *hommes du mouvement* which it is of so much importance that they and their friends should entertain. I am particularly desirous of bringing them into contact with the better members of the Political Union, that they might not suppose our men of action to be all of them like the Revells[15] and Murphys whom they saw and heard on Wednesday last. Yourself and Mr. Fox are [the(?)][16] persons I should most wish them to see. But I do not like to give them a letter of introduction to you without first ascertaining whether it would be agreeable to yourself. Will you therefore oblige me with a line, to say, if possible, that you will allow me to tell them to call upon you, or other-[wise][16] to say that you would rather not. I have not mentioned the matter to them, nor shall I do so until I have the pleasure of hearing from you.

Ever truly yours

J. S. Mill.

Apparently Mr. Taylor at once sent an invitation to the two Frenchmen, who were, however, unable to accept it, and a little later M. Desainteville asked Mrs. Taylor to renew it.

B. E. Desainteville to H. T., September 1832 :[17] De retour de la campagne j'apprends la mort de mon pauvre ami Crawley et j'avai, comme vous pouvez le concevoir, le cœur brisé. Le volume des œuvres de Platon que je vous ai prête lui appartient et je vous serai infinitement obligé, si vous n'en faites plus usage, de me l'envoyer, afin de le restituer à qui de droit.

Mill me parait extrêmement heureux de la cordialité avec laquelle M. Taylor, qu'il estîme beaucoup, l'a reçu et j'en ressens moi-même la plus vive satisfaction. Il me dit que MM. Bastide et Dussard n'ont pas perdu l'espoir que vous renouvellerez l'aimable invitation que vous avez eu l'extrême bonté de leur faire et que des circonstances tout à fait indépendants d'eux ne leur ont pas permis d'accepter: or, comme Mill quitte Londres vendredi prochain, auriez vous la bonté de prier de Mr. Taylor d'inviter ces messieurs avec Mill à prendre le thé jeudi prochain chez vous? cela contenterai tout le monde.

Je me fais un véritable plaisir de vous envoyer çi-joint le dernier numéro de St. [?] qui contient le discours de l'excellent M. Fox avec des observations sur lui qui me font bien plaisir.

J'ai l'honneur d'etre, madame,
V.t.h.e.t.b.A.
B. E. Desainteville

During 1832 and the years immediately following the one common interest in which we can follow Mill's and Mrs. Taylor's activities are their contributions to Fox's *Monthly Repository*. This journal Fox had bought in 1831, perhaps with financial help from Mr. Taylor, after he had already been editing it for three years, and for a time Mrs. Taylor lent the help of her pen to assist him in the effort of turning it from a denominational organ into a general literary and political periodical. Practically all her known publications appeared in the *Monthly Repository* for 1832, and in the following year Mill also became a regular contributor and at the same time entered a new field as a critic of poetry.

Mrs. Taylor's contributions[18] of 1832 include her three printed poems, probably written some time before and already mentioned, six reviews of books and one small essay. It cannot be said that there is anything very remarkable about her prose compositions of this time. They begin in May with a review of Sarah Austin's translation of Prince Puckler-Muskau's *Tour of a German Prince* where she finds something to praise because 'in this land of caste he avows his sympathy with the *paria*'.[19] In June appeared a somewhat more ambitious discussion of Mrs. Trollope's *Domestic Manners of the Americans* with which she dealt severely:

'It has unfortunately chanced that, with few exceptions, the descriptions of the United States have been those of persons either of small intellect, and incapable, with their best efforts, of judging between that which is essential and that which is accidental, as instance Basil Hall; or, worse, those whose prejudices make their principles and whose long-formed habits of subserviency make them fancy servility refinement and its absence coarseness; and of this latter class is the author before us.'[20]

Three more reviews by Mrs. Taylor, like the others well written and expressing strong radical sentiments, appeared in July and September,[21] and in November followed one more, of a translation[22] of B. Sarrans' *Louis Philippe and the Revolution of 1830* in which one is inclined to detect signs of Mill's hand, though it may be that merely his writings on the subject had served as a model. The review ends:

'There can be no doubt that the state of things in France is again slowly tending towards a great moral or physical revolution. That the former may suffice, all friends of humanity must desire; but, should that force of itself be insufficient to produce agreement between the spirit of the government and the spirit of the time, they will not be true friends of humanity who shall not welcome any power which, by means of some evil, may work the regeneration of the people who head the political regeneration of Europe. As needful is it to be kept in mind by nations, as by individuals, *Aide toi, le ciel t'aidera.*'[23]

Mrs. Taylor's last known contribution to the *Monthly Repository*, in December, is a pleasant little essay on the rival attractions of 'The Seasons' of which the only noteworthy passage is perhaps the startling assertion that

'flowers are Utilitarians in the largest sense. Their very life is supported by administering to the life of others—producers and distributors, but consumers only of what, unused, would be noxious.'[24]

Mill's contributions are more interesting, even from our particular point of view. When, early in 1832, Fox had first urged him to contribute he had committed himself no further than to a guarded half-promise that whenever he had anything suitable he would be glad to let Fox have it for the *Monthly Repository*.[25] The first result of this was an essay ' On Genius' which appeared in the form of a Letter to the Editor in September 1832.[26] But his regular contributions did not begin until his article 'What is Poetry' appeared in January of the following year.[27]

There could be little doubt that this new strong interest was due to Mrs. Taylor's influence even if we had not Mill's own statement that this was so. Before that time he had appeared to his friends as a distinctly unpoetical nature[28] and in his account of his discovery of Wordsworth he himself explains Wordsworth's appeal to him by the fact that Wordsworth was 'the poet of unpoetical natures'.[29] In another available fragment of that early draft of the *Autobiography* which has already been mentioned Mill says[30]:

'The first years of my friendship with her were in respect of my own development mainly years of poetic culture. . . . I did cultivate this taste as well as a taste for paintings and sculpture and did read with enthusiasm her favourite poets, especially the one whom she placed far above all others, Shelley.'

From a much later source we know that among Shelley's poems they particularly admired the 'Hymn to Intellectual Beauty', and the same authority reports that their strong preference for Shelley was accompanied by an equally strong aversion to Byron, the lowness of whose ideals Mill deplored while Mrs. Mill then described the popular enthusiasm for him as 'a mere popular delusion'.[31]

Of the two essays of poetry which were among the first fruits of Mill's new interest it has not unjustly been said that

'while clear and strenuous as most of his thoughts were, [they] are neither scientifically precise, nor do they contain any notable new idea not previously expressed by Coleridge—except perhaps the idea that emotions are the main link of association in the poetic mind: still his working out of the definition of poetry, his distinction between novels and poems, and between poetry and eloquence, is interesting as throwing light upon his own poetical susceptibilities. He holds that poetry is the "delineation of the deeper and more secret workings of human emotions".'[32]

In Mill's next excursion into criticism of poetry it is fairly certain that Mrs. Taylor took a direct part; and, although it saw the light of print only in recent times, it was destined to play some role in the development of a major poet. Robert Browning had some years before, when still a boy, made the acquaintance of W. J. Fox and the Misses Flower. Eliza Flower is even reputed to have inspired both Browning's lost early poem *Incondita* and his *Pauline*, the first of his poems to be printed. When it appeared in March 1833, Browning turned to Fox for help in making it known, and Fox not only reviewed it himself in the *Monthly Repository* but also passed a copy on to Mill for review elsewhere. A short article which Mill wrote on it for the *Examiner* could not be inserted[33] and an attempt to alter and enlarge it for Tait's *Edinburgh Magazine*[34] met with no better fate. This article is lost. But Mill also freely annotated his copy[35] on the margin, marking 'all the passages where the meaning is so imperfectly expressed as not to be easily understood', and summed up his opinion on the flyleaf. Some of these marginal notes are in a different hand, which is almost certainly Harriet Taylor's, and though the notes which can be ascribed to her with any confidence do not go beyond short exclamations like 'most beautiful' and 'deeply true', there can be little doubt that she and Mill fully discussed the poem before Mill returned the annotated copy to Fox with the remark that 'On the whole the observations are not flattering to the author—perhaps too strong in the *expression* to be shown to him'.[36] The copy nevertheless reached Browning soon afterwards and the young poet was so deeply mortified by the criticism that he resolved never again by premature publication to expose himself to similar censure. Although Mill's critique has been printed in the standard Life of Robert Browning, it has never been included in any publication concerning Mill and therefore may be given a place here[37].

'With considerable poetic powers, the writer seems to me possessed with a more intense and morbid self-consciousness than I ever knew in any sane human being. I should think it a sincere confession, though a most unlovable state, if the "Pauline" were not evidently a mere phantom. All about her is full of inconsistency—he neither loves her nor fancies he loves her, yet insists upon *talking* love to her. If she *existed* and loved him, he treats her most ungenerously and unfeelingly. All his aspirings and yearnings and regrets point to other things, never to her; then he *pays her off* toward the end by a piece of flummery amounting to the modest request that she will love him and live with him and give herself up to him *without* his *loving her*—moyennant quoi he will think her and call her everything that is handsome, and he promises her that she shall find it mighty pleasant. Then he leaves off by saying that he knows he shall have changed his mind by to-morrow, and "despite these intents which seem so fair," but that having been thus visited once no doubt she will be again—and is therefore "in perfect joy", bad luck to him! as the Irish say. A cento of most beautiful passages might be made from this poem, and the psychological history of himself is powerful and truthful—*truth-like* certainly, all but the last stage. That, he evidently had not yet got into. The self-seeking and self-worshipping state is well described—beyond that, I should think the writer has made, as yet, only the next step, viz. into despising his own state. I even question whether part even of that self-disdain is not *assumed*. He is evidently *dissatisfied*, and feels part of the badness of his state; he does not write as if it were purged out of him. If he once could muster a hearty hatred of his selfishness it would go: as it is, he feels only the *lack* of good, not the positive evil. He feels not remorse, but only disappointment; a mind in that state can only be regenerated by some new passion, and I know not what to wish for him but that he may meet with a *real* Pauline.

'Meanwhile he should not attempt to show how a person may be recovered from this morbid state, for *he* is hardly convalescent, and "what should we speak of but that which we know".'

Mill took a much deeper interest in the other rising great poet of the time, Alfred Tennyson. Although the review of the second volume of Tennyson's poems, on which Mill had been working at about the time when he wrote on Browning, at first did not grow beyond an introduction which he later turned into his second article on poetry for the *Monthly Repository*,[38] it was, when it ultimately appeared two years later,[39] still the first full recognition of a great poet.

That at this time Mill's interests were inspired and shared by Mrs. Taylor we may also feel assured from the closeness of their contacts. At least by the spring of 1833 Mill seems to have been spending most of his free time at the new home of the Taylors at 17 Kent Terrace, Park Road, on the western edge of Regent's Park, to which they had moved from the City at some time during the preceding winter. In reply to W. J. Fox's mentioning that he had hoped to meet Mill there on a certain Wednesday, Mill explained:

J. S. M. to W. J. Fox, 19 May 1833:[40] I seldom go there without special reason on that day of the week for as it cannot be right in the present circumstances to be there every evening, none costs so little to give up than that in which there is much shorter time and that in the presence of others. Had I known of your going I would have gone.

And in another letter to Fox, only a week or two later, Mill said that he was 'going to Kent Terrace today, despite of its being Wednesday'.[41]

During the following summer Mill seems to have continued his visits at some place in the neighbourhood of London at which Mrs. Taylor was staying and there exist a few notes by her to him which may conjecturally be assigned to this period.

H. T. to J. S. M., summer 1833(?).[42] In the beautiful stillness of this lovely country—and with the fresh feeling of all the enjoyment it has been to him—and so soon after that which to him is such a quick-passing pleasure—he is perhaps feeling again what he once said to me, that 'the less human the more lovely' I seemed to him. do you remember that my love? *I* have, because I felt that whatever such a feeling was, it was not love—and since how perfectly he has denied it,— or that may not be exactly the feeling, but only his old 'vanity of vanities' may have come back? neither one nor the other would grieve *me*, but for his own dear sake—for me I *am* loved as I desire to be—heart and soul take their rest in the peace of ample satisfaction after how much [?] & care which of that kind at least has passed for ever—o this sureness of an everlasting spiritual home is itself the blessedness of the blessed—& to that being added—or rather that being brought by, this exquisiteness which is & has been each instant since, & seems as if with no fresh food it would be enough for a long life's enjoyment. O my own love, whatever it may or may not be to you, you need never regret for a moment what has already brought such increase of happiness and can in no possible way increase evil. If it is right to change the 'smallest chance' into a '*distant certainty*' it w^d surely show want of intellect rather than use of it to [breaks off before end of page].

H. T. to J. S. M., summer 1833(?).[43] Far from being unhappy or even low this morning, I feel as tho' you had never loved me half so well as last night—& I am in the happiest spirits & *quite* well part of which is owing to that nice sight this morning.

I am taking as much care of your robin as if it were your own sweet self. If I do not succeed in making *this* live I shall think it is not possible to tame a full grown one.

It is very well but so was the other for two days. . . .

Adieu darling. How very nice next month will be. I am quite impatient for it.

These letters may or may not belong to the summer of 1833 when the relation was evidently approaching a new crisis. We can watch some of the developments in Mill's letters to Carlyle, whom he had promised to visit at Craigenputtock during his month's vacation in September. In a letter of 2 August he for the first time hinted mysteriously that this visit would remain in some measure uncertain 'because the only contingency which would prevent it may happen at any time, and will remain possible to the very last'.[44] A month later he wrote that the plan was definitely off:

J. S. M. to Thomas Carlyle, 5 September 1833:[45] There were about twenty chances to one that I should [see you in the autumn], but it is the twenty-first which has taken effect in reality. I was mistaken, too, when I said that if I went not to Craigenputtock I should go nowhere. I am going to Paris; the same cause which I then thought, if it operated at all, would keep me here, now sends me there. It is a journey entirely of duty; nothing else, you will do me the justice to believe, would have kept me from Craigenputtock after what I have said and written so often; it is duty, and duty connected with a person to whom of all persons alive I am under the greatest obligation.

It seems that on the very day when he wrote this letter Mill must have spoken or written to Harriet Taylor more openly than before. All we have is the following note of hers to him, posted on the following day.

H. T. to J. S. M., 6 September 1833:[46] I am glad that you have said it—I am *happy* that you have—no one with any

fineness & beauty of character but must feel compelled to say
all, to the being they really love, or rather with any *permanent*
reservation it is not *love*—while there is reservation, however
little of it, the love is just *so much* imperfect. There has never,
yet, been entire confidence around us. The difference between
you and me in that respect is, that I have always *yearned* to
have *your* confidence with an intensity of wish which has
often, for a time, swallowed up the naturally stronger feeling
—the affection itself—you have not given it, not that you
wished to reserve—but that you did not *need* to give—but
not having that need of course you had no perception that I
had & so you had discouraged confidence from me 'til the
habit of *checking first thoughts* has become so strong that when
in your presence timidity has become almost a *disease* of the
nerves. It would be absurd only it is so painful (?) to notice
in myself that every word I ever speak to you is detained a
second before it is said 'til I am quite sure I am not by impli-
cation asking for your confidence. It is but that the only
being who has ever called forth all my faculties of affection
is the only one in whose presence I ever felt constraint.[47] At
times when that has been strongly felt I too have doubted
whether there was not possibility of disappointment—that
doubt will never return. You can scarcely conceive dearest
what *satisfaction* this note of yours is to me for I have been
depressed by the fear that I w^d wish most altered in you, you
thought quite well of, perhaps the best in your character. I
am quite sure that want of energy is a defect, would be a
defect if it belonged to the character, but that thank Heaven
I am sure it does not. It is such an opposite to the sort of
character.

Yes—these circumstances *do* require greater strength than
any other—the greatest—that which you have, & which if
you had not I should never have loved you, I should not love
you now. In this, as in all these important matters there is no
medium between the *greatest*, *all*, and none—anything less
than all being insufficient. There might be just as well none.

If I did not know them to be false, how heartily I should scorn such expressions, 'I have ceased to will'! Then to wish? for does not wish with the power to fulfil constitute will?

It is false that 'your strength is not equal to the circumstances in which you have placed' yourself.—It is quite another thing to be guided by a judgement on which you can rely and which is better placed for judgement than yourself.

Would you let yourself 'drift with the tide whether it flow or ebb' if in one case every wave took you further from me? Would you not put what strength you have into resisting it? Tell me—for if you would not, how happens it that you will to love me or any (?).

However—since you tell me the evil & I believe that evil, I may truly believe the good—and if all the good you have written in the last two or three notes be *firm truth*, there is good enough, even for me. The most horrible feeling I ever know is when for moments the fear comes over me that *nothing* which you say of yourself is to be absolutely relied on —that you are not sure even of your strongest feelings. Tell me again that it is not.

If it were certain that 'whatever one thinks best the other will think best' it is plain there could be no unhappiness—if that were certain want of energy could not be felt, could not be an evil, unless both wanted energy—the only evil there could be for me is that you should *not* think my best your best—or should not agree in my opinion of my best.

dearest I have but five minutes in w^h to write this or I should say more—but I was obliged to say something before tomorrow. t'was so long to wait dearest.

Of what must have preceded this we get a glimpse from a letter by Mill to Fox, written on the next day, in which he suggests that he might transfer to Fox's *Monthly Repository* the paper on Poetry which he had thought of putting at the head of the review of Tennyson.

J. S. M. to W. J. Fox, Saturday, 7 September 1833:[48] If you like the idea, and if you see *her* before Monday, will you mention it to her—you know it is hers—if she approves, it shall be yours. I shall see her on Monday myself, and then I shall speak of the matter to her. [Ye][49]s—she is like hers[elf][49] if she is ever out of spirits it is always something amiss in *me* that is the cause—it is so now—it is because she sees that what ought to be so much easier to me than to her, is in reality more difficult—costs harder struggle—to part company with the opinion of the world, and with my former modes of doing good in it. however, thank Heaven, she does not doubt that I can do it.

It seems that as the outcome of long discussions Mr. Taylor had been persuaded to agree to an experimental separation from his wife for six months, and in the course of September Mrs. Taylor left for Paris. Mill followed her there on the 10th of October for a stay of somewhat over six weeks. One of the letters which he wrote thence to Fox has been preserved and must be quoted in full.

J. S. M. to W. J. Fox, Paris, 5 or 6 November 1833:[50] I could have filled a long letter to you with the occurrences and feelings and thoughts of any one day since I have been here— this fortnight seems an age in mere duration, and *is* an age in what it has done for us two. It has brought years of experience to us—good and happy experience most of it. We never could have been so near, so perfectly intimate, in any former circumstances—we never could have been together as we have been in innumerable smaller relations and concerns— we never should have spoken of all things, in all frames of mind, with so much freedom and unreserve. I am astonished when I think how much has been restrained, how much untold, unshewn and uncommunicated till now—how much which by the mere fact of its being spoken, has disappeared —so many real unlikenesses, so many more false impressions of unlikeness, most of which have only been revealed to me since they have ceased to exist or those which still exist have ceased to be felt painfully. Not a day has passed without removing some real & serious obstacle to happiness. I never thought so humbly of myself compared with her, never thought & felt myself so little worthy of her, never more keenly regretted that I am not, in some things, very different for her sake.—yet it is so much to know as I do now; that almost all which has ever caused her any misgivings with regard to our fitness for each other was mistaken in point of fact—that the mistakes no longer exist—& that she is now (as she is) quite convinced that we are perfectly suited to pass our lives together—better suited indeed for that perfect than for this imperfect companionship. There will never again I believe be any obstacle to our being together entirely, from the slightest doubt that the experiment would succeed with respect to ourselves—not, as she used to say, for a short time, but for our natural lives. And yet—all the other obstacles or rather the one obstacle being as great as ever—our futurity is still perfectly uncertain. She has decided nothing except what has always been decided—not to renounce the liberty of sight—and it does not seem likely that anything will be decided until the end of the six months, if even *then* finally. For me, I am certain that whatever she decides will be wisest and rightest, even if she decides what was so repugnant to me at first—to remain here alone—it is repugnant to me still —but I can now see that perhaps it will be best—the future will decide that.

When will you write again—she shewed me your letter— it is beautiful in you to write so to any one, but who could write otherwise to her?

I am happy, but not *so* happy as when the future appeared surer.

I had written thus far before receiving your letter, and I am glad of it. I have now taken a larger sheet and copied the above unto it.

Your letter does indeed show that you do not 'at all understand her state' and never have understood it—this I have only lately begun to suspect, & never was quite sure of it till now—and I see that under the presumption that you were more aware than I perceive you are of the real state of her feelings, I myself have said and written things which have confirmed you in the wrong impression.

You seem to think that she *was* decided, and *is* now undecided—that the state of feeling which led to the separation has been as you say 'interrupted' and is to be 'recommenced'. Now this is an incorrect and so far a lower idea of her than the true one—she *never* had decided upon anything except not to give up either the feeling, or the power of communication with me—unless she did so it was *Mr. Taylor's* wish, and seemed to be necessary to his comfort that she should live apart from him. When the separation had actually taken place the result did as you say seem certain—not because we had willed to make it so, but because it seemed the necessary consequence of the new circumstances if the feelings of all continued the same. This was the sole cause & I think cause enough for the hopefulness and happiness which I felt almost all that month and which must have made a false impression on you. I never felt sure of what was to be after the six months, but I felt an immense increase of the chances in my favour. When I came here, I *expected* to find her no more decided than she had always been about what would be best for all, but *not* to find her as for the first time I did, doubtful about what would be best for our *own* happiness—under the influence of that fact and of the painful feelings it excited, I wrote to you. *That* doubt, thank heaven, lasted but a short time—if I had delayed my letter two days longer I should never have sent it.

If Mr. Taylor feels as you believe he does, he has been very far from telling her 'all he feels'; for his last letter to her, which came by the same post as this of yours (the first she has ever shewed me) is in quite another tone. He is most entirely mistaken in all the facts. Her affection to him, which originated in gratitude for his affection & kindness, instead of being weakened by this stronger feeling, has been greatly *strengthened*, by so many new proofs of *his* affection for *her*, &

by the unexpected & (his nature considered) really admirable generosity & nobleness which he has shewn under so severe a trial. Instead of *reviving* in absence, her affection for him has been steady throughout; it is of quite another character from *this* feeling, & therefore does not in the least conflict with it *naturally*, & now when circumstances have thrown the two into opposition she can no more overcome, or wish to overcome the one, than the other. The difference is, that the one, being only affection, not *passion*, would be satisfied with knowing him to be happy though away from her—but if the choice were absolutely between giving up the stronger feeling, & making him (what he says he should be) durably wretched, I am quite convinced that either would be [more(?)][51] than she could bear. I know it is the common notion of passionate love that it sweeps away all other affections—but surely the *justification* of passion, & one of its greatest beauties & glories, is that in an otherwise fine character it weakens *no* feeling which deserves to subsist, but would naturally strengthen them all. Because her letters to Mr. Taylor express the strong affection she has always felt, and he is no longer seeing, every day, proof of her far stronger feeling for another, he thinks the affection has *come back*—he might have seen it quite as plainly before; only he refused to believe it. *I* have seen it, and felt its immense power over her, in moments of intense excitement with which I am sure he would believe it to be utterly incompatible.

Her affection for him, which has always been the principle, is now the sole obstacle to our being together—for the present there seems absolutely no prospect of that obstacle's being got over. She believes—& she knows him better than any of us can—that it would be the breaking up of his whole future life—*that* she is determined never to be the cause of, & I am as determined never to urge her to it, & convinced that if I did I should fail. Nothing could justify it but 'the most distinct perception' that it is not only 'necessary to the happiness of both', but the only means of saving both or either from insupportable unhappiness. That can never be unless the alternative were entire giving up. I believe he is quite right in his impression that the worst for him which is to be expected at the end of the six months is her remaining permanently here. She will, if it is in human power to do so, make him understand the exact state of her feelings, and will as at present minded, give *him* the choice of every possible arrangement except entire giving-up, with the strong wish that her remaining here may be his choice; with a full understanding however that the agreement whatever it be, is to be no longer binding than while it is found endurable. This seems but a poor result to come of so much suffering & so much effort, but for *us* even so the gain is great.

She has seen and approved all that precedes, therefore it is as much her letter as mine. So now you know the whole state of the case.

She is on the whole far happier than I have ever known her, and quite well physically though far from strong—I have many anxious thoughts of how she is to bear the being again alone with so little of hope to sustain her. I am so convinced of all I have written above, that if the final decision were already made (whatever it might be) I am certain that the fact of Mr. Taylor's being to be here so soon after I am gone would be a real & great good to her—but *now*, I am afraid unless she sees her way clearly to some tolerably satisfactory arrangement in the first few days of his visit she will only be made more unhappy by being made to feel more keenly the impossibility of avoiding great unhappiness to him.

You know, perhaps, that her brother has been here—nothing could have been better or sweeter than all he said & did—he was even *friendly*.

Can I do anything for you here—see anyone, or bring over anything for you—I shall leave Paris probably Friday week.

It is idle, almost, to *say* any thanks for all you are saying and doing for our good & for such part of the interest you feel in it as regards me personally—I may be able some time or other to make some return to you for it all, more than by invoking as I do all the blessings earth is heir to upon you.

Yours
J. S. M.

A small slip of paper which was probably enclosed with this letter carried a note from Mrs. Taylor to Fox and Eliza Flower:[52]

I had written to you dearest friends both,—as you are— but now that I have seen that letter of yours, I cannot send mine. It is sad to be misunderstood by you—as I have been before—but it will not be always so—my own dear friends. O what a letter (?) was that! but my head & soul bless you both.

He tells you quite truly our state—all at least which he attempts to tell—but there is so much more might be said— there has been so much more pain than I thought I was capable of, but also O how much more happiness. O this being seeming as tho God had willed to show the type of the possible elevation of humanity. To be with him wholly is my ideal of the noblest fate for all states of mind and feeling which are lofty & large & fine, he is the companion spirit and heart desire—we are not alike in trifles only because I have so much more frivolity than he. Why do you not write to me my dearest Lizzie? (I never wrote that name before) if you w^d say on the merest scrap what you are talking about what the next sermon is about where you walked to, & such like, how glad I should be! You must come here—it is a most beautiful paradise. O how happy we might all be in it. You will see it with me, bless you! won't you?

When Mill returned to London about 20 November he at once saw Fox and a few days later again wrote to him.

J. S. M. to W. J. Fox, London, 22 November(?) 1833:[53]
I have the strongest wish, and some hope, that there will some day arrive a sketch of Paris, in the manner of some

of your local sketches—if there does, it will be the most
beautiful thing ever written—she has spoken quite enough
to me at different times, to show what it would be.

Have you seen Mr. Taylor? he has received a letter by
this time, part of which she has sent to me, and which if he
was still in the state in which you last saw him, will certainly
put him completely out of it. Ed. Hardy[54] while he confirms
all you told me of the impression her precious letter made
upon him when it came, bringing back his old hopes and
theories, affirms positively that all this had quite gone off
before he received any other letter, & that his acquiescence in
her return to him is *not* given under the influence of those
hopes and theories but of a real intention of being with her as
a *friend* and *companion*. His conduct & feelings *now*, will
shew whether this is correct. I shall be anxious to know your
impression when you shall have seen him in his present state.

It seems he had written to her *again* since I left Paris—she
writes 'I had yesterday one of those letters from Mr. Taylor
which make us admire & love him. He says that this plan &
my letters have given him delight—that he has been selfish
—but in future will think more for others & less for himself
—but still he talks of this plan being good *for all*, by which
he means *me*, as he says he is sure it will "prevent after
misery" & again he wishes for complete confidence. I have
written exactly what I think, without reserve.'

We do not know what 'this plan' was, but apparently some sort of
compromise solution was agreed upon not long after. From another
letter by Mill to Fox written within a week of this[55] we learn that
Mill still did not expect to remain in England and for this reason felt
unable to pursue a suggestion of taking a share in the control of the
Examiner, which was in difficulties. At the same time, in a very full
report to Carlyle on conditions in Paris,[56] which the latter intended to
visit, Mill expressed the hope of seeing him there in the following
summer. It seems however that Mrs. Taylor returned to England long
before the end of the six months and probably even before the end of
1833. The understanding seems to have been that while Mr. Taylor

agreed to the continuance of the friendship, the external appearances of married life should be preserved. Perhaps it was to this date that Mrs. Taylor referred when, some twenty years later, she gave a foreign visitor emphatically to understand that since the beginning of her friendship with Mill she had been to neither of the two men *more* than a *Seelenfreundin*.[57] We do not know whether it was already at that time or only a few years later that she commenced to live most of the time in the country[58] with her small daughter, only occasionally visiting Kent Terrace, while the two boys were apparently placed in some boarding school.

Chapter Three

ON MARRIAGE AND DIVORCE
about 1832

THE situation and the natural inclinations of both parties must have combined from the beginning to make the position of women and their position in marriage one of the main topics of common interest to Mill and Harriet Taylor. The principles at issue are not touched upon in any of the early letters which have survived, but we have two manuscript essays which they wrote for each other at a very early date. Since Mill's and an earlier draft of Harriet Taylor's are on paper watermarked '1831' and a later version of hers on paper watermarked '1832' we shall probably not go far wrong in attributing them to the latter year. Mill's is much the longer and may be given first. It tends to confirm his claim in the *Autobiography* that contrary to what an uninformed person would probably suspect, this was not one of the subjects on which he was mainly indebted to her for his ideas. He says there that

'it might be supposed, for instance, that in my strong convictions on the complete equality in all legal, political, social and domestic relations, which ought to exist between men and women, may have been adopted or learnt from her. This was so far from being the fact, that those convictions were among the earliest results of the application of my mind to political subjects, and the strength with which I held them was, I believe, more than anything else, the originating cause of the interest she felt in me. What is true is, that until I knew her, the opinion was in my mind, little more than an abstract principle. . . . I am indeed painfully conscious of how much of her best thoughts on the subject

I have failed to reproduce, and how greatly that little treatise [*The Subjection of Women*] falls short of what would have been if she had put on paper her entire mind on this question, or had lived to revise and improve, as she certainly would have done, my imperfect statements of the case.'[1]

Here are his ideas on the subject as he expressed them for his friend about thirty-seven years before he stated them in print:

She to whom my life is devoted has wished for written exposition of my opinions on the subject which, of all connected with human Institutions, is nearest to her happiness. Such as that exposition can be made without *her* to suggest and to decide, it is given in these pages: she, herself, has not refused to put into writing for *me*, what she has thought and felt on the same subject, and *there* I shall be taught, all perhaps which I have, and certainly all which I have not, found out for myself. In the investigation of truth, as in all else, 'it is not good for man to be alone'. And more than all, in what concerns the relations of Man with Woman, the law which is to be observed by both should surely be made by both; not, as hitherto, by the stronger only.

How easy would it be for either me or you, to resolve this question for ourselves alone! Its difficulties, for difficulties it has, are such as obstruct the avenues of all great questions which are to be decided for mankind at large, & therefore not for natures resembling each other, but for natures or at least characters tending to all the points of the moral compass. All popular morality is, as I once said to you, a compromise among conflicting natures; each renouncing a certain portion of what its own desires call for, in order to avoid the evils of a perpetual warfare with all the rest. That is the best popular morality, which attains this general pacification with the least sacrifice of the happiness of the higher natures; who are the greatest, indeed the only real, sufferers by the compromise; for *they* are called upon to give up what would really make them happy; while others are commonly required only to restrain desires the gratification of which would bring no real happiness. In the adjustment, moreover, of the compromise, the higher natures count only in proportion to their number, how small! & to the number of those whom they can influence: while, the conditions of the compromise weigh heavily upon them in the states (?) of their greater capacity of happiness, & its natural consequence, their keener sense of *want* and disappointment when the degree of happiness which they know would fall to their lot but for untoward external circumstances, is denied them.

By the higher natures I mean those characters who from the combination of natural & acquired advantages have the greatest capacity of feeling happiness, & of bestowing it. Of bestowing it in two ways: as being beautiful to contemplate, & therefore the natural objects of admiration and love; and also as being fitted, and induced, by their qualities of mind and heart, to promote by their actions, & by all that depends upon their will, the greatest possible happiness of all who are within the sphere of their influence.

If all persons were like these, or even would be guided by these, morality would be very different from what it must now be; or rather it would not exist at all as morality, since morality and inclination would coincide. If all resembled you, my lovely friend, it would be idle to prescribe rules for them: By following their own impulses under the guidance of their own judgment, they would find more happiness, and would confer more, than by obeying any moral principles or maxims whatever; since these cannot possibly be adapted beforehand to every peculiarity of circumstance which can be taken into account by a sound and vigorous intellect *worked* by a strong *will*, and guided by what Carlyle calls 'an open loving heart'. Where there exists a genuine and strong desire to do that which is most for the happiness of all, general rules are merely aids to prudence, in the choice of means; not peremptory obligations. Let but the desires be right, and the 'imagination lofty and refined': & provided there be disdain of all false seeming, 'to the pure all things are pure'.

It is easy enough to settle to moral bearings of our question upon such characters. The highest natures are of course impassioned natures; to such, marriage is but one continued act of self-sacrifice where strong affection is not; every tie therefore which restrains them from seeking out and uniting themselves with some one whom they can perfectly love, is a yoke to which they cannot be subjected without oppression: and to such a person when found, they would, natural superstition apart, scorn to be united by any other tie than free and voluntary choice. If such natures have been healthily developed in other respects, they will have all other good and worthy feelings strong enough to prevent them from pursuing this happiness at the expense of greater suffering of others: & that is the limit of the forbearance which morally ought in such a case to enjoin.

But will the morality which suits the highest natures, in this matter, be also best for all inferior natures? My conviction is that it will: but this can be only a happy accident. All the difficulties of morality in any of its brands, grow out of the conflict which continually arises between the highest morality & even the best popular morality which the degree of development yet achieved by average human nature, will allow to exist.

If all, or even most persons, in the choice of a companion of the other sex, were led by any real aspiration towards, or sense of, the happiness which such companionship in its best shape is capable of giving to the best natures, there would never have been any reason why law or opinion should have set any limits to the most unbounded freedom of uniting and separating: nor is it probable that popular morality would ever, in a civilized or refined people, have imposed any restraint upon that freedom. But, as I once said to you, the law of marriage as it now exists, has been made *by* sensualists, and *for* sensualists and *to bind* sensualists. The aim & purpose of that law is either to tie up the sense, in the hope by so doing, of tying up the soul also, or else to tie up the sense because the soul is not cared about at all. Such purposes never could have entered into the minds of any to whom nature had given souls capable of the higher degrees of happiness: nor could such a law ever have existed but among persons to whose natures it was in some degree congenial, & therefore more suitable than at first sight may be supposed by those whose natures are widely different.

There can, I think, be no doubt that for a long time the indissolubility of marriage acted powerfully to elevate the social position of women. The state of things to which in almost all countries it succeeded, was one in which the power of repudiation existed on one side but not on both: in which the stronger might cast away the weaker, but the weaker could not fly from the stronger. To a woman of impassioned character, the difference between this and what now exists, is not worth much; for she would wish to be repudiated, rather than to remain united only because she could not be got rid of. But the aspirations of most women are less high. They would wish to retain any bond of union they have ever had with a man to whom they do not prefer any other, and for whom they have that inferior kind of affection which habits of intimacy frequently produce. Now, assuming what may be assumed of the greater number of men, that they are attracted to women solely by sensuality, or at best by a transitory *taste*; it is not deniable, that the irrevocable vow gave to women, when the passing gust had blown over, a permanent hold upon the men who would otherwise have cast them off. Something, indeed *much*, of a community of interest, arose from the mere fact of being indissolubly united: the husband took an interest in the wife as being *his* wife, if he did not from any better feeling: it became essential to his respectability that his wife also should be respected; and commonly when the first revulsion of feeling produced by satiety, went off, the mere fact of continuing together if the woman had anything lovable in her & the man was not wholly brutish, could hardly fail to raise up some feeling of regard & attachment. She obtained also, what is often far more precious to her, the certainty of not being separated from the children.

Now if this be all that human life *has* for women, it is little enough: and any woman who feels herself capable of great happiness, and whose aspirations have not been artificially checked, will claim to be set free from *only* this, to seek for more. But women in general, as I have already remarked, are more easily contented, and this I believe to be the cause of the general aversion of women to the idea of facilitating divorce. They have a habitual belief that their power over men is chiefly derived from men's sensuality; & that the same sensuality would go elsewhere in search of gratification, unless restrained by law & opinion. They on their part, mostly seek in marriage, a home, and the state or condition of a married woman, with the addition or not as it may happen, of a splendid establishment &c. &c. These things once obtained, the indissolubility of marriage renders them sure of keeping. And most women, either because these things give them all the happiness they are capable of, or from the artificial barriers which curb all spontaneous movements to seek their greatest felicity, are generally more anxious not to peril the good they have than to go in search of a greater. If marriage were dissoluble, they think they could not retain the position once acquired; or not without practicing upon the attention of men by those arts, disgusting in the extreme to any woman of simplicity, by which a cunning mistress sometimes established & retains her ascendancy.

These considerations are nothing to an impassioned character; but there is something in them, for the characters from which they emanate—is not that so? The only conclusion, however, which can be drawn from them, is one for which there would exist ample grounds even if the law of marriage as it now exists were perfection. This conclusion is, the absurdity and immorality of a state of society & opinion in which a woman is at all dependent for her social position upon the fact of her being or not being married. Surely it is wrong, wrong in every way, & on every view of morality, even the vulgar view—that there should exist any motives to marriage except the happiness which two persons who love one another feel in associating their existence.

The means by which the condition of married women is rendered artificially desirable, are not any superiority of legal rights, for in that respect single women, especially if possessed of property, have the advantage: the civil disabilities are greatest in the case of the married woman. It is not law, but education and custom which make the difference. Woman are so brought up, as not to be able to subsist in the mere physical sense, without a man to keep them: they are so brought up as not to be able to protect themselves against injury or insult, without some man on whom they have a special claim, to protect them: they are so brought up, as to have no vocation or useful office to fulfil in the world, remaining single; for all women who are educated to be married, & what little they are tought deserving the name useful, is chiefly what in the ordinary course of things will not come into actual use, unless nor until they are married. A single woman therefore is felt both by herself & others as a kind of excrescence on the surface of society, having no use or function or office there. She is not indeed precluded from useful & honorable exertion of various kinds: but a married woman is *presumed* to be a useful member of society unless there is evidence to the contrary; a single woman must establish what very few either women or men ever do establish, an *individual* claim.

All this, though not the less really absurd and immoral even under the law of marriage which now exists, evidently grows out of that law, and fits into the general state of society of which that law forms a part, nor could continue to exist if the law were changed, & marriage were not a contract at all, or were an easily dissoluble one: The indissolubility of marriage is the keystone of woman's present lot, and the whole comes down and must be reconstructed if that is removed.

And the truth is, that this question of marriage cannot properly be considered by itself alone. The question is not what marriage ought to be, but a far wider question, what woman ought to be. Settle that first, and the other will settle itself. Determine whether marriage is to be a relation between two equal beings, or between a superior & an inferior, between a protector and a dependent; & all other doubts will easily be resolved.

But in this question there is surely no difficulty. There is no natural inequality between the sexes; except perhaps in bodily strength; even that admits of doubt: and if bodily strength is to be the measure of superiority, mankind are no better than savages. Every step in the progress of civilization has tended to diminish the deference paid to bodily strength, until now when that quality confers scarcely any advantages except its natural ones: the strong man has little or no power to employ his strength as a means of acquiring any other advantage over the weaker in body. Every step in the progress of civilization has similarly been marked by a nearer approach to equality in the condition of the sexes; & if they are still far from being equal, the hindrance is not now in the difference of physical strength, but in artificial feelings and prejudices.

If nature has not made men and women unequal, still less ought the law to make them so. It may be assumed, as one of those presuppositions which would almost be made weaker by anything so ridiculous as attempting to prove them, that men and women ought to be perfectly coequal: that a woman ought not to be dependent on a man, more than a man on a woman, except so far as their affections make them so, by a voluntary surrender, renewed and renewing at each instant by free & spontaneous choice.

But this perfect independence of each other for all save

affection, cannot be, if there be dependence in pecuniary circumstances; a dependence which in the immense majority of cases must exist, if the woman be not capable, as well as the man, of gaining her own subsistence.

The first and indispensable step, therefore, towards the enfranchisement of woman, is that she be so educated, as not to be dependent either on her father or her husband for subsistence: a position which in nine cases out of ten, makes her either the plaything or the slave of the man who feeds her; & in the tenth case, only his humble friend. Let it not be said that she has an equivalent and compensating advantage in the exemption from toil: men think it base & servile in men to accept food as the price of dependence, & why do they not deem it so in women? solely because they do not desire that women should be their equals. Where there is strong affection, dependence is its own reward: but it must be voluntary dependence; & the more perfectly voluntary it is, the more exclusively each owes every thing to the other's affection & to nothing else,—the greater is the happiness. And where affection is not, the woman who will be dependent for the sake of a maintenance, proves herself as low-minded as a man in the like case—or *would* prove herself so if that resource were not too often the only one her education has given her, & if her education had not also tought her not to consider as degradation, that which is the essence of all prostitution, the act of delivering up her person for bread.

It does not follow that a woman should *actually* support herself because she should be *capable* of doing so: in the natural course of events she will *not*. It is not desirable to burthen the labour market with a double number of competitors. In a healthy state of things, the husband would be able by his single exertions to earn all that is necessary for both: & there would be no need that the wife should take part in the mere providing of what is required to *support* life: it will be for the happiness of both that her occupation should rather be to adorn & beautify it. Except in the class of actual day-labourers, that will be her natural task, if task it can be called, which will in so great a measure be accomplished rather by *being* than by *doing*.

We have all heard the vulgar talk that the proper employment of a wife are household superintendance, and the education of her children. As for household superintendance, if nothing be meant but merely seeing that servants do their duty, that is not an occupation; every women that is capable of doing it at all can do it without devoting anything like half an hour every day to that purpose peculiarly. It is not like the duty of a head of an office, to whom his subordinates bring their work to be inspected when finished: the defects in the performance of household duties present *themselves* to inspection: skill in superintendance consists in knowing the right way of noticing a fault when it occurs, & giving reasonable advice & instruction how to avoid it: and more depends on establishing a good *system* at first, than upon a perpetual and studious watchfulness. But if it be meant that the mistress of a family shall herself do the work of servants, *that* is good & will naturally take place in the rank in which there do not exist the means of hiring servants; but nowhere else.

Then as to the education of children: if by that term be meant, instructing them in particular arts or particular branches of knowledge, it is absurd to impose that upon mothers: absurd in two ways: absurd to set one-half of the adult human race to perform each on a small scale, what a much smaller number of teachers would accomplish for all, by devoting themselves exclusively to it; and absurd to set all mothers doing that for which some persons must be fitter than others, and for which average mothers cannot possibly be *so* fit as persons trained to the profession. Here again, when the means do not exist for hiring teachers, the mother is the natural teacher: but no special provision needs to be made for that case. Whether she is to teach or not, it is desirable that she should *know*; because knowledge is desirable for its own sake; for its uses, for its pleasures, & for its beautifying influence when not cultivated to the neglect of other gifts. What she knows, she will be able to teach to her children if necessary: but to erect such teaching into her occupation whether she can better employ herself or not, is absurd.

The education which it *does* belong to mothers to give, and which if not imbibed from them is seldom obtained in any perfection at all, is the training of the affections: & through the affections, of the conscience, & the whole moral being. But *this* most precious, & most indispensable part of education, does not take up *time*; it is not a business, an occupation; & a mother does not accomplish it by sitting down with her child for one or two or three hours to a task. She effects it by being with the child; by making it happy, and therefore at peace with all things; by checking bad habits in the commencement & by loving the child & by making the child love her. It is not by particular effects, but imperceptibly & unconsciously that she makes her own character pass into the child; that she makes the child love what she loves, venerate what she venerates & imitate as far as a child can her example. These things cannot be done by a hired teacher; & they are better & greater than all the rest. But to impose upon mothers what hired teachers *can* do, is mere squandering of the glorious existence of a woman fit for a woman's highest destiny. With regard to such things, her part is to see that they are rightly done, not to do them.

The great occupation of woman should be to *beautify* life: to cultivate, for her own sake & that of those who surround her, all her faculties of mind, soul, and body; all her powers of enjoyment, & powers of giving enjoyment; & to diffuse beauty, elegance, & grace, everywhere. If in addition to this the activity of her nature demands more energetic and definite employment, there is never any lack of it in the world: If she loves, her natural impulse will be to associate her existence with him she loves, and to share *his* occupations; in which, if he loves her (with that affection of *equality* which alone deserves to be called love) she will naturally take as strong an interest, & be as thoroughly conversant, as the most perfect confidence on his side can make her.

Such will naturally be the occupations of a woman who has fulfilled what seems to be considered as the end of her existence and attained what is really its happiest state, by uniting herself to a man whom she loves. But whether so united or not, women will never be what they should be, nor their social position what it should be, until women, as universally as men, have the power of gaining their own livelihood: until, therefore, every girl's parents have either provided her with independent means of subsistence, or given her an education qualifying her to provide those means for herself. The only difference between the employments of women and those of men will be, that those which partake most of the beautiful, or which require delicacy & taste rather than muscular exertion, will naturally fall to the share of women: all branches of the fine arts in particular.

In considering, then, what is the best law of marriage, we are to suppose that women already are, what they would be in the best state of society; no less capable of existing independently & respectably without men, than men without women. Marriage, on whatever footing it might be placed, would be wholly a matter of choice, not, as for a woman it now is, something approaching to a matter of necessity; something, at least, which every woman is under strong artificial motives to desire, and which if she attain not, her life is considered to be a failure.

These suppositions being made: and it being no longer any advantage to a woman to be married, merely for the sake of being married: why should any woman cling to the indissolubility of marriage, as if it could be for the good of one party that it should continue when the other party desires that it should be dissolved?

It is not denied by anyone that there are numerous cases in which the happiness of both parties would be greatly promoted by a dissolution of marriage. We will add, that when the social position of the two sexes shall be perfectly equal, a divorce if it be for the happiness of either party, will be for the happiness of both. No one but a sensualist would desire to retain a merely animal connexion with a person of the other sex, unless perfectly assured of being preferred by that person, above all other persons in the world. This certainty never can be quite perfect under the law of marriage as it now exists: it would be nearly absolute, if the tie were merely voluntary.

Not only there are, but it is in vain to hope that there will not always be, innumerable cases, in which the first connexion formed will be one the dissolution of which if it *could be*, certainly would be & ought to be, effected: It has long ago been remarked that of all the more serious acts of the life of a human being, there is not one which is commonly performed with so little of forethought or consideration, as that which is irrevocable, & which is fuller of evil than any other acts of the being's whole life if it turn out ill. And this is not so astonishing as it seems: The imprudence, while the contract remains indissoluble, consists in marrying at all: If you *do* marry there is little wisdom shewn by a very anxious & careful deliberation beforehand: Marriage is really, what it has been sometimes called, a lottery: & whoever is in a state of mind to calculate chances calmly & value them correctly, is not at all likely to purchase a ticket. Those who marry after taking great pains about the matter, generally do but buy their disappointment dearer. Then (?) the failures in marriage are such as are naturally incident to a first trial: the parties are inexperienced & cannot judge. Nor does this evil seem to be remediable. A woman is allowed to give herself away for life, at an age at which she is not allowed to dispose of the most inconsiderable landed estate: what then? if people are not to marry until they have learnt prudence, they will seldom marry before thirty: can this be expected, or is it to be desired? To direct the immature judgment, there is the advice of parents and guardians: a precious security! The only thing which a young girl can do, worse than marrying to please herself, is marrying to please any other person. However paradoxical it may sound to the ears of those who are reputed to have grown wise as wine grows good, by *keeping*, it is yet true, that A, an average person can better know what is for his own happiness, than B, an average person can know what is for A's happiness. Fathers & mothers as the world is constituted, do not judge more wisely than sons & daughters, they only judge differently: & the judgments of both being of the ordinary strength, or rather of the ordinary weakness, a person's own self has the advantage of a considerable greater number of *data* to judge from, & the further one of a stronger interest in the subject. Foolish people will say, that being interested in the subject is a disqualification: strange that they should not distinguish between being interested in a cause as a party before a judge, i.e. interested in deciding one way, right or wrong,—& being interested as a person is in the management of his own property, interested in deciding right. The parties themselves are only interested in doing what is most for their happiness; but their relatives may have all sorts of selfish interests to promote by inducing them to marry or not to marry.

The first choice, therefore, is made under very complicated disadvantages. By the facts of its being the *first* the parties are necessarily inexperienced in the particular matter: they are commonly young (especially the party who is in the greatest peril from a mistake) and therefore inexperienced in the knowledge & judgment of mankind & of themselves generally: and finally they have seldom had so much as an opportunity offered them of gaining any real knowledge of each other, since in nine cases out of ten they have never been once in each other's society completely unconstrained, or without consciously or unconsciously acting a part.

The chances therefore are many to one against the supposition that a person who requires, or is capable of, great happiness, will find that happiness in a first choice: & in a very large proportion of cases the first choice is such that if it cannot be recalled, it only embitters existence. The reasons, then, are most potent for allowing a subsequent change.

What there is to be said in favor of the indissolubility, superstition apart, resolves itself into this that it is highly desirable that changes should not be frequent, & desirable that the first choice should be, even if not compulsorily, yet very generally, persevered in: That consequently we ought to beware lest in giving facilities for retracting a bad choice, we hold out greater encouragement than at present for making such a choice as there will probably be occasion to retract.

It is proper to state as strongly as possible the arguments which may be advanced in support of this view in question.

Repeated trials for happiness, and repeated failures, have the most mischievous effects on all minds. The finer spirits are broken down, & disgusted with all things: their suscepti- bilities are deadened, or converted into sources of bitterness, & they lose the power of being ever *contented*. On the com- moner natures the effects produced are not the less deplor- able. Not only is their capacity for happiness worn out, but their morality is depraved: all refinement & delicacy of char- acter is extinguished; all sense of any peculiar duties or of any peculiar sacredness attaching to the relation between the sexes is worn away: & such alliances come to be looked upon with the very same kind of feelings which are now connected with a passing intrigue.

Thus much as to the parties themselves: but besides the parties there are also to be considered their children: beings who are wholly dependent both for happiness and for excel- lence upon their parents: & who in all but the extreme causes of actual profligacy, or perpetual bickering and discussion, *must* be better cared for in both points if their parents remain together.

So much importance is due to this last consideration, that

I am convinced, if marriages were easily dissoluble, two persons of opposite sexes who unite their destinies would generally, if they were wise, think it their duty to avoid having children until they had lived together for a considerable length of time, & found in each other a happiness adequate to their aspirations. If this principle of morality were observed, how many of the difficulties of the subject we are considering would be smoothed down! To be jointly the parents of a human being, should be the very last pledge of the deepest, holiest, & most desirable affection: for *that* is a tie which independently of convention, is indeed indissoluble: an additional & external tie, most precious where the souls are already indissolubly united, but simply burthensome while it appears possible to either that they should ever desire to separate.

It can hardly be anticipated, however, that such a course will be followed by any but those who to the greatest loftiness & delicacy of feeling, unite the power of the most deliberate reflexion. If the feelings be obtuse, the force of these considerations will not be felt; & if the judgment be weak or hasty, whether from inherent defect or inexperience, people will fancy themselves in love for their whole lives with a perfect being, when the case is far otherwise, & will suppose they risk nothing by creating a new relationship with that being, which can no longer be got rid of. It will therefore most commonly happen that when circumstances arise which induce the parents to separate, there will be children to suffer by the separation: nor do I see how this difficulty can be entirely got over, until the habits of society allow of a regulated community of living, among persons intimately acquainted, which would prevent the necessity of a total separation between the parents even when they had ceased to be connected by any nearer tie than mutual goodwill, & a common interest in their children.

There is yet another argument which may be urged against facility of divorce. It is this. Most persons have but a very moderate capacity of happiness; but no person ever finds this out without experience, very few even with experience: & most persons are constantly wreaking (?) that discontent which has its source internally, upon outward things. Expecting therefore in marriage a far greater degree of happiness than they commonly find: & knowing not that the fault is in their own scanty capabilities of happiness—they fancy they should have been happier with some one else: or at all events the disappointment becomes associated in their minds with the being in whom they had placed their hopes—& so they dislike one another for a time—& during that time they would feel inclined to separate: but if they remain united, the feeling of disappointment after a time goes off, & they pass their lives together with fully as much happiness as they could find either singly or in any other union, without having undergone the wearing of repeated and unsuccessful experiments.

Such are the arguments for adhering to the indissolubility of the contract: & for such characters as compose the great majority of the human race, it is not deniable that these arguments have considerable weight.

That weight however is not so great as it appears. In all the above arguments it is tacitly assumed, that the choice lies between the absolute interdiction of divorce, & a state of things in which the parties would separate on the most passing feeling of dissatisfaction. Now this is not really the alternative. Were divorce ever so free, it would be resorted to under the same sense of moral responsibility & under the same restraints from opinion, as any other of the acts of our lives. In no state of society but one in which opinions sanctions almost promiscuous intercourse (& in which therefore even the indissoluble bond is not practically regarded), would it be otherwise than disreputable to either party, the woman especially, to change frequently or on light grounds. My belief is that—in a tolerably moral state of society, the first choice would almost always, especially where it had produced children, be adhered to, unless in case of such uncongeniality of disposition as rendered it positively uncomfortable to one or both of the parties to live together, or in case of a strong passion conceived by one of them for a third person. Now in either of these cases I can conceive no argument strong enough to convince me, that the first connexion ought to be forcibly preserved.

I see not why opinion should not act as great efficacy, to enforce the true rules of morality in these matters, as the false. Robert Owen's definitions[3] of chastity & prostitution, are quite as simple & take as firm a hold of the mind as the vulgar ones which connect the ideas of virtue & vice with the performance or non-performance of an arbitrary ceremonial.

The arguments, therefore, in favour of the indissolubility of marriage, are as nothing in comparison with the far more potent arguments for leaving this like the other relations voluntarily contracted by human beings, to depend for its continuance upon the wishes of the contracting parties. The strongest of all these arguments is that by no other means can the condition & character of women become what it ought to be.

When women are merely slaves, to give them a permanent hold upon their masters was a first step towards their evolution. That step is now complete: & in the progress of civilization, the time has come when women may aspire to something more than merely to find a protector. The position of a single woman has ceased to be dangerous & precarious; & the law, & general opinion, suffice without any more special guardianship, to shield her in ordinary circumstances from insult or inquiry: woman in short is no longer a mere property, but a person who is counted not solely on her husband's or father's account but on her own. She is now ripe for equality. But it is absurd to talk of equality while marriage is an indissoluble tie. It was a change greatly for the better, from a state in which all the obligation was on the side of the weaker, all the rights on the side of the physically stronger, to even the present condition of an obligation nominally equal on both. But this nominal equality is not real equality. The stronger is always able to relieve himself wholly or in great measure, from as much of the obligation as he finds burthensome: the weaker cannot. The husband can ill-use his wife, neglect her, and seek other women, not perhaps altogether with impunity, but what are the penalties which opinion imposes on him compared with those which fall upon the wife who even with that provocation retaliates upon her husband? It is true perhaps that if divorce were permitted, opinion would with like injustice, try the wife who resorted to that remedy by a harder measure (?) than the husband. But this would be of less consequence: Once separated she would be comparatively independent of opinion: but so long as she is forcibly united to one of those who *make* the opinion, she must to a great extent be its slave.

Several scraps or drafts of Harriet Taylor on the same subject have been preserved of which the following is the most complete and may well be the one which in fulfilment of her promise she gave to Mill.[4]

If I could be Providence for the world for a time, for the express purpose of raising the condition of women, I should come to you to know the *means*—the *purpose* would be to remove all interference with affection, or with anything which is, or which even might be supposed to be, demonstrative of affection. In the present state of women's mind, perfectly uneducated, and with whatever of timidity & dependence is natural to them increased a thousand fold by their habit of utter dependence, it would probably be mischievous to remove at once all restraints, they would buy themselves protectors at a dearer cost than even at present—but without raising their natures at all. it seems to me that once give women the desire to raise their social condition, and they have a power which in the present state of civilization & of men's characters, might be made of tremendous effect. Whether nature made a difference in the nature of men &

women or not, it seems now that all men, with the exception of a few lofty minded, are sensualists more or less—women on the contrary are quite exempt from this trait, however it may appear otherwise in the cases of some. It seems strange that it should be so, unless it was meant to be a source of power in semi-civilized states such as the present—or it may not be so—it may be only that the habits of freedom & low indulgence on which boys grow up and the contrary notion of what is called purity in girls may have produced the appearance of different natures in the two sexes. As certain it is that there is equality in nothing now—all the pleasures such as they are being men's, & all the disagreeables & pains being women's, as that every pleasure w^d be infinitely heightened both in kind & degree by the perfect equality of the sexes. Women are educated for one single object, to gain their living by marrying—(some poor souls get it without the churchgoing. It's the same way—they do not seem to be a bit worse than their honoured sisters). To be married is the object of their existence and that object being gained they do really cease to exist as to anything worth calling life or any useful purpose. One observes very few marriages where there is any real sympathy or enjoyment or companionship between the parties. The woman knows what her power is and gains by it what she has been tought to consider 'proper' to her state. The woman who w^d gain power by such means is unfit for power, still they do lose (?) this power for paltry advantages and I am astonished it has never occurred to them to gain some large purpose; but their minds are degenerated by habits of dependance. I should think that 500 years hence none of the follies of their ancestors will so excite wonder and contempt as the fact of legislative restraints as to matters of feeling—or rather in the expression of feeling. When once the law undertakes to say which demonstration of feeling shall be given to which, it seems quite consistent not to legislate for *all*, and to say how many shall be seen & how many heard, & what kind & degree of feeling allows of shaking hands. The Turks' is the only consistent mode. I have no doubt that when the whole community is really educated, tho' the present laws of marriage were to continue they would be perfectly disregarded, because no one would marry. The wisest & perhaps the quickest means to do away with its evils is to be found in promoting education—as it is the means of all good—but meanwhile it is hard that those who suffer most from its evils and who are always the best people, should be left without remedy. Would not the best plan be divorce which could be attained by any *without any reason assigned*, and at small expence, but which could only be finally pronounced after a long period? not *less* time than two years should elapse between suing for divorce & permission to contract again—but what the decision will be must be certain at the moment of asking for it—unless during that time the suit should be withdrawn.

(I feel like a lawyer in talking of it only! O how absurd and little it all is!)

In the present system of habits & opinions, girls enter into what is called a contract perfectly ignorant of the conditions of it, and that they should be so is considered absolutely essential to their fitness for it!

But after all the one argument of the matter which I think might be said so as to strike both high & low natures is—who would wish to have the person without inclination? Whoever would take the benefit of a law of divorce must be those whose inclination is to separate and who on earth would wish another to remain with them against their inclination—I sh^d think no one—people sophisticate about the matter now & will not believe that one '*really would wish to go*'! Suppose instead of calling it a 'law of divorce' it were to be called 'Proof of affection'—they would like it better then.

At this present time, in this state of civilization, what evil could be caused by, first placing women on the most entire equality with men, as to all rights and privileges, civil and political, and then doing away with all laws whatever relating to marriage? Then if a woman had children she must take charge of them, women could not then have children without considering how to maintain them. Women would have no more reason to barter person for bread, or for anything else, than have men. Public offices being open to them alike, all occupations would be divided between the sexes in their natural arrangements. Fathers would provide for their daughters in the same manner as for their sons.

All the difficulties about divorce seem to be in the consideration for the children—but on this plan it would be the women's *interest* not to have children—now it is thought to be the woman's interest to have children as so many ties to the man who feeds her.

Love in its true and finest meaning, seems to be the way in which is manifested all that is highest best and beautiful in the nature of human beings—none but poets have approached to the perception of the beauty of the material world—still less of the spiritual—and hence never yet existed a poet, except by inspiration of that feeling which is the perception of beauty in all forms & by all means w^h are given us, as well as by *sight*. Are we not born with the *five* senses, merely as a foundation for others w^h we may make by them —and who extends and refines those material senses to the highest—into infinity—best fulfils the end of creation—that is only saying, *who enjoys most is most* virtuous. It is for *you*— the most worthy to be the apostle of all the highest virtues to teach such as may be tought, that the higher the *kind* of enjoyment, the *greater* the *degree*, perhaps there is but one class to whom this *can* be *tought*—the poetic nature struggling with superstition: you are fitted to be the saviour of such.

Chapter Four

FRIENDS AND GOSSIP
1834–1842

MUCH of the information we have about Mill and Harriet Taylor during the early years after their friendship had become intimate comes at second hand. For a few years in the middle of the 1830's they apparently made little attempt to conceal their intimacy until they became aware of the inevitable gossip which they had caused and withdrew almost completely from all social contacts. At that early stage Mill introduced Mrs. Taylor to a few friends, particularly the Carlyles, and it is from their numerous and in the later years not always too friendly comments that the now generally accepted picture of their relationship is mainly derived. It may be useful to interrupt the presentation of the new manuscript material and to bring together in a separate chapter the more important references by contemporaries.

The story told by John Roebuck, who for about ten years had been one of Mill's most intimate friends and who seems to have been the first with whom he broke completely on account of Mrs. Taylor, is characteristic. Roebuck had been present at the dinner party at which Mill first met Mrs. Taylor, but then lost sight of her until at a party at Mrs. Buller's, the mother of Mill's friend Charles Buller, he one day saw

'Mill enter the room with Mrs. Taylor hanging on his arm. The manner of the lady, the evident devotion of the gentleman, soon attracted universal attention, and a suppressed titter went round the

79

room. My affection for Mill was so warm and sincere that I was hurt by anything which brought ridicule upon him. I saw, or thought I saw, how mischievous might be this affair, and as we had become in all things like brothers, I determined, most unwisely, to speak to him on the subject.'[1]

Roebuck goes on to tell how he went to see Mill at India House to remonstrate with him, how Mill silently listened but by the reception he gave him on the next occasion made it clear that he regarded their friendship at an end.

We do not know precisely when this incident occurred, but by the spring of 1834 the connexion seems to have been freely talked about among Mill's friends. It was the first piece of gossip which the Carlyles then learnt on their return to London after two years' absence. They both in their inimitable ways at once passed on the news to Carlyle's brother in Italy, and then kept him abreast of developments when they themselves made the new acquaintance.

Thomas Carlyle to Dr. John Carlyle, May 1834:[2] Mrs. Austin had a tragical story of his [John Mill's] having fallen *desperately in love* with some young philosophic beauty (yet with the innocence of two sucking doves), and being lost to all his friends and to himself, and what not; but I traced nothing of this in poor Mill; and even incline to think that what truth there is or was in the adventure may have done him good. Buller also spoke of it, but in the comic vein.

Jane Carlyle to Dr. John Carlyle, May 1834: The most important item [of news learnt from Mrs. John Austin] was that a young Mrs. Taylor, tho' encumbered with a husband and children, has ogled John Mill successfully so that he was desperately in love.

Thomas Carlyle to Dr. John Carlyle, 22 July 1834:[3] Our most interesting new friend is a Mrs. Taylor, who came here for the first time yesterday, and stayed long. She is a living romance heroine, of the clearest insight, of the royalest volition, very interesting, of questionable destiny, not above twenty-five. Jane is to go and pass a day with her soon, being greatly taken with her.

Of course, Mrs. Taylor was nearly twenty-seven at the time. Apparently Jane went, and a fortnight later we get another report.

Thomas Carlyle to his Mother, 5 August 1834:[4] We have made, at least Jane has made, a most promising acquaintance, of a Mrs. Taylor; a young beautiful reader of mine and 'dearest friend' of Mill's, who for the present seems 'all that is noble' and what not. We shall see how that wears. We are to dine there on Tuesday and meet a new set of persons, said among other qualities, to be interested in *me*. The editor of the Fox Repository (Fox himself) is the main man I care for.

Thomas Carlyle to Dr. John Carlyle, 15 August 1834:[5] We dined with Mrs. (Platonica) Taylor and the Unitarian Fox (of the Repository if you know it) one day: Mill was also of the party, and the husband, an obtuse, most joyous natured man, the pink of social hospitality. Mrs. Taylor herself did not yield unmixed satisfaction, or receive it. She affects, with a kind of sultana noble-mindedness, a certain girlish petulance, and felt that it did not wholly prosper. We walked home, however, even Jane did, all the way from Regent's Park, and felt that we had done a duty. For me, from the Socinians, as I take it, *wird Nichts*. Here too let me wind up the Radical-Periodical Editorship[6] which your last letter naturally speculates upon. Mill I seem to discern has given it to this same Fox (who has just quitted his preachership and will, like myself, be out on the world); partly I should fancy by Mrs. Taylor's influence, partly as himself thinking him the safer man.

A few weeks later, on the 8th of September, the Carlyles set out to call on Mrs. Taylor, but before reaching her house he broke down on a seat in Regent's Park when[7] 'Mrs. Taylor with her husband make their appearance, walking; pale she, and passionate and sad-looking: really felt a kind of interest in her'.

When shortly afterwards *Sartor Resartus* appeared, a copy was presented to Mrs. Taylor by the author, whose interest in her was however not unmixed with concern for Mill.

Thomas Carlyle to Dr. John Carlyle, 28 October 1834:[8] Mill himself, who were the best of them all [of Mill's usual set] is greatly occupied of late times with a set of quite opposite character, which the Austins and other friends mourn much and fear much over. It is the fairest Mrs. Taylor you have heard of; with whom, under her husband's very eyes, he is (Platonically) over head and ears in love. Round her come Fox the Socinian and a flight of really wretched looking 'friends of the species', who (in writing and deed) struggle not in favour of Duty being *done*, but against Duty of any sort almost being *required*. A singular creed this; but I can assure you a very observable one here in these days: by me 'deeply hated as the GLAR,[9] which is its colour (die seine Farbe ist),' and substance likewise mainly. Jane and I often say: 'Before all mortals, beware of a friend of the species!' Most of these people are very indignant at marriage and the like; and frequently indeed are obliged to divorce their own wives, or be divorced: for though the *world* is already blooming (or is one day to do it) in everlasting 'happiness of the greatest number', these people's own *houses* (I always find) are little Hells of improvidence, discord, unreason. Mill is far above all that, and I think will not sink in it; however, I do wish him fairly far from it, and though I cannot speak of it directly would fain help him out: he is one of the best people I ever saw and—surprisingly attached to *me*, which is another merit.

At the beginning of the next year Mrs. Taylor appears again in the Carlyle letters.

Jane Welsh Carlyle to Dr. John Carlyle, 12 January 1835:[10] There is a Mrs. Taylor whom I could really love, if it were safe and she were willing; but she is a dangerous looking woman and engrossed with a dangerous passion, and no useful relation can spring up between us.

Thomas Carlyle to Alexander Carlyle, 27 February 1835:[11] The party we had at the Taylors' was most brisk, the cleverest (best gifted) I have been at for years: Mill, Charles Buller (one of the gayest, lightly sparkling, lovable souls in the world), *Repository* Fox (who *hotches*[12] and laughs at least), Fonblanque, the *Examiner* editor, were the main men. It does one good; though I buy it dear, dining so late: towards eight o'clock!

These friendly relations could not but be somewhat clouded by the famous incident which occurred a few days later, however admirable the spirit in which Carlyle at first bore the blow. Mill had shortly before borrowed the manuscript of the first volume of Carlyle's *French Revolution* and on 6 March had to go and break to Carlyle the news that the whole manuscript had been accidentally burnt. He arrived at the Carlyle's house in the evening in a carriage with Mrs. Taylor and rushing up the steps alone at first merely begged Mrs. Carlyle to go down and speak to Mrs. Taylor. Although it is probably later embroidery that on first seeing the carriage Mrs. Carlyle exclaimed to her husband, 'Gracious Providence, he has gone off with Mrs. Taylor',[13] this seems indeed to have been so much the first thought of both the Carlyles that they appear to have been curiously relieved when they learnt the true reason for the visit. After Mrs. Taylor drove off Mill sat with the Carlyles until late at night while they did what they could to assure him that the loss was not too serious. Later, however, they seem to have conceived the idea that Mrs. Taylor was responsible for the destruction of the manuscript and their various hints to that effect[14] were later exaggerated by others into the scarcely veiled allegation that Mrs. Taylor had deliberately destroyed it. Any suggestion that Mrs. Taylor was responsible for the accident seems however to be clearly disproved by the very letter of Mill's in which he told Carlyle that Mrs. Taylor had also seen the manuscript and which appears to have been the basis for their later suspicions. Mill, the most truthful of persons, would certainly not have written as he did a few days after the catastrophe in refusing Carlyle's good-natured offer to lend him the manuscript of part of the second volume of the *French Revolution*, 'provided you durst take it'.[15]

J. S. M. to Thomas Carlyle, 10 March 1835[16]: I will not take the Fête des Piques—not that I believe such a thing could possibly happen again, but for the sake of retributive justice

I would bear the badge of my untrustworthiness. If however you would give me the pleasure of reading it give it to Mrs. Taylor—in her custody no harm could come to it—and I can read it aloud to her as I did much of the other—for it had not only the *one* reader you mention but a second just as good.

Carlyle, however, seems not to have accepted this suggestion and Mill to have seen no more in manuscript. For a while cordial relations continued not only with Mill but also with Mrs. Taylor.[17] But after 1835 Mrs. Taylor's illness and absence from town during the greater part of the year prevented much further contact and perhaps there also occurred about that time a definite clash between the two ladies which strained the relations. Something like that at least is suggested in Carlyle's *Reminiscences* when he says that Mrs. Taylor had

'at first considered my Jane to be a rustic spirit fit for rather tutoring and twirling about when the humour took her; but got taught better (to her lasting memory) before long.'[18]

Mill's regular visits and Sunday walks with Carlyle, however, continued for some years. In the spring of 1836 we find Mrs. Carlyle greatly concerned about the news of two of their 'dearest friends' John Mill and John Sterling being 'dangerously ill'.[19] A little later, soon after James Mill's death and shortly before Mill left for France in the summer of the same year, Carlyle visited the Mills at their summer house in Mickleham near Dorking in Surrey and sent a full report to his wife in Scotland.

Thomas Carlyle to Jane Welsh Carlyle, Chelsea, 24 July 1836:[20] There was little sorrow visible in their house, or rather none, nor any human feeling at all; but the strangest *unheimlich* kind of composure and acquiescence, as if all human spontaneity had taken refuge in invisible corners. Mill himself talked much, and not stupidly—far from that— but without emotion of any discernible kind. He seemed to me withered into the miserablest metaphysical *scrae*,[21] body and mind, that I had almost ever met with in the world. His eyes go twinkling and jerking with wild lights and twitches; his head is bald, his face brown and dry—poor fellow after all. It seemed to me the strangest thing what this man could want with me, or I with such a man so *unheimlich* to me. What will become of it? Nothing evil; for there is and there was nothing dishonest in it. But I think I shall see less and less of him. Alas, poor fellow! It seems possible too that he may not be very long seeable: that is one way of its ending.

It is difficult to remember that Mill, of whom Carlyle here speaks, had only a few weeks before completed his thirtieth birthday. Mrs. Carlyle's reply to this deserves also to be quoted.

Jane Welsh Carlyle to Thomas Carlyle, 2 August 1836:[22] Poor Mill! He really seems to have '*loved and lived*'; his very intellect seems to be failing him in its strongest point:—his implicit admiration and subjection to you.

For a time after Mill's departure what news Carlyle had about his movements on the Continent came at second hand and Carlyle lost no time in passing on the gossip which made the round.

Thomas Carlyle to John Sterling, 3 October 1836:[23] Mill, they say, writes from Nice: he is not going into Italy, owing to the Cholera and quarantine: his health is little, and but a little, improved. Mrs. Taylor, it is whispered, is with him, or near him. Is it not strange, this pining away into dessication and nonentity, of our poor Mill, if it be so, as his friends all say, that his charmer is the cause of it? I have not seen any riddle of human life which I could so ill form a theory of. They are innocent says Charity: they are guilty says Scandal: then why in the name of wonder are they dying broken-hearted? One thing only is painfully clear to me, that poor Mill is in a bad way. Alas, tho' he speaks not, perhaps his tragedy is more tragical than that of any of us: this very item that he does not speak, that he never could speak, but was to sit imprisoned as in the thick ribbed ice, voiceless, uncommunicating, is it not the most tragical circumstance of all?

Six days later, however, a long and friendly letter was despatched by Carlyle to Mill at Nice on the urging of their common friend Horace

Grant.[24] On Mill's return in November close contacts were promptly resumed and for another year or so, mainly in connexion with the *London and Westminster Review*, continued fairly regular if less cordial than before.

Thomas Carlyle to John Sterling, 17 January 1837:[25] John Mill, as perhaps you know, is home again, in better health, still not in good. I saw him the day before yesterday, sitting desolate under an *Influenza* we all have. I on the whole see little of him. He toils greatly in his Review; sore bested with mismanaging Editors, Radical discrepancies, and so forth. His *Platonica* and he are constant as ever: innocent I do believe as sucking doves, and yet suffering the clack of tongues, worst penalty of guilt. It is very hard; and for Mill especially as unlucky as ever. The set of people he is in is one I have to keep out of. No class of mortals ever profited me less. There is a vociferous platitude in them, a mangy hungry discontent,—their very joy like that of a thing scratching itself under disease of the itch! Mill was infinitely too good for them; but he would have it, and his fate would. I love him much, as a friend *frozen within ice* for me.

In 1838 they evidently drifted apart.[26] When Mill left again for Italy at the end of that year he seems to have given the Carlyles as his other friends to understand that he was going to Malta, but as both Carlyle's brother John and John Sterling were at Rome[27] at the time and seem to have seen Mill, the pretence, if kept up at all, cannot have been effective for long. Though Carlyle, once more at the urging of Horace Grant, sends a long epistle to Rome,[28] his comments to Sterling when he meets Mill some time after the latter had returned are in a changed tone.

Thomas Carlyle to John Sterling, 29 September 1839:[29] Mill, whom I had not seen till that day (before yesterday) at the India House, was looking but indifferently; he confessed not to be sensibly better at all by his last year's journeying. Mrs. Taylor he further volunteered to tell me, is not living in the old abode in the Regent's Park, but in Wilton Place, a street where as I conjecture there are mainly wont to be *Lodgings*. Can it be possible? Or if so, what does it betoken. I am truly sorry for Mill: he has been a most luckless man since I came hither, seeming to himself all the way to be a lucky one rather.

This is a rather bad instance of careless gossip on the part of Carlyle. It is true that after her return from Italy Mrs. Taylor lived for a time at 24 Wilton Place, Belsize Square. But so did Mr. Taylor.[30] They had probably either let or closed their house in Kent Terrace because of Mrs. Taylor's long absence, or the house was merely being redecorated. There is no sign whatever that in town Mrs. Taylor ever lived apart from her husband, although of course her stays in her husband's house seem to have been little more than occasional visits between her sojourns in the country.

In 1841 Mill appears to have sent to Carlyle Sarah Flower Adams' drama *Vivia Perpetua* with a request to express his opinion on it to Mrs. Taylor, but before Carlyle can write to her he has to enquire from Mill her address.[31] In the following year Mrs. Taylor approached Carlyle in a different matter.

H. T. to Thomas Carlyle:[32] Walton, July 9 (1842)/Dear Mr. Carlyle/I am going to ask you to do for me what if you consent to, I shall feel to be a great favour.

It is to be trustee to a little settlement made at the time of my marriage upon me & upon the children. of the present two trustees, one, a Mr. Travers, a brother in law of Mr. Taylor's, is going to leave England to live abroad & I am anxious to have the vacancy filled so that I shall leave this portion of my young ones interests in the surest hands. Au reste it is a very simple matter & could in no way cause any trouble or inconvenience, otherwise I should hardly feel entitled to ask it. May I hope that you will not disappoint me in this?

Dear Mr. Carlyle

Most truly y[rs]

H. Taylor

Pray present my kind regards to Mrs. Carlyle. Mr. Taylor joins in this request and proposes to take an early opportunity for calling at Chelsea to make it in person.

In reply to this and to Mr. Taylor's personal appeal Carlyle could truthfully plead in a letter of four days later that Mrs. Taylor could not find 'any person, possessed of common sense and arrived at years of discretion, who is so totally unacquainted with every form of what is called Business' as he himself was.[33] To make sure that he would escape the unwelcome burden he offered to walk over from Richmond to her house at Walton to talk the matter over. This produced an invitation and Carlyle together with Mill spent two days at Walton.[34]

Although a few more notes were exchanged between Mill and Carlyle after this, and an inscribed copy of *Past and Present* was sent by the author to Mrs. Taylor when it appeared in 1843,[35] the relations seem to have become very superficial even before at last some of Carlyle's talk about them came to their ears. In October 1846 the break became open: when Carlyle went to call on Mill at India House to ask him to a dinner he was giving in honour of an American visitor, and met Mill on the way in the street, 'he received me like the very incarnation o' the East Wind, and refused my invitation peremptorily.'[36] That seems for many years to have been the end of their regular intercourse.[37] After Mill's marriage some superficial contacts appear to have been resumed and even the two ladies once more to have met. At least Mrs. Carlyle's last recorded comment on Mrs. Mill seems to refer to some date after the Mills were married. In a conversation with Gavan Duffy in 1851 she described Mrs. Mill as

'a peculiarly affected and empty body. She is not easy unless she startles you with unexpected sayings. If she was going to utter something kind and affectionate, she speaks in a hard, stern voice. If she wants to be alarming or uncivil, she employs the most honeyed and affectionate tones. "Come down to see us" she said one day (*mimicking her tone*), "You will be charmed with our house, it is so full of rats." "Rats!" cried Carlyle, "Do you regard *them* as an attraction?" "Yes" (*piano*), "They are such dear, innocent creatures." '[38]

Carlyle never seems to have quite understood that it had been his unrestrained talk about Mill and Mrs. Taylor which had caused the estrangement, and even many years later his remarks to C. E. Norton when he received the news of Mill's death show that he only half suspected what was undoubtedly the truth:

'Many's the time I've thought o' writin' to him and sayin' "John Mill, what is it that parts you and me?" But that's all over now. Never could I think of the least thing, unless maybe it was this. One year the brother o' that man Cavaignac who was ruler for a time in France,— Godefroi Cavaignac, a man o' more capacity than his brother,—was over here from Paris, an' he told me o' meeting Mill and Mrs. Taylor somewhere in France not long before, eatin' grapes together off o' one bunch, like two love birds. And his description amused me, and I repeated it, without thinking any harm, to a man who was not always to be trusted, [Charles Buller], a man who made trouble with his tongue, and I've thought he might perhaps have told it to Mill, and that Mill might have fancied that I was making a jest o' what was most sacred to him; but I don't know if it was it, but it was the only thing I could ever think of that could ha' hurt him.[39]

Carlyle's letters show that this was probably not the only occasion when he had talked rather freely on the matter. It seems at any rate that at some time in the middle 'forties Mill and Mrs. Taylor had suddenly become aware of the talk that was going on about them and not only broke radically with all those whom they suspected of gossip but altogether withdrew from society. To have offended in this con-nexion was the one thing that Mill never forgave. His intimate motherly friend Sarah Austin, who had taught him German when he was fifteen and whom for twenty years afterwards he had regularly addressed in his frequent letters as his *Liebes Mütterlein*, he seems to have regarded, probably with some justification, as the chief offender. She was not only well known as a gossip but also in a special position to know since for some years the Austins had lived at Regent's Park with their garden adjoining that of the Taylors and separated from it only by a hedge through which the children were constantly creeping.[40] In her case the ban was so complete that the mere fact that the Austins had come to live in the neighbourhood was in 1848 sufficient reason for Mrs. Taylor not wishing again to go to Walton.[41] Even after his wife's death, in 1859, when John Austin died, Mill could still not bring himself to write to her an ordinary letter of condolence but wrote instead to her granddaughter Janet Duff Gordon (a girl of seventeen living at the time with Mrs. Austin), who later described how 'the evidently intentional slight cut her to the heart'.[42]

Another old acquaintance who had even better grounds for knowing the whole history of the relationship and who talked freely about it, Harriet Martineau, became the object of Mill's most intense dislike. Two other ladies who at one time had known Mill well, Mrs. Grote and Harriet Baring (Lady Ashburton), fared not much better. And a number of other persons appear for the same reason to have been placed under a complete ban.

Chapter Five

THE YEARS OF FRIENDSHIP
1834–1847

THE survey of the accounts given by contemporaries has led us far beyond the date at which we interrupted the presentation of the main documents. We must return to the time when, after Harriet Taylor's return from Paris, some new *modus vivendi* was agreed between her and her husband. It seems not probable, however, that the more stable form which her relationship to Mill ultimately assumed was at once found. The few fragments of correspondence which we have for the years immediately following this return give glimpses of recurring internal and external difficulties. Very few of the notes which seem to belong to the next two or three years can be dated with certainty. But what is probably the earliest happens to be dated.

H. T. to J. S. M. (?), 20 February 1834:[1] Happiness has become to me a word without meaning—or rather the meaning of the word has no existence in my belief. I mean by Happiness the state wh I can remember to have been in when I consciously used the word—a state of satisfaction, by *satisfaction* meaning not *only* the *mind made up*, not only having *conviction* of some sort on every large subject, but *cheerful* hopeful *faith* about all wh I could contemplate and not understand & this along with the great & conscious enjoyment from my own emotions and sensations—that

91

happiness I had often a year ago—I believe that if the world were as well directed as human beings might direct it, & may be expected to direct it, that all might be *Happy*, in proportion to their capacity for Happiness & that those with *great* capacity might be actually happy—live in a satisfied state, without need for more but with, for their *forward* view, a placid contemplation of the probability of still greater capacity in some other existence—I do not believe I shall ever again feel that—the *most* this world can do for me is to give present enjoyment sufficient to make me forget that there is nothing else worth seeking—for the great mass of peoples I think wisdom would be to make the utmost of sensation while they are young enough & then die—for the very few who seem to have an innate incomprehensible capacity of emotion, more enjoyable than any sensation but consistent (?) with & adding to all pleasurable sensation for *such if* such there be wh. I greatly doubt, *their* wisdom like the others is to *live out* their pleasures & die—*now* I believe that such being w^d not c^d not live out those enjoyments but that I think is because they come to them late thro' struggle & suffering generally, wh gives an artificial depth and tenacity to their feeling, for those who come to such feelings at all are those of the most imagination—& so hold them firmest. I do not believe *affection* to be natural to human beings—it is an instinct of the lower animals for their young—but in humans it is a made up combination of feelings & associations wh will cease to exist when artificiality ceases to exist. only passion is natural that is temporary affection—but what we call affection will continue so long as there is dependance.

During the next few months some passages of Mill's letters to W. J. Fox give us some indication of the prevailing state of affairs. The other two members of the group mentioned in the first were probably Eliza and Sarah Flower.

J. S. M. to W. J. Fox, about April 1834:[2] I hope we shall meet oftener—we four or rather five—as we did on Tuesday

I have been made most uncomfortable
all day by your dear letter sweet & loving
as it was dearest one – because of your
having had that pain – & because of
my having given you pain. You cannot
imagine dearest how very much it grieves
me now when even a small thing goes wrong
now that thank heaven it does not often
happen so, & therefore always happens
unexpectedly. As for my saying "do not let us
talk of that now" & I have not the remotest
recollection of my having said so, or what it was
that I did not want to talk about – but
I am sure that it was something which I
considered to bee settled & done with long ago,
& therefore not worth talking any more about,

a reason which you yourself so continually
express ~~as your reason~~ for not explaining
to me or telling me about impressions of yours
the uncertainty about the nature of which is
tormenting me — & I have latterly learnt
sufficient selfsacrifice, sometimes to yield to
that feeling, & ~~never~~ leave off asking you
questions which you tell me it is unpleasant
to you to answer. But whatever it was
that we were talking about on the common
I am sure if I had thought that anything
remained to be said about it, much more
if I had thought that such a matter as
whether we ~~could~~ can or cannot be in complete
sympathy, had depended on what remained
unsaid, I should have been a great deal
more anxious to have ~~the whole subject~~ everything said,
than you would have been to say it.
O my own love, if you were beginning to
say something which you had been
thinking of for days or weeks, why did

you not tell me so? Why did you not
make me feel that you were saying what
was important to you, & what had not
been said or had not been exhausted
before? I am writing you know in complete
ignorance about what it was — but I am
sure I have tormented you enough & long enough
by refusing to acquiesce in your seemingly
determined resolution that there should be
radical differences of some sort in some of
our beliefs. & now having found, & convinced
you, that there are none that need make
us unhappy, I have learnt from you to be
able to bear that there should be some — consisting
chiefly in the want of some feelings in me which
you have. But I thought we perfectly knew
& understood what those were, & that neither
of us saw any good in discussing them further.
& when I ask you questions which you do not
like to answer, ~~know were~~ it is only
to know what is paining you at the time —

not meaning to discuss feelings any more if it is feelings & not facts that are annoying you

I know darling it is very doubtful if you will get this before I see you – but I cannot help writing it & perhaps I shall feel easier afterwards. at present I feel utterly unnerved & quite unfit for thinking or writing or any business – but I shall get better. & dont let it make you uncomfortable mine own –

o you dear one

my own adored one!

—I do not see half enough of you—and I do not, half enough, see *anybody* along with her—*that* I think is chiefly what is wanting now—that, and other things like it.

J. S. M. to W. J. Fox, 26 June 1834:[3] Our affairs have been gradually getting into a more & more unsatisfactory state— and are now in a state which, a very short time ago, would have made me quite miserab[le] but now I am altogether in a higher state than I was & better able to conquer evil & to bear it. I will tell you all about it some day—perhaps the first time we meet—but by that time perhaps the atmosphere will be clearer.—adieu—

I have not spoken to you about our affairs lately, as I did while she was away; partly because I did not need so much to give confidence & ask support when she was with me, partly because I know you disapprove & cannot enter with the present relation between her & me & him. but a time perhaps is coming when I shall need your kindness more than ever—if so, I know I shall always have it.

The remaining notes exchanged between Mill and Mrs. Taylor which seem to belong to this time must be given in a more or less arbitrary order.

J. S. M. to H. T.:[4] I have been made most uncomfortable all day by your dear letter sweet & loving as it was dearest one—because of your having had that pain—& because of my having given you pain. You cannot imagine dearest how very much it grieves me now when even a small thing goes wrong now that thank heaven it does not often happen so, & therefore always happens unexpectedly. As for my saying 'do not let us talk of that now' I have not the remotest recollection of my having said so, or what it was that I did not want to talk about—but I am sure that it was something which I considered to be settled & done with long ago, & therefore not worth talking any more about, a reason which you yourself so continually express for not explaining to me or telling me about impressions of yours, uncertainty about the nature of which is tormenting me—& I have latterly learnt sufficient selfsacrifice, sometimes to yield to that feeling, & leave off asking you questions which you tell me it is unpleasant to you to answer. But whatever it was that we were talking about on the common I am sure if I had thought that anything remained to be said about it, much more if I had thought that such a matter as whether we can or cannot be in *complete* sympathy, had depended on what remained unsaid, I should have been a great deal more anxious to have everything said, than you would have been to say it. O my own love, if you were beginning to say something which you had been thinking for days or weeks, why did you not tell me so? why did you not make me feel that you were saying what was important to you, & what had not been said or had not been exhausted before? I am writing you in complete ignorance about what it was—but I am sure that I have tormented you enough & long enough by refusing to acquiesce in your seemingly determined resolution that there *should be* radical differences of some sort in some of our feelings, and now having found (?), & convinced you, that there are none that need make us unhappy, I have learnt from you to be able to bear that there should be some—consisting chiefly in the want of some feelings in me which you have. But I thought we perfectly knew & understood what those were, & that neither of us saw any good in discussing them further—& when I ask you questions which you do not like to answer, it is only to know what is paining you at the time—not meaning to discuss feelings any more if it is feelings and not facts that are annoying you.

I know darling it is very doubtful if you will get this before I see you—but I cannot help writing it & perhaps I shall feel easier afterwards. at present I feel utterly unnerved & quite unfit for thinking or writing or any business—but I shall get better, & don't let it make you uncomfortable mine own— o you dear one.

Below the last four words which Mill had enclosed between two lines at the foot of his letter there is a further line in Harriet Taylor's hand: 'my *own adored* one!'.

H. T. to J. S. M.:[5] I don't know why I was so low when you went this morning. I was so LOW I could not bear your going my darling one: yet I should be well enough accustomed to it by now. O you dear one! dear one!

They are not coming to-day nor at all at present & I am not sorry for it. I shall get on very well, I have no doubt until Thursday comes & *you*. I wish tomorrow were Thursday, but I do not wish you were coming before Thursday because I know it would be so much harder to bear afterwards.

If I knew where at Sevenoaks L[izzie] & Sallie are I would go in the chaise & see them. but that will do any time.

Be well & happy dearest—but *well* before everything. dearest I cannot express the sort of degout I feel whenever there comes one of those sudden cessation of life—my only spiritual life—being much with you—but never mind—it is all well & right & very happy as it is. only I long unspeakably for Saturday. This place is very lovely but it both looks & feels to me quite lifeless. farewell Darling mine.

H. T. to J. S. M.:[6] This is one thing so perfectly admirable to me, that you never in any mood, doubt the worth of enjoyment or the need of happiness—one less fine w^d undervalue what he had not reached. does not this prove that you have the poetic principle? for me my hope is so living and healthy that it is not possible to me to doubt that it will increase more and more until it assumes some new and higher form—going on towards perfection.

Those words yesterday were *cold* and distancing, *very*, at *first*. Do you not know what it is to receive, with an *impulse* of thankfulness and joy and comfort, the packet which proves at first sight only a collection of *minerals*—one feels somewhat like a *mineral*—but this comes and must come from the uncongenial circumstances—the circumstances wh *tend* to

95

elate or to despond do not come at the same time to both—
and tho' such things in no degree *alter* ones mind, they *have*
their effect in deciding which state of mind shall be for the
time uppermost—and always will have as long as it pleases
Heaven to endow us with a body and senses.

Yes—dearest friend—things as they are now—bring to
me, besides *moments* of quite complete happiness, a *life* &
how infinitely to be preferred before all I ever knew! I never
for an instant could wish that this had never been on my own
account, and only on yours if you c^d think so—but why do I
say *mine* & *yours*, what is good for the one must be so for the
other & will be so always—*you* say so—& whatever of sadness there may sometimes be, is only the proof of how much
happiness there *is* by proving the capacity for so much more.

You say that what you think virtue, 'the wise and good'
who have long known and respected you, wont think vice—
How can you think people wise, with such opposite notions?
You say too that when those who profess different principles
to the vulgar, *act* their principles, they make all worse whom
they do not make better & I understand you to believe that
they would make many worse and few better in your own
case—Is not this then the 'thinking with the wise and acting
with the vulgar' principle? And does not this imply compromise & insincerity? *You* cannot mean that, for that is both
base & weak—if made a rule and not an occasional hard
necessity.

I was not *quite* wrong in thinking you feared opinions—I
never supposed you dreaded the opinions of fools but only of
those who are otherwise wise & good but have not your
opinions about [?].

Two more notes by Mrs. Taylor are both on paper watermarked
1835 and were probably written in that or the following year.

H. T. to J. S. M.:[1] Tuesday evening/Dearest—You do
not know me—or perhaps more truly you do not know the

best of me—I am not one to 'create chimeras about nothing'
—you should know enough about the effects of petty annoy-
ances to know that they are wearing & depressing not only
to body but to mind—these, on account of our relation, I
have & you have not—& these make me morbid—but I can
say most clearly & surely that I am *never* so without being
perfectly conscious of being so—that I always know that in a
better state of health all those morbid & weakly feelings &
views & thoughts would go. So far from your two instances
being like this—those women took the life with the men they
loved at once as a desperate throw without knowing anything
of those men's characters—if I had done that do you think
that I should not have been blindly devoted? of course I
should—in such a case the woman has absolutely nothing to
make life of but blind implicit devotion—it is not true that
my character is 'the extreme of anxiety and uneasiness'—if
my circumstances do not account to you for all or more of
anxiety & uneasiness which I show to you, why there is
nothing to be said about that—you do not know the natural
effect of those circumstances. If it is true that so long as you
concealed your feelings from me for fear of paining me, I can
only say I am sorry for it because I know you too well not to
know that no real feelings of yours would ever pain me. Then
as to your inquiring of how I should like that you sh^d go for
a walk without me I can only say that I am not a fool & I
should laugh at, or very much dislike the thought, that you
sh^d make your 'life obscure insignificant & useless' pour les
beaux yeux & I cannot think it was consistent with love to be
able to think or wish that. If it is true, & I suppose you know
yourself, that then 'you would never speak a true word again'
never 'express natural liking' never 'dare to be silent or tired'
why I can but say that if you would take such a life as that
you must be mad. That one *might* never be wholly satisfied
with the finite is possible but I do not believe that I sh^d ever
show that—I think it would & must be true of persons of
intellect & cultivation without acute feelings—but I have

always observed where there is strong feeling the interests of feeling are always paramount (?) & it seems to me that personal feeling has more of infinity in it than any other part of character—no ones *mind* is *ever* satisfied, nor their imagination nor their ambition—nor anything else of that class—but feeling *satisfies*—All the qualities on earth never give happiness without personal feeling—personal feeling always gives happiness with or without any other character (?). The desire to give & to receive feeling is almost the whole of my character.

With the calmest, coldest view I believe that my feeling to you would be enough for my whole life—but of course only if I were conscious of having a good feeling.

I have always seen & balanced in my mind all these considerations that you write about therefore they do not either vex or pain me. I know *all about* all these chances—but I know too what you do not, but what I have always told you, that once having accepted that life I should make the very best of it. I used long ago to think that in that case I would have occasional fits of the deepest depression, but that they would not affect *our* happiness, as I should not let you see them—for long now I have been past thinking that. I shall always show you & tell you *all* that I feel. I always do, & the fact that I do so proves to me that I should have but little that was painful to show. as to the rash & blind faith & devotion of those women you instance look at the result to them! & that is the natural result of such an engagement entered into in that way. If when first I knew you I had given up all other life to be with you *I* sh^d gradually have found if *not* that you did not love me as I thought at least that you were different to what I had thought & so been disappointed —there would never be disappointment now. I do not know if 'such a life never succeeds' I feel quite sure that it would succeed in our case. You may be quite sure that if I once take that life it will be *for good*.

With not only all that you write—but more *all* that can be

said, fully before me I should without hesitation say '*let it be*',
I do not hesitate about the certainty of happiness—but I do
hesitate about the rightfulness of, for my own pleasure, giving up *my* only earthly opportunity of 'usefulness'. *You* hesitate about your usefulness & that however greater in amount
it may be, is certainly not like mine *marked out* as duty. I
should spoil four lives & injure others. This is the only
hesitation. When I am in health & spirits I see the possibili-
ties of getting over this hesitation. When I am low & ill I see
the improbabilities. Now I give pleasure around me, I make
no one unhappy, & I am happy tho' not happiest myself. I
think any systematic middle plan between this & all impracticable. I am much happier not seeing you continually here,
because then I have habitually enough to make me able to
always be wishing for more, when I have that more rarely it
is in itself an object & a *satisfaction*.

I think you have got more interest in all social interests
than you used to have, & I think you can be satisfied as I can
at present perhaps with occasional meeting—but then for
every moment of my life you are my one sole interest &
object & I would at any instance give up all, were it ten
thousand times as much, rather than have the chance of one
iota of diminution of your love.

This scrawl literally in the greatest haste—because you
said write—but in the morn I shall see you. *mine*.

H. T. to J. S. M.:[3] Wednesday/Dear one—if the feeling
of this letter of yours were your *general* or even *often* state of
mind it would be very unfortunate for—may I say *us*—for
me at all events. Nothing I believe could make me love you
less but certainly I should not admire one who could feel in
this way except from mood. Good heaven have you at last
arrived at fearing to be '*obscure & insignificant*'! What *can* I
say to that but 'by all means pursue your brilliant and important career'. Am *I* one to choose to be the cause that the
person I love feels himself reduced to 'obscure & insignifi-

cant'! Good God what has the love of two equals to do with making obscure & insignificant. if ever you *could* be obscure & insignificant you *are* so whatever happens & certainly a person who did not feel contempt at the very idea the words create is not one to brave the world. I never before (for years) knew you to have a mesquin feeling. It is a horrible want of unanimity between us—I know what the root (?) is, I have not the least desire either to brave it or to court it—in no possible circumstances sh^d I ever do either—those imply some *fellow-feeling* with it & that I have only in case I could do it or any individual of it any good turn—then I should be happy for the time to be at one with it—but it is to me as tho' it did not exist as to any ability to hurt me—it could not & I never could feel at variance with it. how I long to walk by the sea with you & hear you tell me the whole truth about your feelings of this kind. There seems a touch of Common Place vanity in that dread of being obscure & insignificant— you will never be that—& still more surely *I* am not a person who in any event could give you cause to feel that *I* had made you so Whatever you think I could never be either of those words.

I am not either *exceedingly* hurt by your saying that I am an anxious and uneasy character. I know it is false and I shall pity you if . . .[9]

From the winter of 1835–6 illness becomes a constant feature in the lives both of Mill and Mrs. Taylor, never again quite to disappear. Mrs. Taylor appears to have been in delicate health even for some time before this, but the first references to this occur only about that time: 'She is well, that is as well as she ever is,' wrote Mill to W. J. Fox on 2 February 1836,[10] adding that he himself was still out of health. He had been suffering from a nervous head complaint affecting his eyes since the end of the preceding year and his family and his friends seem to have attributed this to the continued emotional strain. His father, already confined at home by his last illness, wrote on 9 March 1836 to his younger son James, who shortly before had left for India, that 'John is still in a rather pining way; though as he does not choose to tell the cause of his pining, he leaves other people to their conjecture.'[11] That the suspected cause was avoided by the family as a subject of conversation is only too likely from the story told by Bain that James Mill, on learning of John's connexion with Mrs. Taylor, had 'taxed him with being in love with another man's wife. He replied, he had no other feelings towards her, than he would have towards an equally able man. The answer was unsatisfactory, but final.'[12]

At the same time it seems that the heavy burden of work which John Mill had carried for years and continued to impose upon himself provides a sufficient explanation for the breakdown of his health. Just then the absence of his father from India House had thrown still more work on him after for a year, in addition to his normal activities, he had acted as editor of the new *London Review* and in consequence of the inefficiency of his subordinate, the nominal editor,[13] had had to run the journal practically single-handed. For some time he tried to get over his illness by allowing himself occasional short breaks, such as an excursion to Gravesend with Carlyle, at which, as the latter tells us, Mill hoped 'to go and "get better" (in six and thirty hours) at a place out there; and would not go without me'.[14] Later in the spring however he was forced to spend some weeks at Brighton, from where he was apparently brought back by the approaching death of his father. James Mill died on 23 June and we have seen how sadly changed Carlyle found Mill's appearance shortly afterwards. Soon he was ordered away for three months by his doctor and at the end of July he took his two young brothers Henry and George to the Continent. In Paris they met Mrs. Taylor with her son Herbert and probably also the two younger children, who had travelled two days ahead of them. To the first reports which George and Henry Mill sent home to their sisters John added a few lines on the same sheet.

J. S. M. to Clara Mill, Paris, 3 August 1836:[15] One having written to W[illie] & one to H[arriet] I must write to Clara —so here goes—We are all quite as well, perhaps rather better than was to be expected. George & Henry do not seem at all struck with Paris—they are I think too young to care much about it or to be impressed by it at all. They seemed pleased with the country, & on the whole the excursion has been hitherto tolerably successful. But the only piece of thorough solid delight that George seemed to have was in meeting with a playfellow about his own size[16] whom he likes & who likes him very much. Nothing is settled yet about our travelling further—it is not finally settled whether we shall go alone or with our friends here, much less when we shall go & how—the places are all taken by the diligence for nearly a week to come, & posting so far is very expensive —but we shall see. One thing seems certain—that both Derry & I can stand travelling. we have not tried any night work to be sure yet. we will write again from Geneva.

ever affectionately yours

J. S. M.

The two parties proceeded to Geneva and Lausanne where Henry and George Mill and probably the Taylor children remained while Mill and Mrs. Taylor went on to Northern Italy. As they left Lausanne his brothers reported home that[17] 'his head is most obstinate; those same disagreeable sensations still, which he has tried so many ways to get rid of, are plaguing him'. Three weeks later Henry passes on news received from Italy:[18] 'John wrote us a very desponding letter, saying that if he had to go back without getting well, he could not again go to the India House, but must throw it up, and try if a year or two of leisure would do anything.' After spending two months in Piedmont and on the bay of Genoa, and after they had been prevented from going further south by the quarantine imposed because of an outbreak of cholera, John Mill and Mrs. Taylor returned to Switzerland via Milan and the Italian lakes. At the end of October they picked up the children at Lausanne, and early in November[19] Mill at least was back in London and at his work at India House, in only slightly better health and with his head in particular no better than before. It was from this time that 'he retained to the end of his life an almost ceaseless spasmodic twitching over one eye'.[20]

For some months after his return Mill was exceedingly busy working up arrears at India House. He had been absent in effect for five months and during his absence had been promoted, on the death of his father, to the third place in the Examiner's Office. His salary had in consequence risen to £1,200 a year, the figure at which it remained for the next eighteen years.

But most of Mill's energies during the little over two years which separate this from the next long Continental journey were devoted to the editorship of the *London and Westminster Review*. The death of his father had made it possible for him to free it from the all too close connexion with the more doctrinaire type of Utilitarianism and to use it as a vehicle for inspiring into the Radical movement his own somewhat different ideals. Especially in 1838, after he had bought the *Review* from Sir William Molesworth and when he devoted it largely to the support of Lord Durham's Canadian mission, in the hope that Lord Durham would become the leader of a new Radical movement, his interests were more deeply engaged in current politics than almost at any other period of his life, excepting only the years of the Reform agitation.

There can be little doubt that Mrs. Taylor interested herself in Mill's editorial activities but there is little evidence to show how far this interest went. That she was currently reputed to exercise some influence on the policy of the *Review* appears from the story told by Mrs. Carlyle that their friend Godefroy Cavaignac used to call Mrs. Taylor 'the Armida of the "London and Westminster".'[21] Cavaignac, the elder brother of General Louis Cavaignac, was then living in London as a refugee and probably contributed to the *Review* and thus presumably knew why he compared Mrs. Taylor to the beautiful enchantress of Tasso's *Gerusalemme Liberata* who estranged crusading knights from their duty and who to that generation had become a familiar figure through the operas of Gluck and Rossini. But the only document referring to Mrs. Taylor's connexion with the *Review* is a letter of hers to her husband, answering an inquiry on behalf of some of his Italian friends. John Taylor, who had introduced Mazzini to Carlyle in the preceding year,[22] seems to have continued to exert himself on his behalf and for other political refugees, and on one of his visits to his wife in the neighbourhood of London to have charged her with an inquiry in their interest. On the next day, a Saturday, when Mill probably arrived, Mrs. Taylor replied.

H. T. to John Taylor, 23 September 1837:[23] My dear John,/I find that Usilio's[24] article is to be in the next number of the 'London'—Robertson it seems meets the contributors at the publishers Hooper Pall Mall—& Mr. Mill went in there as he passed a day or two since & found both Usilio & Mazzini there with Robertson—he had a good deal of talk

with both of them & liked both very much—he has undertaken to do all the revising that is necessary to Usilio's article
& has engaged him to write another on new Italian books &
Mazzini to write one on Italian politics since 1830 at which
time he was involved in them.[25] I do not know how they are
paid but I believe at the old rate of 16 gui[s] the sheet, & I do
not know how soon. There seems by a letter from Greece in
the Chronicle yesterday[26] to be a man named Usilio engaged
in politics there—perhaps it is a brother or relation of this
man.

I hope you had a pleasant ride yesterday. I am quite well.
I hope you will soon come again, before long. Good bye

Your affectionate

H. T.

Mill on this occasion probably spent the beginning of a short
vacation with Mrs. Taylor since a few days later he wrote to Robertson[27] from a walking tour in South Wales which lasted into October.

Of the several notes and fragments of notes by Harriet Taylor to
Mill which appear to belong to these years the only two which seem
to be complete may be inserted here:

H. T. to J. S. M.:[28] I went this morning there in the hopes
of your word (?) my delight & there it was—believe all I can
say when I tell you how happy I am, that is, how happy you
make me.

This sweet letter (?) has been with me at every moment
since I had it & it keeps me *so* well *so* happy *so* in spirits—but
I cannot tell thee how happy it made me when first I read it
on the highest point (?) of the nice common with those
glorious breezes blowing—It has been like an equinoctial
tempest here ever since you left. Mama and C[aroline] are
here—I like it & it does me good—in the absence of the only
good I ever wish for.

Thank God however the promised summer which was to
be so much is come & will be all it was to be—has been
already so much. I am to see you on Saturday, indeed I could
not get on without.

I cannot write better to-day—tho' I never *felt* better or more.

Adieu my only & most precious—till Saturday—Dear Saturday!

H. T. to J. S. M.:[29] You will want to know how she is before you go shall you not dear—so I write—I want so much to hear how you got on last night that you were not tired or uncomfortable in that, I should think, very tiresome expedition. I did so hate you leaving me—yet that little visit made me very happy—perhaps that is the reason I am better as I am this morning—not very much but really *somewhat* better & that *is* much.

I do not think I shall see you before Tuesday—that is a terrible long time, but it does not feel to me longer than Monday. It is your going away that makes it feel so long but that cannot be avoided. Only do *you* my darling be well & happy & I shall be well as I am happy, the happiest possible, (*no* not *possible*—there *is* a happier possibility always)—but I am perfectly happy. I do not see exactly how to manage going to the sea—so I give it up at present.

When I think that I shall not hold your hand until Tuesday the time is so long & my hand so uselsss. Adieu my delight.

> je baise tes jolies pattes
> > *cher cher cher*

Towards the end of 1838 both Mill and Mrs. Taylor were again ailing seriously and preparing for a long journey to Italy. Mill was suffering from pains in the chest and severe dyspepsia, and although his family does not seem to have regarded his illness as very serious,[30] some of his friends had already little doubt that he was threatened with consumption. Both Mill and Mrs. Taylor appear this time to have taken great care not to let it be known that they were to travel together. Mill let it be understood that he was going to Malta,[31] while Mrs. Taylor was ostensibly proposing to visit one of her brothers and his Italian wife at Pisa.[32] None of the letters and other documents of the period make any allusion to the joint journey, but the complete identity of the itinerary,[33] so far as it is known, could leave no doubt about it even if Mill had not sixteen years later in his letters to his wife from Naples referred to their earlier joint visit.[34]

Mrs. Taylor and her daughter Helen, then a little over seven years old, were just before Christmas taken by Mr. Taylor as far as Paris and Mill apparently joined them there a few days later. The following letter to his mother was sent a day or two after his arrival.

J. S. M. to Mrs. James Mill:[35] Paris/28th Dec.ʳ 1838/ Dear mammy/Please send the first page of this scrawl to Robertson[36]—it saves double postage.

I am about as well, I think, as when I left London. I had a wretched passage—for want of water the boat could not get into Boulogne till half past two in the morning—it set off at ½ past eight & spent the whole 18 hours in going as slowly as it could. My already disordered stomach stood the sickness very ill & I arrived very uncomfortable & was forced to start for Paris a very few hours afterwards. The first day I was uncomfortable enough, but as the effect of the sea went off I got better & arrived at Paris after 30 hours of the diligence much less unwell than I thought I possibly could. Unless I could have got to Marseilles by the 30th it was no use getting there before the 9th so I don't start till Sunday morning & shall not travel any more at night, but post to Chalons (expensive as it is) & then go down the Soane & Rhone to Avignon. Letters put in the post on the 2nd directed to M. J. S. Mill Poste Restante à Marseille France, will be sure to reach me in time. After that direct Poste Restante à Pise, Italie.—I cannot tell if I shall have time to write to you from Marseille but I will endeavour. The weather has not got very cold yet & I dare say I shall get into the mild climate first.

They call England's a bad climate but the north and east of France have certainly a worse. What I most dread is the sea passage from Marseille to Leghorn—seasickness is so bad with me now. Love to all—

your affectionately
J. S. Mill

From a letter of Mrs. Taylor's to her husband from Chalons on 3 January[37] we know that she had left Paris on the same Sunday, 30 December, which Mill had set for his departure, and had travelled in extremely cold weather via Fontainebleau, Sens and Auxerre and was to continue down the rivers to Marseilles and thence by sea to Leghorn. In Pisa[38] her brother and sister-in-law proved to be away and the journey was soon continued to Rome and, after only a short stop, to Naples where they spent most of February. During a fortnight's stop at Rome on the return journey in the early part of March Mill reports home on the state of his health.

J. S. M. to ?, Rome, 11 March 1839:[39] I have returned here after passing about three weeks very pleasantly at Naples, and the country about it. I did not for some time get any better, but I think I am now, though very slowly, improving, ever since I left off animal food, and took to living almost entirely on macaroni. I began this experiment about a fortnight ago, and it seems to succeed better than any of the other experiments I have tried.

Ten days later on the way north another report is rather more gloomy.

J. S. M. to ?, 21 March 1839:[40] As for me I am going on well too—not that my health is at all better; but I have gradually got quite reconciled to the idea of returning in much the same state of health as when I left England; it is by care and regimen that I must hope to get well, and if I can only avoid getting worse, I shall have no great reason to complain, as hardly anybody continues after my age to have the same vigorous health they had in early youth. In the meantime it is something to have so good an opportunity of seeing Italy.

From the last part of the journey we have a few observations by Mrs. Taylor pencilled in a notebook[41] which for the earlier part gives merely the names of some of the places visited. Florence is described as

quite worthy of its reputation for beauty—the valley so exactly the right size to frame the city, which from whatever point of view one sees it is very beautiful. The best view is from the bank of the Arno opposite the Corsini, in the evening. The Appenines are less beautifully shaped here than at any point at which I have seen them. I think the view of Florence from Fiesole the least pretty, as I think Fiesole the least pretty suburb of Florence. it quite agrees with Continental notions of country going that even the plague should drive Boccaccio's company no further than Fiesole. Florence is the most indeed the only middle age looking place in Italy.

There are also some brief comments on the galleries and similar notes on Bologna, Padua and Venice where the party arrived in the middle of May.

J. S. M. to Mrs. James Mill.[42] Venice/19th May 1839/ My dear mother—I have been some days in this strange & fine old place, the most singular place in Italy—& write to say that I am going to set out almost immediately on my return. I shall go by the Tyrol, & through Germany slowly; if you write very soon, write to Mannheim; if not, to Brussels. As to how far the object of my journey has been attained, that is rather difficult to say, & I shall probably be able to say more about it after I have been for some time returned & have resumed my regular occupations. I certainly have not recovered my former health; at the same time I have no very troublesome complaint & no symptoms at all alarming & I have no doubt that by proper regimen & exercise I shall be able to have as good health as people generally have, though perhaps never again so good a digestion as formerly. In this however I shall be no worse off than three fourth of all the people I know. I am not in the least liable to catch cold—I never was less so in my life, & all idea of the English climate being dangerous for me may be entirely dismissed from all your minds. I shall in time find out how to manage myself— indeed I think I have in a great measure found it out already. —I have found no letters at Venice except one old one from Robertson. I do not know if any have been written but I shall leave word to send them after me to Munich where at any rate I hope to find some. Will you show this or tell the contents of it to Grant & thank him warmly from me for his unwearied obligingness & kindness—& will you or the boys tell Mr. Robertson that his letter without date, but bearing I think the postmark 1st April, & directed to Rome, did not for some reason or other reach me there, but has followed me here, & is the last I have had from him & I am hoping for another with fresher news about himself & all other matters —also that I have not yet seen the review, for although they take it at the reading room in Florence, they had not yet got the last number. I have been unusually long without English news having neither had any letters nor seen any newspapers but of very old date. But I shall make it all up six weeks hence.—I have had a most pleasant stay in Italy & may say that I have seen it pretty thoroughly—I have left nothing out except Sicily, & a few stray things here & there. I have been last staying at the baths of Albano in the Euganean hills, not far from Padua—most lovely country, more of the English sort than Italy generally is—but the weather for a month past has been as bad as a wet English summer except that it has never been cold. Italy is a complete disappointment as to climate—not comparable as to brightness & dryness to the South of France, though I can easily believe that some parts of it are more beneficial to certain complaints. Among other fruits of my journey I have botanized much, & come back loaded with plants. By the bye among those I want Henry to dry for me, I forgot to mention the common elder. Italy is no disappointment as to beauty, it is the only country I have ever seen which is more beautiful than England—& I have not seen a mile of it that is not beautiful. I expect to enjoy the passage of the Alps exceedingly if the weather will let me, & there seems to-day some chance of its clearing—it is the first day without rain for a fortnight past.—Let me hear from some of you soon.

                                        affectionately
                                        J. S. Mill

From Venice the party proceeded through Bassano and the Val Sugana into the Tyrol where for a short while Mrs. Taylor's notes become a little fuller:

Trent on the Adige most beautiful and imposing as we approached it from Borgo [di Val Sugana—the last stop before Trent]. a very fine town with German spaciousness cleanness & pleasant eatables. delightful to find oneself in Germany again. at Borgo the inn people spoke german & there was german frankness niceness simplicity & honest charges and from an opposite house, for the first time for six months the great pleasure of hearing the sound of german music played with german touch on a german piano-forte. Certainly the Italians have no taste for music.

Taking about a week going over the Brenner to Innsbruck and via Mittenwald into Bavaria the party arrived at the end of May in Munich. Mrs. Taylor's notes conclude:

altogether Munich is a most cheerful happy looking place & if as dissipated as people say presents an argument for dissipation.

The journey through Germany via Heidelberg and Aachen and finally through Brussels to Ostend took another month and Mill arrived in London just in time to resume his duties at India House on July 1st while Mrs. Taylor seems to have gone at once to Brighton.

The years from about 1840 to 1847 are an almost complete blank in our knowledge of Mill's private life and the character of his connexion with Mrs. Taylor. We have scarcely any documents belonging to this period and few other contemporary sources of interest. It is probable that it was at the beginning of this time that they had become aware of the scandalous talk about them, had learnt to exercise caution, and that they withdrew almost completely from society. There were other reasons present with both of them which contributed to this retirement. With the abandonment of the editorship of the *London and Westminster Review* in 1840 Mill had also given up the attempt to inspire an active radical group to effective political action, and thereafter devoted all his free time to the composition of his major theoretical treatises. The *Logic* was completed at the end of 1841, although it appeared only in March 1843, and part of it was rewritten in the interval. After some years of abortive endeavour to write a treatise on 'Ethology', he turned in 1845 to work on the *Political Economy*. Severe financial losses which he had suffered through the American repudiation of 1842 forced him to economize and to save in an endeavour to make good losses on the capital which he held in trust for his mother and sisters. This considerably reduced his mobility, and according to Bain,[43] he took no holiday at all during the first three or four years of the decade. He also seems to have suffered during these years renewed bouts of illness.

The forms of his intercourse with Harriet Taylor had by then presumably settled down to a recognized routine. Since the end of the 1830's Mrs. Taylor lived mainly in a house at Walton on Thames where Mill appears regularly to have spent the week-ends. It is to the beginning of this period, more precisely to the summer of 1842 and the following years, that Bain's often quoted story refers, that Mill went regularly to dine with her at her husband's house about twice a week, Mr. Taylor himself dining out. This must have been confined to the short periods of Mrs. Taylor's visits to town, which seem to have been few during the time to which Bain refers. Bain also mentions their attending together Carlyle's courses of lectures which were given in 1838 to 1840. One letter of Mrs. Taylor's referring to the last of these courses has been preserved.

H. T. to Miss Eliza Fox, May or June 1840:[44] My dear Miss Fox, not having heard from L[izzie?] & thinking it a pity the card should lie here idle I sent it on Monday to Miss Gillies. But I know Mr. Mill has one, which I do not think he will use, & which I am sure he will be very glad to send to her.

I am very glad she liked the Lectures; I did not expect it; it is the highest flattery when she *likes*; I heard a *mot* of H. Mar[tineau] very characteristic, she wrote to Mr. Carlyle approving the syllabus but reminding him that he had omitted the 'Hero' as 'Martyr' to which he replied that if he had not considered him that in every situation he should never have thought him worth talking about. Lily has begun many letters to you, so that my paper case is crowded with papers commencing 'dear Tottie' but she has never had courage or industry to complete one which she thinks 'worth sending' having a salutary horror of 'blots' and respect for your critical powers. She sends her love to you. She has often wished for you here. We have had a most lovely season & have enjoyed the sea thoroughly.

We leave this place next week to be nearer town. We shall go to Tunbridge Wells & stay there some weeks, so that we shall see you soon.

Adieu dear.

H. T.

A letter to her husband of about 1840, in which Mrs. Taylor asks for a bundle of manuscript which she left behind in town to be sent to her, 'as I am very busy writing for the printers & want to get some scraps out of that',[45] is the only indication of some literary activity of hers during that period, of the nature of which, however, we know nothing. Her health during the whole of this period seems to have been very poor. In addition to the consumptive tendencies which had shown themselves much earlier, she suffered for a time from some spinal injury suffered in a carriage accident[46] which kept her for long on a sofa and for the rest of her life seems to have been the cause of a recurrent paralysis or at least partial lameness. But her illness seems rarely to have been an obstacle to her travelling, or rather seems to have provided the pretext for moving about restlessly most of the time. Even while in England she appears to have been constantly on the move, not only between her cottage in Walton on Thames and the house in town, but also various places in the South of England.

Her only regular companion in this life was her daughter Helen, only ten years old in 1841, who, it would seem, never went to school,[47] but had to pick up her education from her mother, from travel and voracious reading in English, French and German. It is from the fragments of a diary[48] kept by the young girl that we get most of our information on Mrs. Taylor's mode of life during that time, and, incidentally, reflected in the mind of the precocious girl, probably also some of her opinions. The diary covers part of two Continental journeys, one in June and July 1844 to Normandy, and another during the same months of 1846 to Belgium and up the Rhine. On both these journeys Mill, who was absent from London during the periods in question,[49] may have accompanied them.

Helen Taylor's main interests at that time were the theatre and the drama. We find her constantly writing and acting plays, learning long parts, and at one stage translating Schiller's *Maria Stuart*. Her other reading is surprisingly serious for a girl of fourteen or fifteen, mainly history and religion. At thirteen and a half she complains: 'Why do not people write now? Why is there neither man nor woman who dares to say his opinions openly and so that all may know it? People fancy now that cowardice (of opinion) is prudence, and indifference philosophy.' It is probably also the mother speaking through the daughter when, two years later, Helen Taylor notes: 'Everything of the Germans seems excellent. The other books I have read are never like German full of ideas and truths which instantly light up as a new possession.' Her other great interest, which she shared with her brother Haji, was in the ritual and particularly the music of the Roman Catholic church. Even in England and still more on the Continent she rarely misses an opportunity to attend High Mass and at least at one stage one feels that her sympathy must have extended beyond the external forms of the service.

Haji, the younger of her two brothers, is the only other member of the family who occurs frequently in the diary. The relation of mother and daughter to Herbert, the elder, seems to have been much looser. He evidently was more attached to the father, whom he early assisted and later succeeded in the firm, and from 1846 onwards, when he went for his first long visit to America, he seems to have been overseas a good deal. There is no reference to Mill in the diary, though a few other visitors at Walton (including Carlyle in 1842 and Haji's friend George Mill) are recorded.

Only two notes of Mrs. Taylor to Mill have been preserved from this period. The first seems to be one of the few which Mill deliberately kept because of its content. It refers to his correspondence with the French philosopher Auguste Comte which had started in 1840 and continued fairly actively for about five years. Mrs. Taylor evidently had not seen it until after, in the second half of 1843, it had turned mainly on the position of women, on which the two philosophers strongly disagreed. Of this part of the correspondence Mill not only, against his usual habits, had kept the relevant parts of the drafts of his own letters, but had also copied out Comte's replies and had both sides of the discussion bound up as a volume,[50] clearly for Mrs. Taylor's use. Mill's friend, Alexander Bain, seems to have been allowed to see it before her unfavourable criticism made Mill feel 'dissatisfied with the concessions he had made to Comte' and decide that 'he would never show them to anyone again'.[51] It was probably with the following note that Mrs. Taylor returned the letters to Mill.

H. T. to J. S. M., about 1844:[52] These have greatly surprised and also disappointed me, & also they have pleased me, all this only regarding your part in them. Comte's is what I expected—the usual partial and prejudiced view of a subject which he has little considered & on which it is probable that he is in the same state that Mr. Fox is about religion. If the truth is on the side I defend I imagine C. would rather not see it. Comte is essentially *French*, in the sense in which we think French mind less admirable than English— Anti-Catholic—Anti-Cosmopolite.

I am surprised in your letters to find your opinion undetermined where I had thought it made up—I am disappointed at a tone more than half-apologetic with which you state your opinions. & I am charmed with the exceeding nicety elegance & fineness of your last letter.[53] Do not think that I wish you had said *more* on the subject, I only wish that what was said was in the tone of conviction, not of suggestion.

This dry sort of man is not a worthy coadjutor & scarcely a worthy opponent. with your gift of intellect of conscience & of impartiality is it probable, or is there any ground for supposing, that there exists any man more competent to judge that question than you are?

You are in advance of your age in culture of the intellectual faculties, you would be the most remarkable man of your age if you had no other claim to be so than your perfect impartiality and your fixed love of justice. These are the two qualities of different orders which I believe to be the rarest & most difficult to human nature.

Human nature essentially weak, for when it is not weak by defect of intellect it is almost inevitably weak by excess of the moral or conscientious principle, seems to me to attain its finest expression only when in addition to a high development of the powers of intellect, the moral qualities rise consciously above all—so that the being looks down on his own character with the very same feelings as on those of the rest of the world, & so desiring the qualities he thinks elevated for themselves wholly unmoved by considerations proper to any *portion* of the race, still less so to himself. 'To do justly, to love mercy, (generosity) & to walk humbly before all men' is very fine for the age in which it was produced, but why was it not 'before God' rather than before *all men?*

It makes the sentiment seem rather Greek than Jewish.

It appears to me that the idea which you propose in the division of the functions of men in the general Government proceeds on the supposition of the incapacity or unsuitableness of the same mind for work of active life & for work of reflection & combination, & that the same supposition is sufficient to account for the differences in the characters & apparent capacities of man & women considering that the differences of the occupations in life are just those which you say in the case of men must produce distinct characters (neither you nor Comte seem to settle the other analogous question, whether original differences of character & capacities in men are to determine to which class of workers they are to belong) & there is also to be taken into account the unknown extent of action on the physical & mental powers, of hereditary servitude.

I should like to begin the forming of a book or list of what in human beings must be individual & of in what they may be classified.

I now & then find a generous defect in your mind or yr method—such is your liability to take an over large *measure* of people—sauf having to draw in afterwards—a proceeding more needful than pleasant.

Mrs. Taylor's second note from approximately the same period has survived probably by accident, but may serve as a specimen of their more ordinary correspondence.

H. T. to J. S. M.:[54] a thousand thanks & blessings dearest & kindest one. What a deal of trouble I have made you take —but you think nothing trouble for me *beloved*!

I think I had best not hope to see you to-day *dearest dearest* because Arthur[55] is coming & will be here at the time you would come—but tomorrow *certainly* for I *could not* be longer without. I will get the stupid ticket[56] and we will go for an hour & see our old friend Rhino—will you dear come & take me tomorrow about five?

Yesterday I walked to Norfolk St—they were not there & then Haji and I went to mama at the old place—she was very busy & I helped her all day until ten at night, when I came home—so you see dear all the fatigue that had gone before was little compared to this last—& if I had known what it would be I sh^d not have gone there it was a great deal too much—but I am so perfectly and entirely happy, without one single cloud, that I shall soon get over this merely physical fatigue.

I shall hear from Herby soon & on that will depend if I go to that place again. If he is going on well I shall not go till next week to bring them up. So we can have Sunday if we please love & we will talk of it to-morrow.

Adieu & bless you my perfect one.

Chapter Six

A JOINT PRODUCTION
1847–1849

IN the *Autobiography* Mill says of Mrs. Taylor that
'The first of my books in which her share was conspicuous was
the "Principles of Political Economy". The "System of Logic"
owed little to her except in the minuter matters of composition, in
which respect my writings, both great and small, have largely benefited
by her accurate and clear-sighted criticism. The chapter of the Political
Economy which has had a greater influence on opinion than all the
rest, that on "the Probable Future of the Labouring Classes", is
entirely due to her: in the first draft of the book that chapter did not
exist. She pointed out the need of such a chapter, and the extreme
imperfection of the book without it: she was the cause of my writing
it; and the more general parts of the chapter, the statement and discussion of the two opposite theories respecting the proper condition
of the labouring classes, was wholly an exposition of her thoughts, often
in words taken from her lips. The purely scientific part of the Political
Economy I did not learn from her; but it was chiefly her influence
that gave to the book that general tone by which it is distinguished
from all previous expositions of Political Economy that had any pre-
tensions to being scientific, and which has made it so useful in con-
ciliating minds which those previous expositions had repelled. . . .
What was abstract and purely scientific was generally mine; the
properly human element came from her: in all that concerned the
application of philosophy to the exigencies of human society and progress, I was her pupil, alike in boldness of speculation and cautiousness

of practical judgement. For, on the one hand, she was much more courageous and far-sighted than without her I should have been, in anticipations of an order of things to come, in which many of the limited generalizations now so often confounded with universal principles will cease to be applicable.'[1]

In Mill's hand list of his publications the *Political Economy* is described as 'a joint production with my wife'. The description of one of his publications as a 'joint production' occurs for the first time at the beginning of 1846 with regard to a newspaper article and afterwards with increasing frequency.[2] The *Autobiography* also gives an account of the incredibly short period during which the great treatise was written:

'The Political Economy was far more rapidly executed than the Logic, or indeed than anything of importance which I had previously written. It was commenced in the autumn of 1845, and was ready for the press before the end of 1847. In this period of little more than two years there was an interval of six months during which the work was laid aside, while I was writing articles in the Morning Chronicle (which unexpectedly entered warmly into my purpose) urging the formation of peasant properties on the waste lands of Ireland. This was during the period of the Famine, the winter of 1846–7.'[3]

From an unpublished letter of Mill to H. S. Chapman of 9 March 1847[4] we know that Mill had already completed the first draft, presumably the one without the chapter on 'The Futurity of the Labouring Classes', during the preceding week, that is, even before he had discontinued his intense journalistic activity which in the course of about fifteen months led him to contribute more than sixty articles to the *Morning Chronicle*. The last article of the series appeared in April and Mill then discontinued writing for the press to devote himself entirely to the final revision of the book or, as he says in the letter to H. S. Chapman, 'rather rewriting, which is an indispensible part of anything of importance I write'.

Unfortunately we have practically no documentary evidence of the part which Mrs. Taylor took in the composition of the first edition of the work. What little light the existing papers throw on the period tend on the whole to confirm Mill's account. Apart from the tour of about six weeks to the Rhine and Northern France in June and July 1846, Mrs. Taylor appears to have been in England throughout the

period, living mostly at Walton, but according to her habit constantly
going for short visits to Worthing, Brighton, Ryde and other places
on the South Coast or the Isle of Wight, and only rarely coming to
town. What time she and Mill can have spent together must have
been mainly during week-ends and Mill's vacation. The first mention
of the *Political Economy* in the letters of Mrs. Taylor that have been
preserved occurs towards the end of 1847 when the book was practically finished.

H. T. to John Taylor, Walton, late 1847 :[5] I do certainly look
more like a ghost [than] a living person, but I dare say I shall
soon recover some better looks when we get to Brighton. I
think I shall not be able to go before the end of next week
being just now much occupied with the book.

A letter to her husband of only three or four weeks later refers to
Mill in connexion with another matter which probably arose out of his
recent journalistic activities.

H. T. to John Taylor, Walton (?), 18 January 1848 :[6] Mr.
Mill has just had an overture from Sir. J. Easthope wishing
him to share the proprietorship of the Morn[g] Chronicle. It
seems Easthope has had a quarrel with his son in law Boyle
& which he says it is impossible can be made up—nor can
they go on in the same concern. The quarrel however is not
about the Chroni[e]. but about a will. . . . Easthope says that
100,000 have been divided among the proprietors since he
took it. He has 7-8th and Duncan the bookseller 1-8th. He
offers 3 or 4-8th at 1700 each. He says the Daily News has
made an offer to be sold to the Chronicle but they want too
much. The Tories are very eager to get it. Mr. Mill does not
mean to take it as he thinks part proprietorship would not
ensure the opinion he would take it solely with the object of
advocating—but he is very anxious to save it from the Tories.
It seems Alderman Farebrother[7] has made an offer for it.

Shares enough to constitute a majority would amount to a
large sum. Sir J. Easthope said that L[y] Easthope has one
share which she would not give up.

Easthope says the present sale is 3200 & that it has been done up so far by the Daily News. Yet that paper seems on its last legs. I shall be very sorry if the 'rascally Times' is to become the sole representative of english liberalism!

If this was an attempt to interest Mr. Taylor in the control of the *Morning Chronicle* nothing came of it. Not much later 'the book' again appears in the correspondence between Mrs. Taylor and her husband.

H. T. to John Taylor, about February 1848:[8] I am so taken up with the Book which is near the last & has constantly something to be seen to about binding &c that I could not leave town before the beginning of April if even then.

H. T. to John Taylor, Walton, 31 March 1848:[9] The book on The Principles of Political Economy which has been the work of all this winter is now nearly ready and will be published in ten days. I am somewhat undecided whether to accept its being dedicated to me or not—dedications are not unusual even of grave books, to women, and I think it calculated to do good if short & judicious—I have a large volume of Political Economy in my hands now dedicated to Madame de Sismondi—yet I cannot quite make up my mind —what do you advise—on the whole I am inclined to think it desirable.

The reference to the dedication to Madame de Sismondi is a little disingenuous: it is evidently to the English translation of Sismondi's work which had appeared in the preceding year and which had been dedicated by the translator to the widow of the author.[10] Mr. Taylor's first reaction to this request is not preserved, nor the further note with which Mrs. Taylor followed it up, but their general character can be inferred from the more considered reply John Taylor wrote two days later.

John Taylor to H. T.:[11] Monday 3 April 1848/My dear Harriet,/ I was so much surprised on Saturday when I received your note & found you to be inclined to have the

Book dedicated to you that I could not reply until I had a little time to reflect upon the question, & this I had during a walk to Pall Mall from whence I wrote my letter.—Consideration made me decidly think, as I did at the first moment of reading your letter, that all dedications are in bad taste, & that under our circumstances the proposed one would evince on both author's part, as well as the lady to whom the book is to be dedicated, a want of taste & tact which I could not have believed possible.—Two days have since passed & my conviction remains the same notwithstanding your letter of yesterday.

It is not only 'a few common people' who will make vulgar remarks, but all who know any of us—The dedication will revive recollections now forgotten & will create observations and talk that cannot but be extremely unpleasant to me.

I am very sorry you should be much vexed at my decided opinion. You asked me, 'what do you advise'—and feeling & thinking as I do, that the proposed dedication would be most improper, I felt bound to give my opinion in decided terms, & such as could not be mistaken. I much regret, as I always do, differing in opinion with you. But as you asked me what I advised, I have not hesitated to give my opinion.

No one would more rejoice than I should at any justice & honour done to you—and if I thought my feelings and wishes alone stood in the way of your receiving both, it would be a source of great sorrow to me. But I do not believe that either would result from anything in such bad taste as the proposed dedication would, in my opinion, shew. I can assure you that this subject has given me much anxiety & trouble these last two days,—it is never pleasant to differ with you—most of all upon questions such as this.

Yours affy

J. T.

When the *Principles of Political Economy with Some of Their Applications to Social Philosophy* appeared in April 1848, a limited number of copies had a separate sheet pasted in after the title page, marked 'Gift Copy' in small print at the foot, and bearing the following dedication[12]:

TO

MRS. JOHN TAYLOR

AS THE MOST EMINENTLY QUALIFIED
OF ALL PERSONS KNOWN TO THE AUTHOR
EITHER TO ORIGINATE OR TO APPRECIATE
SPECULATIONS ON SOCIAL IMPROVEMENT,
THIS ATTEMPT TO EXPLAIN AND DIFFUSE IDEAS
MANY OF WHICH WERE FIRST LEARNED FROM HERSELF,

IS

WITH THE HIGHEST RESPECT AND REGARD
DEDICATED.

Some copies, it seems, were distributed by Mrs. Taylor herself and one of them went to the daughter of their old friend W. J. Fox.

H. T. to W. J. Fox:[13] Kent Terrace,/May 10,/1848/Dear Mr. Fox,/I am glad you like the book. It is, I think, full of good things—but I did not suppose you were interested in the subjects which most interest me in it, and I sent it to Miss Fox because when I knew her in her early youth she appeared to interest herself strongly in the cause to which for many years of my life & exertions have been devoted, justice for women. The progress of the race *waits* for the emancipation of women from their present degraded slavery to the *necessity* of marriage, or to modes of earning their living which (with the sole exception of artists) consist only of poorly paid & hardly worked occupations, all the professions, mercantile clerical legal & medical, as well as all government posts being monopolized by men. Political equality would alone place women on a level with other men in these respects. I think the interested or indifferent selfishness of the low reformers would be overmastered by the real wish for greater justice for women which prevails among the upper classes of men, if but these men had *ideas* enough to perceive that society requires the infusion of the new life of the feminine element. The great practical ability of women which is now wasted on worthless trifles or sunk in the stupidities called *love* would tell with most 'productive' effect on the business of life, while their emancipation would relieve the character of men from the deadening & degrading influences of life passed in intimacy with inferiors. But *ideas* are just that needful stock in trade in which our legislators are as lamentably deficient as our Chartists, who with their idea of universal suffrage are too purblind to perceive or too poltron to proclaim that half the race are excluded. I cannot but dissent from an argument you for a moment turned the light of your countenance upon, the first time, I think, you spoke in the house,—to the effect that 'who would be free themselves must strike the blow' or at all events express their desire. This argument appears to be even less appropriate to the case of women than it would have been to that of the negroes by emancipating whom, from her own sense of justice alone, England has acquired the brightest glory round any nation's name. Domestic slaves cannot organize themselves,—each one owns a master, & this mastery which is normally passive would assert itself if they attempted it. The position of women is also *unique*. No other slaves have . . .[14]

H. T. to W. J. Fox:[15] May 12 [1848]/Dear Mr. Fox,/ Your note has given me a genuine & hearty sensation of pleasure. I was going to say it is delightful to find that one has done less than justice to a friend! which you should understand but which I will change into, I am delighted to find that we agree so far.

You must not suppose that I am less interested in the other great question of our time, that of labour. The equalizing among all the individuals comprising the community (varied only by variation in physical capacities) the amount of labour to be performed by them during life. But this has been so well placed on the tapis by the noble spectacle of France ('spite of Pol[l] Eco[y] blunders) that there is no doubt of its continuing *the* great question until the hydra-headed selfishness of the idle classes is crushed by the demands of the lower. The condition of women question goes deeper into the mental and moral characteristics of the race than the other & it is *the race* for which I am interested. God knows if only the people now living or likely to follow such progenitors were what one thought of in any exertion, both common & uncommon sense would make one as utterly and as successfully selfish (for oneself and a little band of friends) as the rest. I fear that if the suffrage is gained by *all* men before *any* women possess it, the door will be closed upon equality between the sexes perhaps for centuries. It will become a *party* question in which only the highminded of the stronger party will be interested for justice. The argument is all in the general principle—and this is neither understood nor cared for by the flood of uneducated who would be let in by the 'male' universal suffrage.

I should have said that the Ded^n. was confined to copies given to friends at my special request & to the great disappointment & regret & contrary to the wish & opinion of the author, my reason being that opinions carry more weight with the authority of his name alone.

Ever Truly Yrs
H. T.

Of the great interest which political events abroad during 1848 must have aroused in Mill and Mrs. Taylor we get only a slight reflection in two of her notes written from the Isle of Wight where she was staying.

H. T. to J. S. M., Ryde, 25 July 1848 :[16] It seems to me that you are the only man with a mind & feeling in this country—certainly in public life there is none possessing the first named requisite. Only think of *Fox* saying that he 'entirely approved & w^d do all in his power to enable the ministers to carry the bill the earliest possible'![17] Is this place hunting of John Bullism—

I am very glad you wrote that to Crowe.[18] It is excellent &
must do some good. I only disagree in the last sentence—but
that does not much matter. How can you '*know*' that a rising
c^d. not succeed—and in my opinion if it did not succeed it
might do good if it were a serious one, by exasperating &
giving fire to the spirit of the people. The Irish w^d I sh^d hope
not be frightened but urged on by some loss of life. However
that is entre nous & is not the thing to say to these dowdies
(?)—the more that it might not prove true. I suppose it is
impossible that Ireland c^d. eventually succeed & if so you
are right. I am disgusted with the mixture of impudence (in
his note and marked passages) & imbecility in the article
which he send of the Reasoner[19] of this *foolish* creature Holyoake. I suppose he must too be answered. What do you think
of the ci-joint notion of an answer? I should like to see your
answer before it goes if quite convenient.

I fancy I sh^d say that the morality of The Reasoner
appears to me as far as *any* meaning can be picked out of the
mass of verbiage (?) in which its opinions on morality are
always enveloped to be as intolerant slavish & selfish as that
of the religion which it attacks, and the arguments used in
the Reasoner against religion are even if possible more foolish & weak than that of its opponents. None of the marked
quotations against people who are afraid to acknowledge
their opinions touch (?) me, in the slightest degree. I am
ready to stand by my opinions but not to hear them traves-
tied, & mixed up with what appears to me opinions founded
on no principles & arguments so weak that I should dread
for the furtherance of my anti religious opinions the imputa-
tion that they do not admit of being better defended.

In the very number you send me of 'The Reasoner' a
vulgar epithet of abuse is applied to the French for having
imageried (?) *Reason* as their head! You say your 'atheism'
does not '*negative*' (I suppose this means in English *deny*) the
worship of a God to set up reason instead? The sentence has
& admits no other meaning.

The fool ought to be sharply set down by *reasons*—but he is such an *excessive* fool & so lost in self sufficiency that he will cavil & prate say what you will. But as I suppose he must have an answer the only plan is to strike hard without laying yourself open. I am glad of the quarrel with him as I am glad not to have your name and influence degraded by such a connection.

The sentence I copied above runs thus—'our atheism is not the' &c 'for it does not negative the worship of God to set up the worship of a harlot'.

What does the fellow mean except by a sideblow to crush those who practise illegally what he practises legally. If he had any *principles* of morality he c^d. not use such an expression. *The fact is* his irreligion like Fox's liberalism is a trade.

Will you please dear keep this note as I have put down my notions about this man.

I am as you see utterly disgusted with the adhesion to Russell of Fox & that is the cause that I can for the first time in my life speak of him without the title of respect. the *tame* & stupid servility. If saying he 'would do all *in his power* to make Russell carry it'—says 'come and buy me' as plainly as words can speak for what c^d. be, or be supposed to be, in his power beyond his vote! It was the roast pig's 'come eat me'.

I was excessively amused by the top paragraph in the Daily News from Paris saying that Proudhon moved that the fiction of the acknowledgement of the being of a God sh^d be erased.[20] It does one good to find one man who dares to open his mouth & say what he thinks on that subject. It did me good, & I need something for the spirits, as did also your note to Crowe—The reading that base selfish & imbecile animal Trench[21] has made my spirits faint. But the 2^d vol. is the corpus delicti. Adio caro carissimo till Sat^y when we shall talk over all these things.

Among[22] other trash did you observe Hume said—'To interfere with the labour of others and to attempt to establish community of property is a direct violation of the funda-

mental laws of society'. What a text this would be for an
article which however no paper would publish. Is not the
Ten Hours' Bill an 'interference &c &c'? Is not the 'interference' with their personal freedom by this Suspension Bill
a 'violation' &c, what is the meaning of 'fundamental laws of
society' the very point in debate on the subject, communism,
on which he professed to be speaking.

Oh English men!
English intellect!

& also might it not be said that if they are justified in interfering with *personal liberty* (a fundamental law if there is any)
would they not be equally justified in enacting a law that all
Irish landlords whatsoever must instantly repair to Ireland?
This w^d. be in accordance with their professed principles of
noble & propertied government in exchange for benefits, of
duties accompanying *rights*—but no; troops & force—but no
interference with the liberty of the propertied or extra con-
stitutional measures for them!

H. T. to J. S. M., Ryde, 27 or 28 July 1848:[23] I am so disgusted with the French Assembly & also with the Daily
News that it makes me sick to think of defending the one or
helping the other. Surely the intense & disgusting vulgarity
of the Daily news might be noticed somewhere. Did you
observe its Paris correspondents notice of Flocon's speech.[24]
Progress of Liberty forsooth advocated by a paper which
applauds the Suspension of the Habeas Corpus—that is to
say the suspension of the boasted freedom of the english constitution the moment the people endeavour to profit by it.
& applauds the exclusion by law of women from clubs! The
last is so monstrous a fact, & involves so completely the
whole principle of personal liberty or slavery for women that
it seems to me a case of conscience & principle to write
specially on it. Certainly I cannot conceive publishing this[25]
or any article in defence of the French revolution unless

accompanied by one specially on the subject of *this act* of the chamber. by such an article you would also have the means of saying out *fully* to the readers of the Daily News that in principle women ought to have votes &c. This would be in some degree pledging the Daily News still more it w^d teach many timid young or poor reformers that such an opinion is not *ridiculous*. It [is] this last that makes the *low* dread to advocate it. Look at that disgusting sentence in their Paris correspondent's letter.

The French article[26] I return with some few pencil marks attached. If you follow it by one on *this* vote of the Assembly & on the true & JUST meaning of Universal Suffrage—on the propriety of keeping that title as best expressive of the true & just principle instead of as some *low-minded* reformers have done merging the principle in the vulgar selfishness of 'manhood suffrage' which I perceive is quite the fashion among the active low reformers.

I confess I prefer an aristocracy of men & women together to an aristocracy of men only—for I think the last is far more sure to last—but all this we have often said. I sh^d be sorry this really excellent article on French affairs sh^d go unless it is to be followed by an attack on the assembly. If you think this can be done & were to do it before Sat^y we could talk it over together but you will scarcely have time.

The note to Holyoake I think is very good bring me the draft again will you? Perhaps you will think it better to leave out about Md^e d'Arusmont.[27] yet I long to give the rascal that retort. The pencil marks on the article are meant only as hints.

I wholly disagree that the influence of Ireland on the english mind is now anti-revolutionary.

'The publication of the *Political Economy* was followed by another very serious breakdown in [Mill's] health. In the summer of 1848, he had a bad accident. Inside the Kensington Grove gate of Hyde

HARRIET TAYLOR

c. 1834

Oil portrait in possession of the Author

HARRIET TAYLOR

c. 1844

Miniatures in the British Library of Political and Economic Science

Park, there is a pump by which he used to cross in order to walk on the grass. One day he trod on a loose brick, and fell heavily on the hip. In treating the hurt, a bella donna plaster was applied. An affection of his eyes soon followed, which he had knowledge enough at once to attribute to the bella donna, and disused the plaster forthwith. For some weeks, however, he was both lame and unable to use his eyes. I never saw him in such a state of despair. Prostration of the nervous system may have aggravated his condition.'[28]

Mrs. Taylor meanwhile, during the summer and autumn of 1848, was moving about in her usual manner between Walton and various places on the South Coast. A number of notes exchanged between her and her husband during these months give us a few glimpses of some of the events.

H. T. to John Taylor, Walton, 20 September 1848 :[29] I must occupy myself seriously in house hunting as we certainly must give up this nice little house the sooner perhaps the better, for they have spoiled the appearance of it now from the outside by poor people's poor little places opposite—and what is another great nuisance I hear that the Austin's have taken a furnished house at Weybridge & like the place so much that they are looking out for a cottage there. I have no doubt this is to be near Clairmont, & for her to make a circle of French people, the Guizots etc. as an attraction to the english. already I hear a number of people going by the railway to call there—and I neither wish to renew the acquaintance nor to seem to avoid it.

At last, at the end of October, Mrs. Taylor settled for two months at Worthing where Mill visited her, probably only for week-ends, but long enough to write there the article in reply to Lord Brougham's attack on the French Revolution of that year, or 'the pamphlet' as he usually refers to it, since he intended to distribute a number of reprints in France. Immediately after Christmas, probably in order that Mill could use the holidays to accompany them part of the way, Mrs. Taylor and her daughter left for the South of France—somewhat to the distress of Mr. Taylor, who had been ailing for some time and, though nobody yet knew the seriousness of his condition, seems to have wished

to know his wife at least in the neighbourhood. But problems arising
out of the presence in London of one of her brothers on a visit from
Australia made Mrs. Taylor insist.

John Taylor to H. T., 2 November 1848:[30] I hear that Geo.
Mill is going to Madeira on Tuesday next. I am glad he is to
go immediately—but I cannot believe he will derive much
benefit from the change—his mind & whole morale is
unhinged and unsettled.

H. T. to John Taylor:[31] Worthing Dec. 19 [1848]/My
dear John/ I am very sorry to find you say *you are sorry* I am
going to Pau. I can assure you I do not do it for my pleasure,
but exceedingly the contrary, & only after the *most* anxious
thought—Indeed I am half killed by *intense anxiety*. The near
relationships to persons of the most opposite principles to my
own produces excessive embarrassments, and this spring it
must be *far* worse than usual owing to the constant presence
in London of A[rthur], whom I must either neglect (which
is very disagreeable to me) or admit into a degree of intimacy
which must inevitably lead to an interference on the part of
Birksgate and either a rupture with them or to discussions &
dissentions which I have not the strength to bear. I feel
scarcely any doubt that A will not stay in England another
winter & I therefore think that my going away for the next
four months would *cut* the difficulties I feel about this spring,
while I should return at a season (May) & in health to exert
myself during the summer months—having got through by
leaving England the otherwise insurmountable difficulty of
those months with A. I think if you turn over in your mind
my circumstances you will see how completely my going is a
matter of expediency. It is the alternative of a rupture
with them which may thus be avoided.—& it is always so
undesirable to make family quarrels if it is possible to avoid
them.

    . . . Your saying that you are sorry I am going has given
me ever since I read your note so *intense* a headache, that I

can scarcely see to write—However it is only one of the vexations I have to bear & perhaps everybody has.

Mill probably accompanied the ladies as far as Paris, from where they proceeded slowly by *diligence* via Orleans and Bordeaux to Pau at the foot of the Pyrenees. Here they stopped for a little over three months. Although a number of Mrs. Taylor's letters from Pau to her husband and her son Algernon are preserved,[32] none of hers then written to Mill are extant and only six of the carefully numbered letters Mill[33] wrote to her twice a week still exist. They give, however, the fullest information we have on the nature of the influence which Mrs. Taylor exercised on the successive revisions of the *Political Economy* and it is largely from them that we must draw whatever inference we can on the part she played in the original composition of the work. The first of Mill's letters which survives is numbered 8.

J. S. M. to H. T.:[33] Saturday/27 Jan^y [1849]/You might well feel that the handwriting would be 'worth having', but instead of there being 'little said' the excessive sweetness & love in this exquisite letter makes it like something dropt from heaven. I had been literally *pining* for it & had got into a state of depression which I do not think I shall fall into again during this absence. When I left you my darling & during all the journey back I was full of life & animation & vigour of wish & purpose, because fresh from being with you, fresh from the influence of your blessed presence & of that extreme happiness of that time which during the last week or fortnight I have hardly been able to conceive that I ever had—much less that I ever should have again—but this angel letter has begun to bring back happiness & spirit & I begin to feel the holiday & journey & that blessed meeting as if they would *really be*—& to feel capable also of being & doing something in the meanwhile which I had entirely ceased to feel. But I am very anxious darling to hear about the lameness & to find that it has got better. I have a very strong feeling about the obstinacy of lameness from the troublesome persistency of this of mine—though it is certainly better—but still it does not go away, nor allow me to take more than a very little exercise—& I feel the effect a little now in general health—the sight too has not quite recovered itself which is an additional teaze, but I am not uneasy about it. The only piece of news is that Austin called yesterday. When he came & during all the time he staid there was a Frenchman with me, a man named Guerry,[34] a statistical man whom Col. Sykes[35] brought to me—the man whose maps of France with the dark & light colours shewing the state of crime instruction etc. in each department you may remember. he was wanting to show me some other maps & tables of his & to ask me about the 'logic' of his plans so he did not go away & the talk was confined to general subjects, except that Austin said he was going to prepare a new edition of his book on jurisprudence on a much enlarged plan & should wish very much to consult me on various matters connected with the application of induction to moral science. Of course I could not refuse & indeed saw no reason for doing so—but as this will lead to his coming again, sending MSS. & so on it both gives an occasion & creates a necessity of defining the relation I am to stand in with respect to them. He said he had after much difficulty and search taken a house at Weybridge & that he liked the place, but he did not (I have no doubt purposely) say anything about wishing that I should visit him there, or anywhere. His talk was free & *éclairé* as it always is with me, much of it about that new publication of Guizot[36] (which I have not read) of which he spoke disparagingly & defended communists & socialists against the attacks contained in it & said he saw no real objection to socialism except the difficulty if not impracticability of managing so great a concern as the industry of a whole country in the way of association. Nothing was said about her or about the copy of the Pol. Ec. but it is necessary to *prendre un parti*. what should it be? I am reading Macaulay's book:[37] it is in some respects better than I expected & in none worse. I think the best character that can be given of it is that it is a man without genius, who has observed what people of genius do when they write history, & tries his very best to do the same—without the amount of painful effort, & affectation, which you might expect & which I did expect from such an attempt & such a man. I have no doubt like all his writings it will be & continue popular—it is exactly au niveau of the ideal of shallow people with a touch of the new ideas—& it is not sufficiently bad to induce anybody who knows better to take pains to lower people's estimation of it. I perceive no very bad tendency in it as yet, except that it in some degree ministers to English conceits.

From a letter by Mrs. James Mill to her children in Madeira, dated four days later, we get further information about John Mill's health.

Mrs. James Mill to Clara and George Mill, Kensington, 31 January 1849:[38] John wishes me to say that he had fully intended to write to you by this mail but that his eyes are bad from the effect of the medicine he took for his Hip, and Alexander whom he saw yesterday says that he must not use them; his hip is still bad so that he cannot walk, it is not worse he thinks, but it is not much better so that he cannot walk either way to the India House, the D[rs] say that it will require time, if he could walk he could go to the country while his eyes are bad, so that it is of no use going—I am going to Lewes[39] to see whether he can recommend a Man to read to John, and to write to his dictation that he may [be] beginning another edition of his book as the other is almost all sold. . . . He wishes me to tell you that he will write to you as soon as he is allowed to use his eyes. We played at cards till 12 o'clock last night and between while he played upon the Piano without music some of his own compositions.

John did after all add a few lines to the letter—on some problem concerning the property of his married sisters for which George acted as trustee.

The first edition of the *Political Economy* (of 1,000 copies) was in fact exhausted in less than a year and the preparation of a second edition was becoming urgent. As Mill explains in the *Autobiography*, the revolution of 1848 had made public opinion more ready to consider novelties and he and Mrs. Taylor had through it acquired a new interest in French socialism:

'In the first edition the difficulties of socialism were stated so strongly, that the tone was on the whole that of opposition to it. In the year or two which followed, much time was given to the study of the best socialist writers on the Continent, and to meditation and discussion on the whole range of topics involved in the controversy: and the result was that most of what had been written on the subject in the first edition was cancelled, and replaced by arguments and reflections which represent a more advanced opinion.'[40]

It is this process which we can follow in part in the letters which follow. The main discussion of socialism is contained in the chapter 'On Property' at the beginning of Book II of the *Political Economy*. The first instalment of the revised proofs (probably in the type of the first edition) which contains this crucial chapter must have gone to Mrs. Mill early in February and we can gather the nature of her comments from Mill's replies.

J. S. M. to H. T.:[41] 15/Monday/19 Febr. [1849]/I received your letter 11 on Saturday & this morning the first instalment of Pol. Ec. This last I will send again (or as much of it as is necesasry) when I have been able to make up my mind about it. The objections are I think very inconsiderable as to quantity—much less than I expected—but that paragraph, p. 248, in the first edit.[42] what you object to so strongly & totally, is what always has seemed to me the strongest part of the argument (it is only what even Proudhon says about Communism)—& as omitting it after it has ever been printed would imply change of opinion, it is necessary to see whether opinion has changed or not—yours has, in some respects at least, for you have marked strong dissent from the passage that 'the necessaries of life when secure of the whole of life are scarcely more a subject of consciousness'[43] &c which was inserted on your proposition & very nearly in your own words. This is probably only the progress we have been always making, & by thinking sufficiently I should probably come to think the same—as is almost always the case, I believe always when we think long enough. But here the being unable to discuss verbally stands sadly in the way, & I am now almost convinced that as you said at first, we cannot settle this 2ᵈ edit. by letter, but now I feel almost certain that we must adjourn the publication of the 2ᵈ edit. to November. In the new matter one of the sentences you have cancelled is a favourite of mine, viz, 'It is probable that this will finally depend upon considerations not to be measured by the coarse standard which in the present state of human improvement is the only one that can be applied to it[44].' what I meant was that whether individual agency or Socialism would be best ultimately (both being necessarily very imperfect now, & both susceptible of immense improvement) will depend on the comparative attractions they will hold out to human beings with all their capacities, both individual and social, infinitely more developed than at present. I do not think it is English improvement only that is too backward to enable this point to be ascertained for if English character is starved in its social part I think Continental is as much or even more so in its individual & Continental people incapable of entering into the feelings which make very close contacts with crowds of other people both disagreeable & mentally & morally lowering. I cannot help thinking that something like what I meant by the sentence ought to be said though I can imagine good reasons for your disliking the way in which it is put. Then again if the sentence 'the majority would not exert themselves for anything beyond this & unless they did nobody else would &c'[45] is not tenable, then all the two or three pages of argument which precede & of which this is but a summary, are false & there is nothing to be said against Communism at all—one would only have to turn round & advocate it—which if done would be better in a separate treatise & would be a great objection against publishing a 2ᵈ edit. until after such a treatise I think I agree in all the other remarks. Fourier if I may judge by Considerant is perfectly right about women both as to equality & marriage—& I suspect that Fourier himself went farther than his disciple thinks prudent in the directness of his recommendations. Considerant sometimes avails himself as Mr. Fox used of the sentimentalities & superstitions about purity, though asserting with it all the right principles. But C[onsiderant] says that the Fourierists are the *only* Socialists who are not orthodox about marriage—he forgets the Owenites, but I fear it is true of all the known Communist leaders in France. he says it specially of Buchez, Cabet, & what surprises one in Sand's 'guide, philosopher & friend' of Leroux. This strengthens one exceedingly in one's wish to [?] the Fourierists besides that their scheme of Association seems to me much nearer to being practicable at present than Communism.—Your letter was delightful—it was so very pleasant to know that you were still better as to general health than I knew before & that the lameness also improves though slowly. I am very glad I did right about Herbert— his conduct on Xmas day & his not writing even to say that he is going to America seem like ostentation of heartlessness & are only as you say to be explained by his being a very great fool (at present) & therefore influenced by some miserably petty vanities and irritabilities. Their not sending George's letter directly is very strange. The pamphlet has gone to Hickson[46]—I had thought of sending one of the separate copies to L. Blanc. Whom else should it go to? To all the members of the Prov. Gov. I think. & as it will not be published till April I had better take the copies to Paris with me & send when there as it saves so much uncertainty and delay. I did see that villainous thing in the Times & noticed that the American had used those words.

J. S. M. to H. T..[47] 16/Wednesday/21 Feb. 1849/I despatched yesterday to the dear one an attempt at a revision of the objectionable passages. I saw on consideration that the objection to Communism on the ground of its making life a kind of dead level might admit of being weakened (though I believe it never could be taken away) consistently with the principles of Communism, though the Communistic plans now before the public could not do it. The statement of objections was moreover too vague & general. I have made it more explicit as well as more moderate; you will judge whether it is now sufficiently either one or the other; & altogether whether any objection can be maintained to Communism, except the amount of objection which, in the new matter I have introduced, is made to the present applicability of Fourierism. I think there can—and that the objections as now stated to Communism are valid: but if you do not think so, I certainly will not print it, even if there were no other reason than the certainty I feel that I never should long continue of an opinion different from yours on a subject which you have fully considered. I am going on revising the book; not altering much, but in one of the purely political economy parts which occurs near the beginning, viz. the discussion as to whether buying goods made by labour gives the same employment as hiring the labourers themselves, I have added two or three pages of new explanation & illustration which I think make the case much clearer.⁴⁸—It is certainly an unlucky coincidence that the winter you have gone away should be so very mild a one here: on Sunday I found the cottage gardens &c as far advanced as they often are only in the middle of April, mezereum, hepaticas, the white arabis, pyrus japonica &c in the fullest flower, the snow ball plant very much in leaf, even periwinkles and red anemones fully out: daffodils I saw only in bud. If it is not checked it will be I think an even earlier spring than the very early one two or three years ago. I shall be able to benefit by it more than I expected in the way of country walks on Sundays although the dimness of sight, slight as it is, interferes not a little with the enjoyment of distant scenery—as I found in that beautiful Windsor Park last Sunday. If it is very fine I think I shall go some Sunday & wander about Combe—it is so full of associations with all I wish & care for. As I have taken care to let my ailments be generally known at the I.H. I have no doubt it will be easy to get a two or three months holiday in the spring if we like: this indeed if I return quite well would make any holiday in the after part of the year impracticable, but need not prevent me from taking two or three days at a time occasionally during a séjour at Ryde or any other place & thus making it a partial holiday there. Unless, which I do not expect, a long holiday soon should be necessary for health, the question ought to depend entirely on what would best suit you—which is quite sure to be most desirable for me. I am in hopes that parties in France are taking a more republican turn than they seemed likely to do—if Napoleon Bonaparte coalesces with Lamartine's party for election purposes there will be a much larger body of sincere republicans in the new assembly than was expected. The Roman republic & the Tuscan Provisional Govt. I am afraid will end in nothing but a restoration by Austria & a putting down of the popular party throughout Italy. I was sorry to see in the feuilleton of the National a very bad article on women in the form of a review of a book by the M. Légouvé (?) who was so praised in La Voix des Femmes.[49] The badness consisted chiefly in laying down the doctrine very positively that women always are & must always be what men make them— just the false assumption on which the whole of the present bad constitution of the relation rests. I am convinced however that there are only two things which tend at all to shake this nonsensical prejudice: a better psychology & theory of human nature for the few; & for the many, more & greater proofs by example of what women can do. I do not think that anything that could be written would do nearly so much good on that subject, the most important of all, as the finishing of your pamphlet—or little book rather, for it should be that.[50] I do hope you are going on with it—gone on with & finished & published it *must be*, & next season too.—Do you notice that Russell in bringing forward his Jew Bill, although he is actually abolishing the old oaths & framing (?) new, still has the meanness to reinsert the words 'on the true faith of a Christian' for all persons except Jews, & justifies it by saying that the Constitution ought not avowedly to admit unbelievers into Parliament.—I have seen very little of the Chairman & Dep. Chairman[51] lately—as to avoid the long staircase I have communicated with them chiefly by others but now being released from restraint I shall take an early opportunity of speaking to Galloway about Haji. I have seen nothing more of Haji any more than of Herbert. Addio (?)[52]

From a letter to her husband of a few days later we see that Mrs. Taylor had some real understanding of economic problems. The gold discoveries to which it refers can then only recently have become known:

H. T. to John Taylor, Pau, 27 February 1849:[53] Do you suppose this Californian discovery will make any change in the value of money for some time to come? If it continues I suppose it will lower the value of fixed incomes, but I suppose benefit trade? If I were a young man I would go there quickly. The most probable chance is that the gold will not continue below the surface—meanwhile there must be fine opportunities for placing *goods*, & especially drugs, in the *placiemento*. are you going to send out quinine.

H. T. to Algernon Taylor, Pau, 6 March 1849:[54] I have not written lately—I have been out of spirits and therefore disinclined to enjoy or to write about the beautiful objects and scenery which form the staple of our quiet life here. The account I hear of George [Mill] and my knowledge of that insidious disease make me very much fear for him, and I most earnestly and anxiously wish that he may live. It is very important in writing to him to say very little about his health, and not to seem to think of it as anything more than a common cough, because if a person thinks themselves consumptive the effect on the spirits has the utmost possible tendency to produce or to accelerate that fatal disease. I think he would much like to hear from you and perhaps you have already written. You might give him a long letter about all sorts of impersonal objects, such as politics—your review and its articles—what you have been reading lately and your opinion thereon—our stay at his place & its scenery, Sinnett's prospects—Herbert's voyage &c. . . . I often wish for you when I see all this beauty and feel that if we live we will sometime see it together, and that 'Ce qui est deferé n'est pas perdu', as the proverb says. I am very glad to hear that Papa is better on the whole but I wish the improvement were quicker. He ought in future to pay due respect to my medical judgement as I have twice anticipated his physician's advice in the last few months! I do hope he will mend more quickly with the finer weather which may be expected in April. . . . I have not read Grote's history, I should think it must be interesting—tho' I think that knowing his 'extreme opinions' I should think it a defect that he does not indicate them more clearly, as there is ample and easy room to do in treating of the Greek Philosophers. extreme timidity is his defect, but this is a great one indeed in a public instructor. Mr. Mill was to write a review of the book in last Sunday's Spectator,[55] which you will like to see. And now dearest Haji, with love to Papa—Adieu.

The five letters which Mill wrote to Mrs. Taylor during these weeks are missing but the next three which are preserved are consecutive.

J. S. M. to H. T.:[56] 22/Wednesday/14 March [1849]/ What a nuisance it is having anything to do with printers. Though I had no reason to be particularly pleased with Harrison, I was alarmed at finding that Parker had gone to another. & accordingly, though the general type of the first edition is exactly copied, yet a thing so important as the type of the heading at the top of the page cannot be got right— you know what difficulty we had before—& now the head-

ings, & everything else which is in that type, they first gave
much too close & then much too wide, & say they have not
got the exact thing, unless they have the types cast on purpose. Both the things they have produced seem to me detest-
able & the worst is that as Parker is sole owner of this edition
I suppose I have no voice in the matter at all except as a point
of courtesy. I shall see Parker today & tell him that I should
have much prefered waiting till another season rather than
having either of these types—but I suppose it is too late now
to do any good—& perhaps Parker dragged out the time in
useless delays before on purpose that all troublesome changes
might be avoided by hurry now. It is as disagreeable as a
thing of that sort can possibly be—because it is necessary
that something should be decided immediately without waiting for the decision of my only guide & oracle. If the effect
should be to make the book an unpleasant object to the only
eyes I wish it to please, how excessively I shall regret not
having put off the edition till the next season. I have had the
proofs of the pamphlet, all but the last few pages. There
seems very little remaining in it that could be further softened
without taking the sting out entirely—which would be a pity.
I am rather against giving away *any* copies, at least for the
present, in England—except to Louis Blanc to whom I suppose I should acknowledge authorship. He has not come near
me—I see he is writing in sundry Communist papers of
which there are now several in London. As a heading *in the
review* I have thought of 'The Revolution of February and
its assailants'—it does not seem advisable to put Brougham's
name at the top of the page—& 'the revolution of February'
or anything of that kind by itself would be tame, & excite no
attention. There is no fresh news of George, nor any incident
of any kind except that Mr. Fox has send me (without any
letter) four volumes of his lectures to the working classes, the
last volume of which (printed this year)[57] has a preface in
which he recommends to the working classes to study Polit.
Economy telling them that they will see 'by the ablest book

yet produced on the subject' that it is not a thing against them but for them—with some other expressions of compliment he prints two paragrs., one of them the strongest there is in the book about independence of women, & tells them in another place though rather by inference than directly that women ought to have the suffrage. He speaks in this preface of 'failing health' & as if he did not expect either to write or to speak in public much more: this may mean little, or very much. I feel now as if the natural thing, the thing to be expected, was to hear of every one's death—as if we should outlive all we have cared for, and yet die early.

Did you notice that most bete & vulgar say by Emerson in a lecture at Boston, about the English?[58] It is hardly possible to be more stupidly wrong—& what sort of people can he have been among when here? The Austrian octroyé federal constitution seems as bad as anything pretending to be a constitution at all now dares to be—the only significant circumstances in it on the side of democracy being that there is no house of Lords nor any mention of nobility or hereditary rank. Here the sort of newspaper discussion which has begun about Sterling's infidelity seems to have merged into a greater scandal about a book by Froude[59]—a brother of the Froude who was the originator of Puseyism. This book was reviewed in the last Spectator I sent to you[60] & that review was the first I had heard & is all I have seen of the book—but the Herald & Standard are abusing the man in the tone of the Dominican inquisition on account of the strong declaration against the inspiration of the Bible which he puts into the mouth of one of his characters, obviously as they say thinking the same himself. It appears the Council of University College had been asked to select a schoolmaster for Hobart Town & had chosen Froude[61] from among a great many candidates & probably some rival defeated candidate has raised this stir. It all, I think, does good, but one ought to see occasionally the things that are written on such matters, in order not to forget the intensity of the vulgar bigotry, or affectation of it, that is still thought to be the thing for the Christian readers of newspapers in this precious country. The Times is quite gentlemanlike in comparison with these other papers when they get on the ground of imputed infidelity or anything approaching it. I suppose they overshoot their mark, but they would scruple nothing in [?] such case.

The next letter is mutilated, most of the first sheet being deliberately cut away, leaving on the first page only a fragment of what was evidently a discussion of the itinerary for the joint return journey from Pau,[62] but carefully preserving the beginning of the discussion of a new paragraph on page two.

J. S. M. to H. T., 17 March (?) 1849:[63] The bargain with Parker is a good one & that it is so is entirely your doing— all the difference between it & the last being wholly your work, as well as the best of the book itself so that you have a redoubled title to your joint ownership of it. While I am on the subject I will say that the difficulty with the printer is surmounted—both he & Parker were disposed to be accomodat ing & he was to have the very same type from the very same foundry today—in the meantime there has been no time lost, as they have been printing very fast without the headings, & will no doubt keep their engagement as to time. You do not say anything this time about the bit of P.E.—I hope you did not send it during the week, as if so it has miscarried—at the rate they are printing, both volumes at once, they will soon want it.

I was wrong in expressing myself in that way about the Athenians,[64] because without due explanation it would not be rightly understood. I am always apt to get enthusiastic about those who do great things for progress & are immensely ahead of everybody else in their age—especially when like the Athenians it has been the fashion to run them down for what was best in them—& I am not always sufficiently careful to explain that the praise is *relative* to the then state & not the *now* state of knowledge & what ought to be improved feeling. I *do* think, however, even without these allowances, that an average Athenian was a far finer specimen of humanity on the whole than an average Englishman —but then unless one says how low one estimates the latter, one gives a false notion of one's estimate of the former. You are not quite right about the philosophers, for Plato *did* condemn those 'barbarisms'.

I regret much that I have *not* put in anything about Palmerston into that pamphlet—I am almost tempted to write an express article in the West^r in order to make him the amende. As you suggested I wrote an article on Russell's piece of meanness in the Jews Bill & have sent it to Crowe from whom I have not yet any answer—there has been no time hitherto fit for its publication—the time will be when the subject is about to come on again in Parl^t, but I fear the article even as 'from a correspondent' will be too strong meat for the Daily News, as it declares without mincing the matter, that infidels are perfectly proper persons to be in parliament. I like the article myself. I have carefully avoided anything disrespectful to Russell personally, or any of the marks, known to me, by which my writing can be recognized.

If I meet Fleming[65] again or am again assaulted on any similar point I will reply in the sort of way you recommend— I dare say the meeting with F. was accidental as it was just at the door of Somerset House where he is Assistant Secretary of the Poor Law Board & just at the time when he would be probably coming out. Ever since I have kept the opposite side.

J. S. M. to H. T.: 24/Wednesday/21 March [1849][66]/ The Pol. Ec. packet came on Monday for which a thousand thanks. I have followed to the letter every recommendation. The sentence which you objected to in toto of course has come quite out.[67] In explanation however of what I meant by it—I was not thinking of any mysterious change in human nature—but chiefly of this—that the best people now are

JOHN TAYLOR

Miniature in the British Library of Political and Economic Science

JOHN STUART MILL
1840
Medallion reproduced from 'The Letters of John Stuart Mill',
ed. by H. S. R. Elliott

necessarily so much cut off from sympathy with the multitudes that I should think they must have difficulty in judging how they would be affected by such an immense change in their whole circumstances as would be caused by having multitudes whom they could sympathize with—or in knowing how far the social feeling might then supply the place of that large share of solitariness & individuality which they cannot now dispense with. I meant one thing more, viz. that as, hereafter, the more obvious & coarser obstacles & objections to the communist system will have ceased or greatly diminished, those which are less obvious & coarse will then step forward into an importance & require an attention which does not now practically belong to them & that we can hardly tell without trial what the result of that experience will be. I do not say that *you* cannot realize & judge of these things—but if you & perhaps Shelley & one or two others in a generation can, I am convinced that to do so requires both great genius & great experience & I think it quite fair to say to common readers that the present race of mankind (speaking of them collectively) are not competent to it. I cannot persuade myself that you do not greatly overrate the ease of making people unselfish. Granting that in 'ten years' the children of the community might by teaching be made 'perfect' it seems to me that to do so there must be perfect people to teach them. You say 'if there were a desire on the part of the cleverer people to make them perfect it would be easy[']
—but how to produce that desire on the part of the cleverer people? I must say I think that if we had absolute power tomorrow, though we could do much to improve people by good laws & could even give them a very much better education than they have ever had yet, still, for effecting in our time anything like what we aim at, all our plans would fail from the impossibility of finding fit instruments. To make people really good for much it is so necessary not merely to give them good intentions & conscientiousness but to unseal their eyes—to prevent self flattery, vanity, irritability & all

that family of vices from warping their moral judgments as those of the very cleverest people are almost always warped now. But we shall have all those questions out together & they will all require to be entered into to a certain depth, at least, in the new book which I am so glad you look forward to as I do with so much interest.—As for news—did you see in the Times Mrs. Buller's death? I suspect it was the very day I wrote last. I have heard nothing of the manner or occasion of it, & had not supposed from anything I had heard before, that there was any likelihood of it. So that volume is closed now completely.[68] I called the other day at Charles Fox's shop to ask the meaning of Mr. Fox's illness & C.F. said he has constant pains in his side which are either heart disease or merely nervous but which are made much worse by public speaking or any other excitement & that is the reason he so seldom speaks in the H.o.C. It is probably mere nervous pain therefore, & not dangerous, but it shews him to be out of health. There were letters from George yesterday of three weeks later date: his report is that he is neither worse nor better, he thinks that he coughs about six or seven times an hour through the 24 hours. He still writes as not at all out of spirits—one expression he uses is that he wants nothing to make him happy but to be able to go up into the mountains, & to have a better prospect of the future—I think he means better *avenir* in case he ultimately recovers—but he seems persuaded that his disease is seldom cured or stopped. I shall write to encourage him for I am convinced it is often stopped though hardly ever cured & I do not yet despair of his case.

Crowe's answer was 'I shall be but too happy to print the article. The Jews Bill is put off till after Easter, but if you will allow me I will insert it immediately.' There is nothing like kicking people of the D[aily] N[ews] sort it appears. I answered telling him if he thought it would be of as much use now as about the time when the bill comes on by all means to print it now. It has not yet made its appearance. The printing of the 2ᵈ edit. goes on satisfactorily in all

respects. Last Sunday I went by railway to Watford &
walked from there to town, indeed more, for the direct road
being by Stanmore I turned off before getting there, to
Harrow, thus lengthening the walk 3 or 4 miles. I think I
must have walked 20 miles, & almost all of it at a stretch,
with occasional short resting on a stile. I confess however
that the miles between Harrow & London were excessively
long, but I felt no kind of inconvenience the next day or since
from the walk. The lameness is now no obstacle at all—the
only obstacle is general weakness, as compared with my state
when in perfect health. The sight remains the same. I look
forward to Saturday with immense pleasure because there is
always a letter. adieu with every good wish.

The last of Mill's letters in this series which has been preserved is
also mutilated. Almost the whole of the first half of the sheet is
deliberately cut away, leaving on the second page[69] only the beginning
of his reply to Mrs. Taylor's comments on the discussion of population
in the chapter on The Remedies for Low Wages towards the end of
the first volume of the *Political Economy*.

J. S. M. to H. T., London, 31 March 1849: The alteration I
have made in the sentence of the P.E. was instead of 'placard
their intemperance' to say 'placard their enormous families'
—it does not read so well, but I think it may do, especially as
the previous sentence contains the words 'this sort of incontinence'—but your two sentences are so very good that as that
sheet is not yet printed, get them in I must & will.[70]—Are
you not amused with Peel about Ireland? He sneers down
the waste lands plan,[71] two years ago, which the timid ministers, timid because without talent, give up at a single sar-
casm from him, & now he has enfanté a scheme containing
that & much more than was then proposed—& the Times
supports him & Ireland praises him. I am extremely glad he
has done it—I can see that it is working as nothing else has
yet worked to break down the superstition about property—
& it is the only thing happening in England which promises

a step forward—a thing which one may well welcome when
things are going so badly for the popular cause in Europe—
not that I am discouraged by this—progress of the right kind
seems to me to be quite safe now that Socialism has become
inextinguishable. I heartily wish Proudhon dead however—
there are few men whose state of mind, taken as a whole,
inspires me with so much aversion, & all his influence seems
to me mischievous except as a potent *dissolvent* which is good
so far, but every single thing which he would substitute
seems to me the worst possible in practice & mostly in principle. I have been reading another volume of Considerant
lately published.[72] he has got into the *details* of Fourierism
with many large extracts from Fourier himself. It was perhaps necessary to go into detail in order to make the thing
look practicable, but many of the details *are*, & all *appear*,
passablement ridicules. As to their system, & general mode
of thought there is a great question at the root of it which
must be settled before one can get a step further. Admitting
the omnipotence of education, is not the very pivot & turning point of that education a moral *sense*—a feeling of duty,
or conscience, or principle, or whatever name one gives it—
a feeling that one *ought* to do, & wish for, what is for the
greatest good of all concerned. Now Fourier, & all his followers, leave this out entirely, & rely wholly on such arrangements of social circumstances as without any inculcation of
duty or of 'ought', will make every one, by the spontaneous
action of the passions, intensely jealous for all the interests of
the whole. Nobody is ever to be made to do anything but act
just as they like, but it is calculated that they will always, in a
phalanstere, like what is best. This of course leads to the
freest notions about personal relations of all sorts, but is it, in
other respects, a foundation on which people would be able
to live & act together? *Owen* keeps in generals & only says
that education can make everybody perfect, but the Fourierists attempt to shew how, & exclude, as it seems to me, one
of the most indispensable ingredients.

What a bathos[73] to turn from these speculations to pinched methodistical England. It is worth while reading the articles in the newspapers about Froude & Sterling[74] to have an adequate idea of what England is. The newspaper talk on the subject having the irresistible attraction of personality still continues, & I have within this week read in shop windows leading articles of two weekly newspapers, the Church & State Gazette & the English Churchman, keeping it up. They have found the splendid mare's nest of the 'Sterling Club'.[75] I remember the foundation of the said club by Sterling himself, very many years before his death—soon after he began to live permanently out of London—though called a club it had neither subscription nor organization, but consisted in an agreement of some 12 or 20 acquaintances of Sterling, the majority resident University people, that there should be one day in the month when if any of them liked to dine at a place in Lincoln's Inn Fields he would have a chance of finding some of the others. I let them put me down as one, & went there, I think three times, with Sterling himself & at his request, in order to pass an evening in his company—the last time being, I believe, in 1838. A few weeks ago I was reminded of the existence of the thing by receiving a printed list of members, in which I was put down with many others a honorary—it has greatly increased in numbers, is composed (in more than one half) of clergymen, including two bishops, Thirlwall and Wilberforce, & I suppose it has organized itself with a regular subscription as it has removed to the Freemason's & has begun sending circulars previous to each dinner. One of these lists fell into the hands of the 'Record' newspaper & combining this with Hare's Life of Sterling it charges Hare, Maurice, Trench, these bishops, & innumerable others with founding a society to honour & commemorate an infidel—& joining for that purpose with persons strongly suspected of being no better than infidels themselves, such as Carlyle & me. It is very amusing that these people who take such care to guard their orthodoxy get nothing by it but to be more bitterly attacked. However it shews what I did not suppose, that it required some courage in a church dignitary to write about a heretic even in the guarded way that Hare did.[76]—

Yesterday Nichol[77] called on me—whom I had not seen since 1840—he is in town for some days or probably weeks & is about to publish a book on America where he has been travelling. As he is a walking man I am going to have a country walk with him tomorrow—my other Sunday walks have been alone. I always have thought him a man of whom something might be made if one could see enough of him—I shall perhaps be able to judge now if my opinion was right, but at all events his book will shew. He has this in his favour at least which is the grand distinction now that he is intensely *forward*-looking—not at all conservative in feeling but willing to be very destructive & now adieu with every possible wish.

On Monday no doubt I shall hear again.

In a letter from her husband received by Mrs. Taylor toward the end of March he seems to have given her a more unfavourable account of the state of his health which caused her some concern but evidently gave no idea of the real gravity of his condition.

H. T. to John Taylor, Pau, 30 March 1849:[78] If I only consulted my own inclination I should come back to England immediately on the receipt of your letter in hopes of being able to be of use to you—the reason I cannot do this is that I have arranged with Mr. Mill to meet me on the 20th of April when he is to have three weeks holiday on account of his health which has been the whole winter in a very precarious state. For the last two months he has been almost unable to read or write & has had to engage a man to read to him & to write from his dictation & both Clark & Alexander the occulist say that a complete change & cessation from all work is absolutely necessary to save his sight—he has had blisters & irritating applications innumerable without any effect and is indeed about half blind. They say that giving up using the eyes & mild weather will cure them as they attribute all the bad symptoms to extreme debility. I shall therefore return with him as far as Paris & I shall get back the earliest that I possibly can in the hopes of being of use to you. I have not been quite well lately having had some return of my stomach derangement, but I am getting better again & the travelling will be sure to do my health good. I feel it a duty to do all in my power for his health & it is unfortunate that he is so much required at the change of direction on 11th April that he cannot leave London before that. He does not tell even his own family *where* he goes for his holiday as I so hate all tittle-tattle. Therefore I do not mention it either except to you. I trouble you with all these particulars because I wish you to know that nothing but a feeling of right would prevent my returning at once.

Mill probably joined Mrs. Taylor and her daughter at Bagnères, where however the party cannot have stayed long since, after an excursion to Cauterets in the High Pyrénées, they were already on their way home at Toulouse on April 29[79] but appear to have spent another fortnight going north via Montauban, Limoges and Chateauroux to Orleans and Paris.

Chapter Seven

JOHN TAYLOR'S ILLNESS AND
DEATH
1849

EITHER in order to avoid travelling together when they were likely to meet acquaintances, or merely because Mrs. Taylor was awaiting a calmer day for crossing the Channel, Mill returned from Paris to London a day or two in advance, with a message for Mr. Taylor that his wife was well and would arrive presently. When at last Mrs. Taylor arrived on 14 May, she found her husband much more gravely ill than she had expected—in fact, as the doctor soon gave her to understand, dying of cancer.

For two months until his death she then devoted all her strength to nursing the invalid. A long series of hastily written notes to Mill give a continuous account of her fluctuating hopes and fears. For some time she refused to accept the scarcely veiled verdict of the doctors and to submit to the inevitable. A great part of her notes to Mill during the first few weeks is concerned with the question of what other doctors to consult and with books on the disease which she studies to discover whether there is any chance of a cure. Nobody who reads the whole set of these notes[1] can doubt the genuineness of her anguish or the exclusiveness of her devotion during these last weeks, when she scarcely sees Mill, to the incessant care of her dying husband. All the following excerpts are taken from these notes to Mill, whose exact dates are mostly uncertain.

H. T. to J. S. M., 28 (?) May 1849:[2] It is extraordinary the hard work both I & L[ily] have gone through & still take each day but I have lost almost all count of the days & know not when is the beginning or end of the week—the whole time passed in soothing the pain by words of sympathy or diverting it by inventing talk or actively engaged in all the incessant operations for relief. He is most patient & firm & endures with the utmost strength & courage—but *why* should he have these torments to endure! what good to anybody is all this—he never hurt or harmed a creature on earth. If they want the life why can't they take it—what useless torture is all this! & he is so sorry & hurt to give so much labour to me—he feels that I am the greatest good to him & feeling that no servant could do what I do for him enables me to keep up. He said 2 days since 'well if ever I *do* recover it will be entirely owing to you'. How cruel to feel that his chance is so slight—alas I feel as if he besides you is the only life I value in this wretched world. He is so thoroughly true direct honest strong & with all the realities of *nice* feelings, as I constantly see now. What a contrast is such a man to the vapid sentimental egotists Stirling, Carlyle, etc., who let inflated conceit of their own assumed superiority run away with all strength and humility.

Early June:[3] You talk of my writing to you 'at some odd time when a change of subject of thought may be rather a relief than otherwise'! *odd time!* indeed you must be ignorant profoundly of all that *friendship* or *anxiety* means when you can use such pitiful narrow hearted expressions. The sentence appears to have come from the pen of one of the Miss Taylors. It is the puerility of thought & feeling of any utterly headless & heartless pattern of propriety old maid.

As to 'odd time' I *told* you that I have not a moment unfilled by things to be done when not actually standing by the bedside or supporting the invalid—& as to 'change of subject of thought a relief'! Good God sh^d you think it a relief to think of somebody else some acquaintance or what not while *I* was dying? If so—but I will say no more about this—only after such a mode of feeling on your part I feel it sacrilegious to enter into any account of what I feel & suffer in this most dreadful & most melancholy & most piteous case—my heart is wrung with indignation & grief.

July 6:[4] This disease seems to combine the evils of consumption with those of acute distress—all the pains of exhaustion by slow wasting away with the terrible local characteristics of its own. So terrible & frightful is this disease that it is something to be glad of that he remains free from pain—only those who have watched with the deep sympathy of true affection & pity can fully estimate the infinite distinction there is between freedom from pain & freedom from suffering. I am sure almost any pain is less bad (tho' not perhaps less hard) to bear than this which he poor poor dear calls so truly dying by inches.

However he has hours of comparative pleasure now—& himself & those who don't hear the medical opinions seems to flatter themselves he may be going on well—but they say that tho' it is a wonderfully easy case of the kind, that others suffer so very much more than he (the truth of which is that no one I sh^d think was ever so well nursed) yet that the result will be the same. For me after two days of feeling ill & knocked up I have now recovered again. I am now feeling scarcely tired.

The certainty of being really of the greatest use & quite indispensable to him (or to any one) gives me a quantity of strength and life—so that I feel sure my health will not suffer —unless indeed the disease is contagious which I dare say it is not—if it were we three who do all for him w^d be sure of it. However never mention this idea to them.

His sisters who come to see him & others say no one w^d think there was illness in his room it is so fresh and gay—& this freshness & cheerfulness I am sure have much to do with his ease & comfort & almost complete freedom from nervous depression. Neither window nor door have been shut either day or night for a month & the sight & scent of fresh flowers & christal iced (?) water & all sorts of nice looking things beguile him into a feeling of pleasure & cheat the low spirits.

So all this incessant attention & effort to keep up his spirits & also the long time it is now since I heard the dreadful truth, has combined to sink the deep grief & indignation I feel below the surface—but I have so much to say to you that no one but you could understand.

What a duping is life & what fools are men who seem bent upon playing into the hands of the mischievous demons! One comfort & hope lies in the fact that the worst they suffer is from their own bad qualities,—but the good suffer with the bad.

Perhaps you will enclose George's letter for H[aji] to me. Tell me how you are. Take care of yourself for the world's sake.

I cannot think how you have been silent all the while about Roman *heroism*—never equalled—& the French utter baseness. I have been longing to write myself—the only person who seems to feel it as strongly as I do is Landor & he seems half-mad.

July 9:[5] Will you send any Mag⁵. or Rev⁵. you have, for him—if you have any that is.

He has got, for July, the New Monthly & the Quarterly— Especially I want the Edinburgh *at the earliest* possible. Don't call again.

You have no notion what a mistake you make in saying that it could be no more contagious than a fractured skull— Any one who saw & watched this & thought so must already have got a fractured skull. I have very little doubt that this is as often contagious as Typhus or plague— It seems very like the latter—probably all are contagious in circumstances—& to persons predisposing or predisposed. However I cannot now give my reasons for this opinion.

I have so very much to say which must wait.

What an iron despotism we live under, & who can wonder that men are bad while they take the government of this world for their model. I am glad to hear that the timid upper classes think the Romans fine—if indeed they do so—but Grote always paints his fine acquaintances couleur de rose.

That they dislike & condemn the French proceedings I have no doubt.

Tocqueville is a notable specimen of the class which includes such people as the Stirlings Romillys Carlyles Austins —the gentility class—weak in moral, narrow in intellect, timid, infinitely conceited & gossiping. There are very few men in this country who can seem other than more or less respectable puppets to us.

Thus gradually, as she resigns herself to the inevitable conclusion of her husband's suffering, other topics begin to enter into Mrs. Taylor's thoughts and her correspondence. The first extraneous subject discussed, apparently still in May, was an application for money to Mill made by G. J. Holyoake to help him in an attempt to obtain a university degree. Mrs. Taylor advised 'to give but not unaccompanied with a suitable lesson on this vain and senseless affectation'[6] and Mill's draft of the reply to Holyoake is fully commented upon by her.

H. T. to J. S. M., May (?) 1849:[7] I think it duty when you tell him you will subscribe as he requests to tell him some of your opinion on the very false and *vicious* sort of note it [his note to Mill] is. I think it is impossible you can agree with the humbug (even when translated into honest expressions it is humbug) that hearing men lecture at London or any other University is a means of improvement of knowledge, of being 'learned', as he so boastfully and vulgarly calls it, such as can never be equalled by reading. That lectures and lecturers such as exist at present are means of improvement superior to all reading. Then this hypocritical cant about 'violating austere incorruptibility'—either the words are useless & therefore insincere braggadacio, or the man is 'violating etc.' by his letter.

The whole thing in an honest man's language amounts to this: I want to get a degree or some other University honour to try to get on in the world. Are you disposed to help me with a little money? This is the whole—while his note is like all his a heap of boastful conceited vulgar insincerity & I wish that he sh^d see or feel that you are not humbugged by him. And this only because it feels to me immoral to let falseness think itself more successful than honesty w^d be with true & intelligent people.

Soon a more important subject arose. Captain Antony Sterling, the brother of Mill's friend John Sterling who had died not long before, was at the time preparing for publication a collection of his brother's letters. This never appeared, though it was later to serve Thomas Carlyle for his *Life of John Sterling*. Apparently Captain Sterling had applied to Mill for permission to include some of his letters to Sterling as well as some passages about him, perhaps those in the correspondence between Sterling and Carlyle which have been quoted earlier.

June.[8] I had said nothing more about those letters lately because I understood from your note a fortnight ago that it was all decided that you meant to leave out all mention of yourself in them & also to withdraw the letters addressed to you. I supposed that this had been done & that the thing was settled. I am quite sure that it ought to be done both in justice & honour and as to the difficulty you find in doing it, that does not seem to me great if, what is not the case, your usual ways were exactly like those of ordinary people. In a matter of taste & one wholly concerning yourself that you should change your mind is certainly not fatally odd.

A further note evidently refers to the letter to be sent to Captain Sterling.

June 30.[9] I think the words which I have put the pencil through are better omitted—but they might with a little alteration be placed at the end?
The *reason* I should give to Capt S. if a reason is asked, is that the way in which you are mentioned in the letters is cal-

culated to give an erroneous impression of you. This is the simple truth. The words I have added at the end do not go quite right but you will make them do so. It is if possible as desirable to get those passages omitted as your own letters. Therefore something of the kind (like the words I have added) should be said.

July 7–8 (?):[10] I have had but a few moments in which to look at those extracts from S's letters. I cannot at all understand, & I mean this wholly *sincerely* and not at all ironically, how you could ever see with complacency or even with indifference such a quantity of misapprehension of your character to be published. I know that you place great vanity in not being vain but with me a love of truth as well as vanity w^d make repugnant to me the myself giving the world an appreciation of me made by an *evident* inferior who makes it with all the air of judging from a height which is conceivable. a second thing which hurts me intensely tho' it does not surprise me is your perfect madness to put your own hand & seal to the mention of your name & character soi-disant appreciatingly by a man who you perceive was weak & foolish enough to be in agreement with his correspondent in *judging* your relation with some unknown woman in unknown circumstances. Of course the old bugbear words 'married woman' were at the bottom of this unanimity of fear & sorrow which these men honoured (or disgraced selon moi) you with. Nowadays I sh^d have thought that with our opinion we must thoroughly despise men who have not got out of that baby morality & intellect. That you c^d be willing to have these things printed hurts me more deeply than anything else I think c^d do. It has disturbed my mind & feelings even amidst these trying days & nights. but if you have engaged yourself about them some of them must stand.

In what was probably the next note a different topic is taken up.

July 10:[11] The enclosed paper marked A I wrote one Sunday some weeks ago but did not send it feeling I had so ill expressed the fullness of my meaning. However another case which I will enclose gives so admirable an occasion for an article in the Daily News on the subject—against legalizing *corporal punishment* ANYWHERE—public or private —that I think it OUGHT to be written.

Mark this case—how there was no *pretence* of brutality or violence in the offence that it sh^d be punished by brutal degradation (you sh^d take care to copy in the report the words *middleaged* man for tho' it adds nothing to *our* feeling it strengthens the case as against the magistrates immensely with the commonalty). Then *do* hit police magistrates in general & Secker in particular as hard as possible—all the *rest* of the subject you will at once see as strongly & clearly as I. How the most brutal attacks of personal violence are sentenced to *imprisonment* only—how you never see a case of that kind met by personal violence i.e. by corporal punishment—how bad & disgusting as corporal punishment is ever—if used it ought to be only for personal violence.

Enclosure A: Sunday evening.

My eye fell just now on the Examiner as it lay open with an account of the trial of the young man who shot at the Queen.

I see it reported that the newly revived barbarous & degrading punishment of flogging which ever since the offence the Newspapers, especially the Examiner, have been gloating over with disgusting toadying satisfaction is said to have been omitted by especial desire of the Queen—now whether this is so or not w^d it not be an excellent opportunity to treat the statement as true—to compliment for refusing so unworthy & disgusting a tribute as the revival of a brute degradation as punishment of offences against her. Pointing out that the offence was not of a Degraded or brutal kind but of a wicked & grave kind, and that flogging is no more fit for it than it w^d be for murder. admiring too the *unsovereignlike* magnanimity of punishing such a serious offence only as if it had been directed against the meanest subject. In fact the punishment is not severe enough.

The second enclosure, probably a clipping from a newspaper, has not been preserved and probably was used by Mill in writing the unheaded and unsigned article which four days later appeared in the *Daily News* of July 14 and is confirmed as Mill's by its inclusion in his hand list of his publications.[12]

Since this is the best illustration we have of the manner in which Mill expanded a brief suggestion of Mrs. Taylor's into an article which he describes as 'a joint production, very little of which was mine', it deserves a little fuller discussion. The magistrate had sentenced to a fine and three months' imprisonment a man for illegally pawning another person's gold watch and had added that if the prisoner omitted to pay the fine and the estimated value of the watch 'within three days of the expiration of his imprisonment he should be once publicly whipped within the precincts of the gaol'. Mill makes this indeed the occasion for a violent onslaught on police magistrates in general and Mr. Secker in particular, but while he in general closely follows Mrs. Taylor's suggestions, he puts the main blame on the state of the law. After complaining that

'Amidst our talk of reformatory treatment we are returning to the most demoralizing, the most brutalizing because the most degrading of punishments, the bastinado',

he proceeds with some comments on the particular case and then continues

'If a brutal punishment can ever be appropriate, it is in a case of a brutal offence. . . . But who ever hears of corporal punishment for assault? One or two months imprisonment is all we hear of in the most atrocious cases; while, if property is in question—if pounds, shillings and pence have been tampered with, years of imprisonment, with hard labour (not to mention transportation) are almost the smallest penalty. And this is not peculiarly the fault of police magistrates. . . . It is the crime more especially of the legislators and of the superior courts. . . . Because persons in the upper and middle ranks are not subject to personal outrage, and *are* subject to having their watches stolen, the punishment of blows is revived, not for those who are guilty of blows, but for middle aged men who pawn watches. Is this to be endured?

'A few weeks ago, the punishment of flogging, in the case of the young man who shot at the Queen, was omitted, it is said, at the special desire of the Queen herself. The forebearance was uncomplimentary to the legislatorial wisdom which had recently enacted that penalty as peculiarly fit for that particular offence: but no one can be surprised by an example of good sense, good taste, and good feeling, given by the Queen.

'The crime of Hamilton was not of a degraded or brutal kind, though of a wicked and grave kind, deserving, in truth, and requiring, a severer punishment than it received. To refuse so disgusting a tribute as the revival of a brutalizing degradation as a punishment for offences against herself, was a worthy lesson to legislators and judges; and it was magnanimity, not like but most unlike a sovereign, to punish so serious an offence only as if it had been directed against the meanest subject. Would that her Majesty would take in hand this vast and vital question of the extinction of personal violence by the best and surest means—the illegalizing of corporal punishment, domestic as well as judicial, at any age. We conscientiously believe that more large and lasting good, both present and future, to the moral and social character of the whole people, would be achieved by such an act of legislation, than fifty years of legislative efforts without it would be required to supply.'

A few days later all other concerns are again suspended by the obvious approach of her husband's end.

July 16:[13] Monday. I have exceedingly wanted to write about many things, but cannot find a moment.

Yesterday & to-day this sad sad tragedy seems drawing to a close in the most piteous yet most patient & calm way.

Alas poor thing what a mocking life has been to him! ending in this fierce contest in which death gains inch by inch!

The sadness & horror of Nature's daily doings exceed a million fold all the attempts of Poets! There is nothing on earth I would not do for him & there is nothing on earth which *can* be done.

Do not write.

July 18:[14] Wednesday. I cannot write much now, not on account of the sorrow & distress for that has been as great for weeks—but I find I am quite physically exhausted & faint after two nights & a day of most anxious and sad watching, ended by his gently breathing the last without a sigh or pang at 3°/ck this morning.—I must defer saying anything till this next week has passed—To me a very painful one—feeling has to remain in abeyance while the many absolutely necessary mechanical details are ordered & attended to by me who never saw anything of the kind before & having no person *whatever* but the three children to advise with—it is the most trying time.

I do not know *where* he should be laid—having no connection with any place—I have thought of either Kensal Green or Hampstead as not too far? Tell me what you think! Write to me enclosed to Herbert at Cross Street.

There is a person here who is médisance personified & just now I w^d not have a shadow of the kind—so for a few days write to me only thus.

July 19:[15] Thursday. I want your opinion which is right & best—about coming to the funeral next Wednesday. I have no doubt your first impression is like mine, to say, *of course* yes—The grounds of all I wish done at this time are twofold—what the world thinks most respectful to him, & what he would have wished. But the latter *in this case* is I think pretty much included in the former, which is the reason I think at all of the former. I wish everything done which can be honourable & respectful to him being the last testimony of the affection I felt & feel for him & of the true & strong respect he has added too so much during this illness—& in all this I know you must truly sympathize. My *first* impression about your coming was a feeling of 'better not' grounded on the sort of distance which of late existed. But now on much consideration it seems to me in the first place that coming is certainly thought a mark of respect? Is it not? and that therefore your not doing so will be a *manque* of that. Then again the public in some degree & *his* public too have heard or are sure

to hear (through Arthur if no other way) of the Dedication
—of our intimacy—& on the side of his relations, nor that I
know of on mine, there does not appear to be any medisance.
(Indeed the kindness & attention to me of all his relations is
as marked as the neglect of these by mine.)

Thus all who know or care to hear anything on the subject
must hear of great intimacy. Does not therefore *absence* seem
much more noticeable than coming? On the other hand
nothing is more true of common world than 'out of sight out
of mind' & thought about it may never occur to any one as
they are principally relations or daily associates who will
come. I fancy Herbert has like him a sort of Ostrich instinct,
like morally timid people, always *not to do*—while my instinct
is always *to do*.

Tell me by a note addressed here what you think or feel
about this.

My first impulse was against—my present is *for*—but the
reasons are so nearly balanced that an opinion of yours would
turn the scale.

Write soon—I will write again too—soon—I have decided for Kensal Green. Tell me if there is *choice* as to situation there? I mean as to *niceness*, I know we can *choose*.

Do you know Gilbert Elliot? The clergyman? Is he not
incumbent somewhere near here? At Kensal Green I believe
one has to find ones own clergyman? Do you know? And
would it be a suitable thing to ask him?

Every detail without exception I have to order as there is
no one here but the three children. Herbert does the speaking to the people. [He (?)] is gone to business to-day. I
thought the inserting it so soon in the Papers very ugly &
unpleasant but Herbert so insisted upon it on account of his
having to reply to so many enquiries, that I gave way—which
I repent. Tell me if it *struck* you as indecent haste?

There is one more letter mainly about the question whether Mill
should attend the funeral, on the whole more against, and it is not
known whether he did. The letter concludes:

July 22:[16] Of feelings & thoughts there is far too much to be said in a note—I must see you soon—it occurs to me that it might be well to go down to Walton to spend next Sunday & that in that case you might come down for the Sunday. As there is no one there but old Mrs. Delarne it w^d not do for any one to sleep there but me & Lily as she is too old to do anything—but even a day would be much after such an interval.

Soon after Mrs. Taylor had another severe breakdown of her health.

When John Taylor's will, made less than five months before his death, was opened, it was found that he had left to his wife a life interest in the whole of his property.

Chapter Eight

MARRIAGE AND BREAK WITH
MILL'S FAMILY
1851

ALTHOUGH nearly two years passed between John Taylor's death and Mill's marriage to Harriet Taylor, the only significant documents which we have for this period are two letters by Mill. The first of these can be dated only approximately.

J. S. M. to H. T., about 1850:[1] thanks dearest dearest angel for the note—what it contained was a really important addition to the letter & I have put it in nearly in your words, which as your impromptu words almost always are, were a hundred times better than any I could find by study. What a perfect orator you would make—& what changes might be made in the world by such a one, with such opportunities as thousands of male dunces have. But you are to me, & would be to any one who knew you, the type of Intellect—because you have all the faculties in equal perfection—you can both think, & impress the thought on others—& can both judge what ought to be done & do it. As for me, nothing but the division of labour could make me useful—if there were not others with the capacities of intellect which I have not, where would be the use of those I have—I am but fit to be one wheel in an engine not to be the self moving engine itself—a real majestic intellect, not to say moral nature, like yours, I can only look up to & admire—but while you can love me as you so sweetly & beautifully shewed in that hour yesterday, I have all I care for or desire for myself—& wish for nothing except not to disappiont you—& to be so happy as to be some good to you (who are all good to me) before I die. This is a graver note than I thought it would be when I began it— for the influence of that dear little hour has kept me in spirits ever since—thanks to my one only source of good.

The second letter raises the subject which during the next few months was to be the occasion for the article on the Enfranchisement of Women. Since the 'Women's Rights Convention' at Worcester, Massachusetts, to which it refers, took place on 23 and 24 October 1850 and was reported in the European edition of the *New York Tribune* on 29 October, it cannot be of a much later date.

J. S. M. to H. T., *October/November 1850*:[2] You will tell me my own dearest love, what has made you out of spirits. I have been put in spirits by what I think will put you in spirits too—you know some time ago there was a Convention of Women in Ohio to claim equal rights—(& there is to be another in May)[3] well, there has just been a Convention for the same purpose in Massachussets—chiefly of women, but with a great number of men, including the chief slavery abolitionists Garrison, Wendell Phillips, the negro Douglas[4] &c. The New York Tribune contains a long report—most of the speakers are women—& I never remember any public meetings or agitation comparable to it in the proportion which good sense bears to nonsense—while as to tone it is almost like ourselves speaking—outspoken like America, not frightened & senile like England—not the least iota of compromise—asserting the whole of the principle & claiming the whole of the consequences, without any of the little feminine concessions & reserves—the thing will evidently not drop, but will go on till it succeeds, & I really do now think that we have a good chance of living to see something decisive really accomplished on that of all practical subjects the most important—to see that will be really looking down from Pisgah on the promised land—how little I thought we should ever see it.

The days seems always short to me as they pass. the time that seems long, the time that I am often impatient of the length of, is the time till spring—the time till we have a home, till we are together in our life instead of this unsatisfactory this depressing coming and going, in which all disagreeables have so much more power than belongs to them, & the atmosphere of happiness has not time to penetrate & pervade in the way I know so well even by the most imperfect experience & which then it will always——

The article which during the following winter grew out of this and finally appeared in the *Westminster Review* for July 1851 is generally described as by Mrs. Taylor. But while this is probably true enough so far as the general argument is concerned, Mill's introduction to the reprint of the article in Volume II of *Dissertations and Discussions* makes one doubt how much it applies to the actual writing.[5] He describes it merely as, unlike the other 'joint productions' of the period, as 'hers in a peculiar sense, my share in it being little more than that of an editor and amanuensis'. The article must have been practically completed by the time when Mill offered it to the editor of the *Westminster Review*:

J. S. M. to W. E. Hickson:[6] India House/3ʳᵈ March 1851/ Dear Hickson—If you are inclined for an article on the Emancipation of Women, a propos the Convention in Massachussets which I mentioned to you the last time I saw you, I have one nearly ready, which can be finished and sent to you within a week, which, I suppose, is in time for your April number.

Very truly yours,

J. S. Mill

To Hickson this must the more have appeared as a definite statement that Mill was himself the author, as they had corresponded a year earlier about the possibility of just such an article. It would seem most unlikely that Mill should have used so definite a form of words if he had not at the time himself so regarded it. Hickson appears at first to have answered that there was not likely to be room for the article in the next issue, and when some days later he asked for the manuscript, Mill had not made enough progress and the article had to wait for the July issue.

It was thus fresh from the work on this article that Mill wrote out that formal promise never to claim any rights that the law of marriage would confer on him which has already appeared in Elliot's edition of his letters:[7]

Being about, if I am so happy as to obtain her consent, to enter into the marriage relation with the only woman I have ever known, with whom I would have entered into that state; & the whole character of the marriage relation as constituted by law being such as both she and I entirely & conscientiously disapprove, for this amongst other reasons, that it confers upon one of the parties to the contract, legal power & control over the person, property, & freedom of action of the other party, independent of her own wishes and will; I, having no means of legally divesting myself of these odious powers (as I most assuredly would do if an engagement to that effect could be made legally binding on me) feel it my duty to put on record a formal protest against the existing law of marriage, in so far as conferring such powers; and a solemn promise never in any case or under any circumstances to use them. And in the event of marriage between Mrs. Taylor and me I declare it to be my will and intention, & the condition of the engagement between us, that she retains in all respects whatever the same absolute freedom of action, & freedom of disposal of herself and of all that does or may at any time belong to her, as if no such marriage had taken place; and I absolutely disclaim & repudiate all pretension to have acquired any *rights* whatever by virtue of such marriage.

6th March 1851   J. S. Mill

About the same time Mill appears to have informed his family of the intended marriage. It must have been then that his mother and his two unmarried sisters, Clara and Harriet, with whom until then he had been living in Kensington, committed the never to be forgiven offence of not at once calling upon the lady whom until then they had not been allowed to know and to whom they had probably not even dared to allude. Very soon after Mrs. Taylor seems to have left London with her younger son and her daughter for Melcombe Regis whence Mill either accompanied or soon followed them to make final arrangements for the wedding. Back in London on 11 April he acknowledged briefly but in fairly cordial terms the congratulations of his married sisters Willie and Jane.[8] 'No one ever was more to be congratulated than I am', he wrote to the latter and to both he explained that he and his wife will try to find during the summer a suitable house a little way out of London and that they did not expect to set up house before the autumn. But in a letter to his brother George in Madeira, though he provided the invalid with news of political developments at home, he made no allusion to the impending marriage.[9]

A few days later he returned to Dorsetshire for a fortnight's leave around Easter and on Easter Monday, 21 April, the ceremony was performed at the Register Office at Melcombe Regis, apparently in the presence of only Algernon and Helen Taylor, who signed as witnesses. A curious ostensible letter by Mill to his wife, of a somewhat later date, which refers to an incident at the ceremony may be inserted here.

J. S. M. to H. M., 13 July 1852: My dearest wife/Though I am persuaded it is unnecessary for any practical purpose, it will be satisfactory to me to put into writing the explanation of an accidental circumstance connected with the registry of our marriage at the Superintendant Registrar's Office at Weymouth on the 21st of April 1851.—Our marriage by the Registrar Mr. Richards was perfectly regular, and was attested as such by Mr. Richards and by the Superintendant Registrar Mr. Dodson, in the presence of both of whom, as well as of the two witnesses, we signed the register. But I was not aware that it was necessary to sign my name at full length, thinking that as in most other legal documents, the proper signature was the ordinary one of the person signing; and my ordinary signature being J. S. Mill, I at first signed in that manner; but on being told by the Registrar that the name must be written at full length, I did the only thing which occurred to me and what I believe the Registrar suggested, that is, I filled in the remaining letters of my name. As there was not sufficient space for them, they were not only written very small and close, but not exactly in a line with the initials and the surname, and the signature consequently has an unusual appearance. The reason must be at once apparent to any one who sees it, as it is obvious that J. S. Mill was written first, and the remainder filled in afterwards. It is almost superfluous to say that this is not stated for your information—you being as well aware of it as myself, but in order that there may be a statement in existence of the manner in which the signature came to present this unusual appearance. It cannot possibly affect the legality of our marriage, which I have not the smallest doubt is as regular and valid as any marriage can be; but so long as it is possible that any doubt could for a moment suggest itself either to our own or to any other minds, I cannot feel at ease, and therefore, unpleasant as I know it must be to you, I do beg you to let us even now be married again, and this time in a church, so that hereafter no shadow of a doubt on the subject can ever arise. The process is no doubt disagreeable, but I have thought much and anxiously about it, and I have quite made up my mind that however annoying the fact, it is better to undergo the annoyance than to let the matt[er][10] remain as it is. Therefore I hope you will comply with my earnest wish—and the sooner it is done the better.

your
J. S. Mill

July 13th 1852
Mrs. J. S. Mill,/Blackheath Park

It does not seem that such a further ceremony as Mill suggested actually took place and it is to be hoped that Mrs. Mill laughed him out of his apprehensions.

Mill was back in London a week after the wedding and very soon after this engaged in reading the proofs of the article on the Enfranchisement of Women which was probably completed during the stay at Melcombe Regis.

The marriage led to the most painful episode in Mill's life, his complete break with his mother and her other children. The real cause of this is obscure and it seems to have been almost as unintelligible to his relations as to us. Twenty-two years later his sister Harriet still could only say that while 'up to the time of his marriage he had been everything to us. . . . It was a frightful blow to lose him at once and forever, without even a word of explanation,—only in evident anger.'[11] The nearest approach to an account of what happened we get in a letter in which his youngest sister tried a few months after the marriage to remonstrate with Mill against his behaviour towards his mother and the two unmarried sisters in London. Mary Colman was then a young woman of thirty-one and since her marriage four years before was living in the country with her growing family. Her husband Charles Colman seems to have belonged to the Calvinistic sect of Plymouth Brethren and Mary herself to have been at least a devout Christian.[12]

Mary E. Colman to J. S. M.:[13] July 18th 1851/My dear John/In thinking over the strange change which appears to have taken place in your character, which has taken place in your conduct towards your family, during the last six months whilst striving to feel indifferent towards you, I felt that even now I loved you too much for such indifference, and I trust that a worthier feeling had gained possession of me, when I determined honestly to write and remonstrate with you on your present conduct. Under these circumstances I could not help recalling the letters which you sent me immediately before my marriage, letters which first made me aware that individually I was an object of no interest to you, that you had no affection for me.

Believe me I bear you no resentment for the bitter pangs which this conviction forced on me by yourself gave me; I *never* felt the least resentfully—I thought that I had perhaps been presumptuous that the expressions of kindness which you had been in the habit of using towards me, the uniform kindness you had shown me, I had no right to suppose proceeded from love to myself, but from a *principle* of not giving others needless pain. I *had* wondered sometimes to see you (in a less degree perhaps) kind to others of whom I had heard you speak in a way which had made me know you did not respect them; I however felt assured that this was from the same principle. Although however I felt no resentment, I felt less respect, I no longer could feel that you were unerring. I felt that you had been needlessly cruel in your *manner* of telling me this, and that however much I might have disappointed you in other respects the love I bore you even if I had been the dirt under your feet deserved it not——

On recovering a little from the *severe* 'agony' (for I *will* tell you the truth) which your letters gave me, letters which you have probably forgotten but which I have never yet had the courage to reopen, I determined that I would never again love you or any human creature to such a degree as to cause me such grief——But now when I find you acting unworthily towards others, I try to feel that your lowering yourself is nothing to me but in vain (?), and a voice within me urges me at least to endeavour to do you the only service that may ever be in my power to tell you the whole truth.

When Clara left this house December last she was congratulating herself in returning to a home, for some reasons which you know, unpleasant to her, that at least your society your kindness would compensate her for all besides. How great then was my surprise to find that you were behaving in the beginning as if she had affronted you in some way that finally after you had announced your intended marriage your behaviour became more extraordinary still, that in fact Clara was suffering intensely, the truth of which when once stated by herself no one would doubt who knew as you do how undemonstrative and uncomplaining she is by nature.

That you showed no interest in them or their concerns, these were negative, but positive acts of unkindness were not wanting. That at last your presence which used always to bring happiness, had become painful to the last degree——
I ask you now yourself if such conduct is worthy of you——

If it would be well if all brothers were to act in the same way. And finally I ask you how you could act so to Clara who valued you not for your reputation or any other advantages which you could bring to her, but for yourself, thoroughly unselfishly. I tell you now and one day you may know yourself that you have cast away a pearl of great price. And for what? What has she done, what has anyone done, what do you alledge. I can find nothing except that my mother did not call on your wife the day after you had announced your engagement, the propriety of which step as a matter of Etiquette remains to be settled. Anyhow however you know full well, that if you had only expressed a wish to my Mother on the subject anything would have been done. But even supposing that their behaviour had been bad which I cannot believe was that any justification for yours.

Before your marriage I trusted that anxiety and the absorbing nature of a very strong attachment might account for your appearing to forget or to be utterly indifferent to their feelings though even you must have known what a blank your mere absence would create.

But since your marriage—How bitterly cruel to refuse to see [?] at the India House, who if she had faults loved you enough to suffer from such a refusal. Then the farce of your fashionable call, at Kensington and your evident dread lest any of your family should show the least affection for you. It was well for Clara that she felt herself unequal weakened by her passage from France, to see you without exhibiting emotion before your wife, since even I determined as I was not to let your conduct influence me in my conduct towards your wife and steeled as I fancied myself, felt a difficulty in bearing the sensation your iciness struck into me.

Again when Clara determined that your conduct should not make her behave ill to your wife called on her, how did you drive her from your door; and poor little Clara King[14] whom your wife had expressed a wish to see and who went anxious to see Hadji and Lilla about whom her Uncle

173

George had written her. Finally your last letter, how needless an insult, and how unworthy of a man of the least sense, in the first place you knew that your sisters would not lie about your wife and if my Mother has ever erred it has been in speaking so warmly in favour of a person of whom personally she knew nothing, and with regard to the piece of mischievous gossip which you chose to believe, I should have thought that you, who have already suffered so much from such things ought to have been the last to have given ear to them.

Do not imagine that I attribute to the influence of your wife this conduct of yours. I have none but good feelings towards her, I was no liar when I told you I wished to know her, I had long wished it, before I ever thought of her becoming your wife—Why were you not open with me, why did you not tell me when you answered my letter, that you did not wish that she should know your sisters, you would have spared yourself and your family much pain.

One word more before I close this letter, which may be the last you ever receive from me; As regards the unfortunate estrangement which has taken place between you and George now for some years, and which was increased by some occurrences which took place when I last saw you at Kensington now more than a year ago, you may remember that *I* was the only one who told you you were unjust in your judgment of him, I knew George better than you did, and I told you you were mistaken. I had known George in his unreserved moments and from childhood and although we had never spoken on the subject I felt convinced that had you not yourself destroyed your influence over him, by showing at some time or other that you were ashamed of him and thought nothing of him, did not love him, you might have led him in any direction, so great was his *respect* for you as a man. But you must have shown him that you were afraid of his disgracing *you*. From such a sway he turned away, had you trusted him as a man, with a noble heart and as he deserved, you would never have had occasion to say he 'never had a character'. I should have told you this had I had an opportunity of being with you alone, at that time—— I tell it you now because it may be my last opportunity.

And now Good Bye. I have prayed that this letter may touch your heart for we differ 'as you observed' in our opinions or rather say convictions, but this difference has not made me love you less, and in striving each day to become more Christian I feel that I shall love you more really.

I finish a painful task with one last request, urging you by the only feeling that now seems remaining to you, 'your love for your wife' not to throw this from you as coming from one of a family now evidently hateful to you, but to read it through without irritation, judge from what motives it has sprung, and ask yourself if your present course is likely to conduce to her happiness.

Ever your aff^{te} Sister
Mary Elizabeth Colman

PS. If this should close all intercourse between us as I think possible it will be to me very painful, but at least the sting will be wanting of thinking that I have shrunk from the duty of honesty towards you.

Mill's reply to this and a further letter from Mary are not preserved. We may however form some conception of their tone when we see the withering replies which Mrs. Mill and Mill himself addressed to his youngest brother George in Madeira. The latter's letter which caused these retorts seems harmless enough, although we do not have the letter to Haji which accompanied it and which apparently gave the main offence.

George Grote Mill to H. M.:[15] Funchal May 20th 1851/ Dear Madam,/Though I have only heard at second hand, of your recent marriage with my brother, and know nothing certain except the bare fact, I will not pass over such an event in silence. My brother wrote to me a letter by the mail of April 9th but not a word wrote he then, had he written before, or has he written since of what I can only conclude he must have thought me either uninterested in, or undeserving to know. I don't know therefore what changes your union will make in your mode of life, if any. It would give me the greatest pleasure to hear that J. was free of the tether which binds *him* to the City & *you* to the neighbourhood of London. Twenty-five years work at the I. House, believe me, is as much as any man can well bear. I fear his generosity in money matters, has made his leaving the office difficult, but surely with his power of work & Established reputation, he could earn enough money by writing for the press much more easily & with much greater advantage to others than by his present employment. I believe his work already published would have given him an income if he had not made such easy bargains with his publishers.

I have not heard how your health is since I saw you in person & though I then thought your looking much stronger than when I had seen you last, you complained of it: pray let me hear sometime or other. If you feel in me any part of the interest which I feel in you all, you will not leave me in entire darkness.

My own health continues pretty good. I am prosecuting the silk business, though it advances slowly towards a profitable conclusion. In the meantime I am endeavouring to earn a little money by writing. I have a long art. in the last No. of the British Quarterly (on volcanoes and earthquakes) but there is nothing original in it.

Believe me/dear Mrs. Taylor (I can't forget the old name)
Yours affect[ly]
Geo G. Mill

As I don't know your present address I send this to Cross St.[16] I am writing to Hadjy./Kind regards to Lily.

H. M. to George Grote Mill, Richmond, 5 July 1851:[17] I do not answer your letter because you deserve it—that you certainly do not—but because tho I am quite inexperienced in the best way of receiving or replying to an affront I think that in this as in all things, frankness and plain speaking are the best rule, as to me they are the most natural—also it is best that every one should speak for themselves. Your letters to me & to Haji must be regarded as one, being on the same subject & sent together to us. In my opinion they show want of truth modesty & justice to say little of good breeding or good nature which you appear to regard as very unnecessary qualities.

Want of justice is shown in suggesting that a person has probably acted without regard to their principles which principles you say you never [?]. Want of modesty in passing judgment on a person thus far unknown to you—want of everything like truth in professing as you do a liking [?] for a person who in the same note you avoid calling by their name using an unfriendly designation after having for years addressed them in to say the least a more friendly way. In fact want of truth is apparent in the whole, as your letters overflow with anger & animosity about a circumstance which in no way concerns you so far anything you say shows & which if there was any truth in your profession of regard sh^d be a subject of satisfaction to you. As to want of the good breeding which is the result of good feeling that appears to be a family failing.

The only small satisfaction your letter can give is the observation that when people desert good feeling they also are deserted by good sense—your wish to make a quarrel [?] with your brother & myself because we have used a right which the whole world, of whatever shade of opinion, accords to us, is as absurd as unjust and wrong.

Harriet Mill

Possibly this letter was never sent and the following of Mill's dispatched instead.

J. S. M. to George Grote Mill, India House, 4 August 1851 :[18]
I have long ceased to be surprised at any want of good sense or good manners in what proceeds from you—you appear to

be too thoughtless or too ignorant to be capable of either—but such want of good feeling, together with such arrogant assumption, as are shown in your letters to my wife & to Haji I was not prepared for. The best construction that can be put upon them is that you really do not know what insolence & presumption are: or you would not write such letters & seem to expect to be as well liked as before by those to whom & of whom they are written. You were 'surprised', truly, at our marriage & do not 'know enough of the circumstances to be able to form an opinion on the subject'. Who asks you to form an opinion? An opinion on what? Do men usually when they marry consult the opinion of a brother twenty years younger than themselves? or at my age, of any brother or person at all? But though you form no 'opinion' you presume to catechize Haji respecting his mother, & to call her to account before your tribunal for the conformity between her conduct & her principles—being at the same time as you say yourself, totally ignorant what your principles are. On the part of any one who avowedly does not know what her principles are, the surmise that she may have acted contrary to them is gratuitous impertinence. To every one who knows her it would be unnecessary to say that she has, in this as in all things, acted according to her principles. What imaginary principles are they which should prevent people who have known each other the greater part of their lives, during which her & Mr. Taylor's house has been more a home to me than any other, and who agree perfectly in all their opinions, from marrying?

You profess to have taken great offence because you knew of our intended marriage 'only at second hand'. People generally hear of marriages at 'second hand', I believe. If you mean that I did not write to you on the subject, I do not know any reason you had to expect that I should. I informed your mother & sisters who I knew would inform you & I did not tell them of it on account of any right they had to be informed, for my relations with any of them have been always of too cool & distant a kind to give them the slightest right or reason to expect anything more than ordinary civility from me—& when I did tell them I did not receive ordinary civility in return. In the dissertation on my character with which you favour Haji, you show yourself quite aware that it has never been my habit to talk to them about my concerns —& assuredly the feelings you have shown to me in the last two or three years have not been so friendly as to give me any cause for making an exception. As for the 'mystery' which on my father's authority you charge me with, if we are to bandy my father's sayings I could cite plenty of them about all his family except the younger ones, compared with which this is very innocent. It could be said at all but as a half joke—& every one has a right to be mysterious if they like. But I have not been mysterious, for I had never anything to be mysterious about. I have not been in the habit of talking unasked about my friends, or indeed about any other subject.

J. S. M.

A similar letter appears to have descended on George Mill from Algernon Taylor and a paragraph of his reply to it explains a little further the expressions which had given so much offence.

George Grote Mill to Algernon Taylor; Funchal, 27 September 1851:[19] Believing that your mother would generally rather discourage than encourage the marriage of others I certainly was at first surprised to find her giving so deliberate an example of marriage in her own case; in which moreover there seemed to me less to be gained than in almost any marriage I could think of. I certainly took sufficient interest in both parties to wish to solve the matter in my own mind & fancied (erroneously it now appears) that I might express my feelings to you without giving offence; but you have placed yourself on stilts & decline all confidential intercourse; so the matter ends. As your letter alludes chiefly to your mother I must observe that you ought to know that I am quite incapable of being impertinent to her, a charge which I think you might leave her to make when she finds any impertinence in my letters to her.

Here this particular correspondence presumably ended and there was probably little more intercourse between J. S. Mill or his wife and young George Mill until three years later the latter put an end to his life shortly before he would inevitably have died of consumption. But his sisters Clara and Harriet in London and Mary Colman, urged on by their mother, continued their efforts at a reconciliation.

Clara Esther Mill to J. S. M.:[20] 4 Westbourne Park Villa/ March 3rd [1852]/Dear John/I am sorry to hear from my Mother that you considered I had been wanting in civility to Mrs. Mill, I certainly never meant to be so, nor indeed do I think I have, though it is evident that you have had a strong impression that such was the case with the family ever since your marriage—quite erroneously however I believe. I am entirely at a loss to imagine in what my incivility has consisted. I (and I alone of those in this house) have seen your correspondence with Mary & George in which you state clearly enough your opinions of us all, and that there are some of us, myself among the rest, whom you hold in the same estimation as my father did. I cannot therefore be the acquaintance of a person who 'only deserves common civility from you' which you seek for your wife, especially as you do it not on the score of relationship. What then am I to understand? You are, to use George's words 'a great and good man' and you see farther than I do. I do not therefore pretend to judge you, I only cannot understand you, but under such circumstances to have any personal intercourse with you, could only be painful, and tho' I by no means admit that I deserve your contempt, I do not conceive that my acquaintance can be of any importance to your wife. We did not seek each other's acquaintance before her marriage nor ever should have done so—on what ground then begin it now?

This may after all not be the subject of your complaint—

nor is it of much consequence, we have failed to understand each other in an apparent intimacy of 40 years it is therefore a hopeless case, and with sorrow but most decidedly I wish to give up the appearance.

C. E. Mill

After drafting a reply to this[21] Mill seems to have confined himself to answer it and a similar note from his sister Harriet in a brief letter to his mother.

J. S. M. to Mrs. James Mill, India House, 5 March 1852:[22] My dear Mother/I received yesterday two most silly notes from Clara & Harriet filled with vague accusations. They say that when you called at the I.H. on Monday I 'complained to you of their incivility to my wife'. I did no such thing. Another charge is that I repeated idle gossip in a note to you last summer—this is untrue. George Fletcher called at the I.H. a day or two before I wrote that note to you & asked after my wife saying he was sorry to hear she was not well. I asked where he had heard that; he said he was told so at Kensington, & this I mentioned in my note to you; no one else had anything to do with it. This was not 'gossip'.

I hope you are not the worse for your journey to I.H.

Y^{rs} aff^y

J. S. M.

Chapter Nine

ILLNESS
1851–1854

I T was probably only after their return from a holiday in France and Belgium in September 1851 that Mill and his wife set up house together. Blackheath Park, where they had taken a house, was then still a rural district at the outskirts of London and the house itself facing 'a wide open space of rolling meadow bounded far off by a blue outline of distant hills'.[1] It was accessible from London only by railway and, although Mill made the daily train journey to the City, this placed them effectively outside the social contacts of the metropolis. The efforts of some old friends, such as Lord Ashburton,[2] to make the marriage the occasion for drawing them back into social life, proved unavailing, while others appear deliberately to have omitted even the ordinary courtesy calls.[3] Their only guests, usually for weekends, seem to have been a few old friends such as W. J. Fox and his daughter or an occasional foreign scholar. Even fairly close friends of the period, such as the philosopher Alexander Bain, apparently were never asked to Blackheath Park during Mrs. Mill's life, and Mill himself never went into society, except six or seven times a year to the meetings of the Political Economy Club where he frequently opened the discussions.[4] The other members of the household were Mrs. Mill's two younger children, Algernon and Helen Taylor. Her elder son, Herbert, who had taken over his father's business, remained in town and appears to have married soon afterwards.

Of the daily routine of the life at Blackheath Park we get a glimpse in a passage of a letter by Helen Taylor to her mother written a few years later at the beginning of her first prolonged absence.

Helen Taylor to H. M., Newcastle, 23 November 1856:[5] I
like to think about nine o'clock that you are talking with
him. I feel very unhappy at three because you are at dinner
and I am not there to help you. I grow impatient at five
because he has not come in but at six it is pleasant to think
that he is making tea and you have got my letter [which he
has brought home].

A different recollection by Algernon Taylor which shows Mill in a
little known role may also be given a place here:

'Mr. Mill, who used, now and then, to perform on the piano, but
only when asked to do so by my mother; and then he would at once
sit down to the instrument, and play music entirely of his own composition, on the spur of the moment: music of a singular character,
wanting, possibly, in the finish which more practice would have im-
parted, but rich in feeling, vigour, and suggestiveness: the performer
taking for his theme, may be, the weird grandeur of cloud and storm,
the deep pathos of a dirge, the fierce onset of the battlefield, or the
triumphant, joyous time of a processional march. When he had
finished, my mother would, perhaps, enquire what had been the idea
running in his mind, and which had formed the theme of the im-
provisation—for such it was, and a strikingly characteristic one too.'[6]

The quiet and retired life to which Mill and his wife had hoped to
settle down did not long remain undisturbed, however. Probably even
the first two years, for which we have practically no documents, were
clouded by ill health. But these years were still a time of fairly normal
activities. Of the very small amount of publications listed by Mill for
this period it is stated of an article in the *Morning Chronicle* of
28 August 1851, on the need for protection of wives and children from
brutal husbands and fathers, that 'like all my newspaper articles on
similar subjects, and most of my articles on all subjects, [it] was a joint
production with my wife';[7] and with regard to the small pamphlet on
the same subject printed for private distribution in 1853[8] the same list
says: 'In this I acted chiefly as amanuensis to my wife'. Of Mill's only
major publication of these years, the article on 'Whewell's Moral
Philosophy', which he contributed to the *Westminster Review*, with its
strong attack on Whewell's intuitionist theory of morals, we can at
least be certain that it had Mrs. Mill's full sympathy. During the seven

and a half years between their marriage and Mrs. Mill's death only one other more substantial article appeared, the article on Grote's *History of Greece* to which we shall have to refer presently. Most of what he wrote then appeared only at a later date.

The first major task to which the Mills turned after commencing life at Blackheath Park was the thorough revision of the *Political Economy* for the third edition which appeared in the spring of 1852. It is the most comprehensive revision the book underwent and represents a considerable further advance towards socialism. But as they were together at the time we have no documents to show us the part Mrs. Mill took in the task.

In 1853 not only Mrs. Mill's health, which had been precarious so long, was decidedly deteriorating, but Mill himself was also showing increasing signs of serious illness. Towards the end of August he took his wife to Sidmouth in Devonshire, where she stayed for a short period while Mill returned to his work at India House. Of the five of Mill's letters to her written to Sidmouth which are extant,[9] one may be given in full.

J. S. M. to H. M.: India House/Aug. 29, 1853/ This is the first time since we were married my darling wife that we have been separated & I do not like it at all—but your letters are the greatest delight & as soon as I have done reading one I begin thinking how soon I shall have another. Next to her letters the greatest pleasure I have is writing to her. I have written every day since Friday [August 26] except the day there was no post—I am glad the cause of your not getting Saturday's letter was the one I guessed & that you did get it at last. This time I have absolutely nothing to tell except my thoughts, & those are wholly of you. As for occupation, after I get home I read as long as I can at the thick book[10]—yesterday evening I fairly fell asleep over it, but I shall read it to the end, for I always like to get to the latest generalizations on any scientific subject & that in particular is a most rapidly progressive subject just at present & is so closely connected with the subject of mind & feeling that there is always a chance of something practically useful turning up. I am very much inclined to take the Essay on Nature[11] again in hand & rewrite it as thoroughly as I did the review of Grote[12]—that is what it wants—it is my old way of working & I do not think I have ever done anything well which was not done in that way. I am almost sorry about the engagement with Lewis[13] about India as I think it would have been a much better employment of the time to have gone on with some of our Essays. We must finish the best we have got to say, & not only that, but publish it while we are alive. I do not see what living depository there is likely to be of our thoughts, or who in this weak generation that is growing up will even be capable of thoroughly mastering & assimilating your ideas, much less of re-originating them—so we must write them & print them, & then they can wait until there are again thinkers. But I shall never be satisfied unless you allow ou[r][14] best book the book which is to come, to have our *two* names on the title page. It ought to be so with everything I publish, for the better half of it all is yours, but the book which will contain our best thoughts, if it has only one name to it, that should be yours. I should like everyone to know that I am the Dumont & you the originating mind, the Bentham, bless her!

I hope the weather has improved as much with you as it has here—but it does not look settled yet—with all loving thoughts and wishes

J. S. Mill

In signing this letter with his full name Mill departed for once from an almost invariable practice of himself and his wife, whose letters to each other generally lacked both the usual commencement and signature.

As Mrs. Mill's health apparently had not improved at Sidmouth and Mill's condition was getting worse, they were soon after ordered abroad by their doctor. Mill obtained leave of absence for the last three months of the year, which they spent at Nice. Although they themselves long refused to believe it, they were evidently both in fairly advanced states of consumption and this appears to have been sufficiently apparent to Mill's friends at India House to make them doubt whether they would ever see him again. At Nice Mrs. Mill had a severe hæmorrhage of which she nearly died and Mill's own symptoms continued to get worse, but he still tried to convince himself that it was not the fatal 'family disease', as he calls it in the *Autobiography*, of which his father and two of his brothers had died.[15] At the end of the year he even returned to London and his work at India House after he had taken Mrs. Mill to Hyères where she was to stay until the beginning of the spring. All but two of the thirty-eight carefully numbered letters written by Mill to her during this period have been preserved. They give a minute picture of the progressive deterioration of his health during the next few months. Of Mrs. Mill's pencilled notes which he received in reply we have only one, because Mill burnt all the others at her request.

Mill's return to London in the middle of the winter took him almost ten days and must have put no small strain on the invalid. First by diligence to Marseilles, then by train to Avignon and again by diligence and omnibus to Lyons and Chalons, and finally with the railroad to Paris and Boulogne; he had the extra misfortune of being snowed up in the train for twenty-four hours on the last lap of this journey. The first letter from London, written on the day of his arrival, reports on the return home and to India House.

J. S. M. to H. M., India House, 6 January 1854: [Ellice] as well as Hill Thornton & others asked the questions that might be expected about your health & in a manner which showed interest—Peacock[16] alone asked not a single question about your health & hardly about mine but struck into India House subjects & a visit he had from James.[17] Grote & Prescott[18] called together today, as they said to inquire whether I was returned & very warm, especially Grote, in their expressions of sympathy & interest about your illness. It is odd to see the sort of fragmentary manner in which news gets about—Grote had heard of you as dangerously ill but not of my being ill at all, & of your illness as a fever but not of the rupture of a blood vessel. Grote is vastly pleased with the article in the Edinburgh—a propos I found here a letter from Mrs. Grote, of complimentation on the article, which though little worthy of the honour of being sent to you

I may as well inclose. The impudence of writing to me at all
& of writing in such a manner is only matched by the excessive conceit of the letter. Grote alluded to it saying that Mrs.
Grote had written to me after reading the article—I merely
answered that I had found a note from her on arriving.

Two days later Mill commenced the 'experiment' of trying to note
down in a little book 'at least one thought per day which is worth writing down'. These notes, which he continued during the whole period
of his wife's absence, have been printed in full forty years ago.[19] But as
some of them gain new significance and poignancy from the knowledge
of the circumstances under which they were written, some passages
from this 'diary' will be reproduced here together with the extracts
from the letters.

J. S. M.'s Diary, 9 January, 1854: What a sense of protection is given by the consciousness of being loved, and what
an additional sense, over and above this, by being near the
one by whom one is and wishes to be loved the best. I have
experience at present of both these things; for I feel as if no
really dangerous illness could actually happen to me while I
have her to care for me; and yet I feel as if by coming away
from her I had parted with a kind of talisman, and was more
open to the attacks of the enemy than while I was with her.

J. S. M. to H. M., India House, 9 January 1854: The
Kensington letters I inclose, as it is best you should see all
that comes from that quarter—& along with them a note I
have just written to my mother. I have looked through the
Edinburgh Review for October—the article on Grote reads,
to my mind, slighter & flimsier than I thought it would.
There is another article by Greg on Parl^y reform[20] shewing
that he had seen our letter to Ld Monteagle[21] (the one Marshall writes about) for he has adopted nearly every idea in the
letter almost in the very words, & has also said speaking of
the ballot, that it is within his knowledge that some to whom
ballot was once a sine qua non, now think it would be 'a step
backward' the very phrase of the letter. He goes on to attack

the ballot with arguments some of them so exactly the same as those in our unpublished pamphlet[22] (even to the illustrations) that one would think he had seen that too if it had been physically possible. Though there are some bad arguments mixed yet on the whole this diminishes my regret that ours was not published. It is satisfactory that those letters we took so much trouble to write for some apparently small purpose (?), so often turn out more useful than we expected. Now about reviewing Comte:[23] the reasons *pro* are evident. Those *con* are, 1. I don't like to have anything to do with the name or with any publication of H. Martineau. 2dly the West^r though it will allow I dare say anything else, could not allow me to speak freely about Comte's atheism, & I do not see how it is possible to be just to him, when there is so much to attack, without giving him praise on that part of the subject. 3dly, as Chapman is the publisher he doubtless wishes, & expects, an article more laudatory on the whole, than I sh^d be willing to write. You dearest one will tell me what your perfect judgment & your feeling decide.

J. S. M. to H. M., Blackheath Park, 16 January 1854: About Mrs. Grote's letter, my darling is I daresay right. It did not escape me that there was that amende, & I should have felt much more indignant if there had not. But what was to my feeling like impudent, though impudent is not exactly the right word, was, that after the things she has said & done respecting us, she should imagine that a tardy sort of recognition of you, & flattery to me, would serve to establish some sort of relation between us & her. It strikes me as déplacé to answer the letter, especially so long after it was written, but her having made this amende might make the difference of my asking how she is, at least when he mentions her. That is about as much, I think, as her good intentions deserve.—I will, dear, say to Grote what she wishes, & the best opportunity will be the first time he writes a note to me in that form. I do not, and have not for years, addressed him as *Mr.*—& it is very dull of him not to have taken the hint.—I am getting on with India house work but the arrear will take me a long time—I worked at it at home all yesterday (Sunday) & got through a good deal. Sunday, alas, is not so different from other days as when she is here —though more so than when I am quite with her. I am reading, in the evenings, as I said I would do, Sismondi's Italian Republics which I read last in 1838, before going to Italy. Having seen many of the places since makes it very interesting.

I. H. 17th. This morning I watched the loveliest dawn & sunrise & felt that I was looking directly to where she is & that that sun came straight from her. And now here is the Friday's letter which comes from her in a still more literal sense. I am so happy that the cough is better & that she is in better spirits. How kindly she writes about the keys, *never mind* darling. I have bought one set of flannels since. I am glad she likes the note to Sykes. As for Chapman's request, the *pro* was the great desire I feel to atone for the overpraise I have given Comte & to let it be generally known to those who know me what I think on the unfavourable side about him. The reason that the objection which you feel so strongly & which my next letter afterwards will have shown that I felt too, did not completely decide the matter with me, was that Chapman did not want a review of this particular book, but of *Comte* & I could have got rid of H.M.'s part in a sentence, perhaps without even naming her. I sh^d certainly have put Comte's own book at the head along with hers & made all the references to *it*. But malgré cela I disliked the connexion, & now I dislike it still more, & shall at once write to C. to refuse—putting the delay of an answer upon my long absence so that he may not think I hesitated.

J. S. M.'s Diary, 19 January 1854: I feel bitterly how I have procrastinated in the sacred duty of fixing in writing, so that it may not die with me, everything that I have in mind which is capable of assisting the destruction of error and prejudice and the growth of just feelings and true opinions. Still more bitterly do I feel how little I have done as an interpreter of the wisdom of one whose intellect is as much profounder than mine as her heart is nobler. If I ever recover my health, this shall be amended; and even if I do not, something may, I hope, be done towards it, provided a sufficient respite is allowed me.

J. S. M. to H. M., India House, 20 January 1854: I write every evening in the little book. I have been reading the Essay on Nature as I rewrote the first part of it before we left & I think it very much improved & altogether very passable. I think I could finish it equally well.

J. S. M. to H. M., 23 January 1854: I too have thought very often lately about the life & am most anxious that we should complete it the soonest possible. What there is of it is in a perfectly publishable state. As far as the writing goes it could be printed tomorrow—& it contains a full writing out as far as anything can write out, what you are, as far as I am competent to describe you, & what I owe to you—but, besides that until revised by you it is little better than unwritten, it contains nothing about our private circumstances, further than shewing that there was an intimate friendship for many years, & you only can decide what more is necessary or desirable to say in order to stop the mouths of enemies hereafter. The fact is that there is about as much written as I *can* write without your help & we must go through this together & add the rest to it at the very first opportunity—I have not forgotten what she said about bringing it with me to Paris.

Meanwhile Mill's health was getting constantly worse, though for a time his doctor continued to assure him that there was 'no organic disease'.

J. S. M. to H. M., 29 January 1854: I have been feeling much (I must have been incapable of feeling anything if I did not) about the shortness and uncertainty of life & the wrongness of having so much of the best of what we have to say, so long unwritten & in the power of chance—& I am determined to make a better use of what time we have. Two years, well employed, would enable us I think to get most of it into a state fit for printing—if not in the best form for popular effect, yet in the state of concentrated thought—a sort of mental pemican, which thinkers, when there are any after us, may nourish themselves with & then dilute for other people. The Logic & Pol. Ec. may perhaps keep their buoyancy long enough to hold these other things above water till there are people capable of taking up the thread of thought & continuing it. I fancy I see one large or two small posthumous volumes of Essays, with the Life at their head, & my heart is set on having these in a state fit for publication quelconque, if we live so long, by Christmass 1855; though not then to be published if we are still alive to improve & enlarge them. The first thing to be done & which I can do immediately towards it is to finish the paper on Nature, & this I mean to set about today, after finishing this letter—being the first Sunday that I have not thought it best to employ in I.H. work. That paper, I mean that part of it rewritten, seems to me on reading it to contain a great deal which we want said, said quite well enough for the volume though not so well as we shall make it when we have time. I hope to be able in two or three weeks to finish it equally well & then to begin something else—but all the other subjects in our list will be much more difficult for me even to begin upon without you to prompt me. All this however is entirely dependent on your health continuing to go on well, for these are not things that can be done in a state of real anxiety. In bodily ill health they might be.

In a later part of the same letter, written on the next day, Mill returns to the subject:

It is a pleasant coincidence that I should receive her nice

say about 'Nature' just after I have resumed it. I shall put those three beautiful sentences about 'disorder' verbatim into the essay. I wrote a large piece yesterday at intervals (reading a bit of Sismondi whenever I was tired) & I am well pleased with it. I don't think we should make these essays very long, though the subjects are inexhaustible. We want a compact argument first, & if we live to expand it & add a longer dissertation, tant mieux: there is need of both.

The 'three beautiful sentences' about disorder are probably those which occur on pp. 30 and 31 of the posthumous edition of the essay:

'Even the love of "order" which is thought to be a following of the ways of Nature, is in fact a contradiction of them. All which people are accustomed to deprecate as "disorder" and its consequences, is precisely a counterpart of Nature's ways. Anarchy and the Reign of Terror are overmatched in injustice, ruin, and death, by a hurricane and a pestilence.'

J. S. M. to H. M., *7 February 1854:* I finished the 'Nature' on Sunday as I expected. I am quite puzzled what to attempt next—I will just copy the list of subjects we made out in the confused order in which we put them down. Differences of character (nation, race, age, sex, temperament). Love. Education of tastes. Religion de l'Avenir. Plato. Slander. Foundation of Morals. Utility of religion. Socialism. Liberty. Doctrine that causation is will. To these I have now added from your letter, Family, & Conventional (?). It will be a tolerable two years work to finish all that. Perhaps the first of them is the one I could do most to by myself, at least of those equally important.

Diary, 8 February 1854: I would not, for any amount of intellectual eminence, be the only one of my generation who could see the truths which I thought of most importance to the improvement of mankind. Nor would I, for anything which life could give, be without a friend from whom I could learn at least as much as I could teach. Even the merely intellectual needs of my nature suffice to make me hope that

I may never outlive the companion who is the profoundest and most far-sighted and clear-sighted thinker I have ever known, as well as the most consumate in practical wisdom. I do not wish that I were so much her equal as not to be her pupil, but I would gladly be more capable than I am of thoroughly appreciating and worthily reproducing her admirable thoughts.

J. S. M. to H. M., 10 February 1854: You will be surprised when I tell you that I went again to Clark[24] this morning—& I am afraid you will think I am fidgety about my ailments, but the reverse is the case, for I never was so much the opposite of nervous about my own health, & I believe whatever were to happen I should look it in the face quite calmly. But my reason for going to day was one which I think would have made you wish me to go—namely the decided & unmistakable appearance of blood in the expectoration. Clark however on my describing it to him does not think it of any importance, but thinks it is very likely not from the lungs, & even if it does come from them, thinks it is from local & very circumscribed congestion not from a generally congested state. Very glad was I to hear of anything which diminishes the importance of bleeding in a chest case. I knew before that it is not at all a sure sign of consumption, as it often accompanies bronchitis—which is the real technical name of my cough, though it sounds too large & formidable for it. I am very well convinced, since Clark thinks so, that I am not in a consumption at present, however likely this cough is to end in that—for it seems to resist all the usual remedies. The favourable circumstance is that none of my ailments ever seem to yield to remedies, but after teazing on for an unconscionable time, go away or abate of themselves —as perhaps this will if all goes well with my dearest one. Indeed if I had belief in presentiments I should feel quite assured on that point, for it appears to me so completely natural that while my darling lives I should live to keep her company. I have not begun another Essay yet, but have read through all that is written of the Life—I find it wants revision, which I shall give it—but I do not well know what to do with some of the passages which we marked for alteration in the early part which we read together. They were mostly passages in which I had written, you thought, too much of the truth about my own defects. I certainly do not desire to say more about them than integrity requires, but the difficult matter is to decide how much that is. Of course one does not, in writing a life, either one's own or another's, undertake to tell everything—& it will be right to put something into *this* which shall prevent any one from being able to suppose or to pretend, that we undertake to keep nothing back. Still it va sans dire that it ought to be on the whole a fair representation. Since things appear to be on looking at them now to be said very crudely, which does not surprise me in the first draft, in which the essential was to say everything somehow, sauf to omit on general subjects, I find there is a great deal of good matter written down in the Life which we have not written anywhere else, & which will make it as valuable in that respect (apart from its main object) as the best things we have published. But of what particularly concerns *our* life there is nothing yet written, except the descriptions of you, & of your effect on me; which are at all events a permanent memorial of what I know you to be, & of (so far as it can be shown by generalities) of what I owe to you *intellectually*. That, though it is the smallest part of what you are to me, is the most important to commemorate, as people are comparatively willing to suppose all the rest. But we have to consider, which we can only do together, how much of our story it is advisable to tell, in order to make head against the representations of enemies when we shall not be alive to add anything to it. If it was not to be published for 100 years I should say, tell all, simply & without reserve. As it is there must be care taken not to put arms into the hands of the enemy.

Mrs. Mill's reply to this is the only one of her letters from this period which has been preserved.

H. M. to J. S. M., Hyères, 14 and 15 February 1854:[25] I do not think you at all fidgetty about your illness dear, and I never should think you too much so. I never feel objections to anything you do but when I think it tends to increase an ailment. I think (you may be sure) that you were quite right to go to C. about that bleeding, but I cannot help believing that the practice of looking at the expectoration in the morning, is itself in great measure the cause of there being any expectoration at all. I cannot but think that if you tried as earnestly as I have done since Octr to avoid any expectoration that you could lose the habit altogether as I have done. I am far more anxious about your health than about my own, and the more because I do not think a continental life would suit you. You would soon miss the stimulus and excitement of the daily intercourse with other men to which you are accustomed. However you must be the only judge on that subject and you are not likely to have to decide it at present at least. I hope you have not taken cold again—here after a cold east wind last Friday and Sat. on Monday the bright sky suddenly darkened and a snow storm more violent than we have them in England covered the whole town and country with deep snow in about an hour. Last night it froze hard and they express great fear for the olives. To-day the sun has melted the snow, tho' not in shady places, and it continues very cold. I do not feel at all the worse for the cold, but it is true it has not lasted long as yet. They say here that March is a cold windy month. After the bad days I had last week, I have been something better again, as I see I always am after an unusually bad week.

About the Essays dear, would not religion, the Utility of Religion,[26] be one of the subjects you would have most to say on—there is to account for the existence nearly universal of some religion (superstition) by the instincts of fear, hope and mystery etc., and throwing over all doctrines and theories, called religion, and devices for power, to show how religion and poetry fill the same want, the craving after higher objects, the consolation of suffering, the hope of heaven for the selfish, love of God for the tender and grateful —how all this must be superseded by morality deriving its power from sympathies and benevolence and its reward from the approbation of those we respect.

There, what a long winded sentence, which you could say ten times as well in words half the length. I feel sure dear that the Life is not half written and that half that is written will not do. Should there not be a summary of our relationship from its commencement in 1830—I mean given in a dozen lines—so as to preclude other and different versions of our lives at Kis^n (?) and Wal^n—our summer excursions, etc. This ought to be done in its genuine truth and simplicity— strong affection, intimacy of friendship, and no impropriety. It seems to me an edifying picture for those poor wretches who cannot conceive friendship but in sex—nor believe that expediency and the consideration for feelings of others can conquer sensuality. But of course this is not my reason for wishing it done. It is that every ground should be occupied by ourselves on our own subject.

I thought so exactly as you did about that trash in the Ex[aminer] about the Russell letters[27]—she was an amiable woman as there are, only a good deal spoilt, hardened by puritanism, who was excessively in love with her husband (though she did not admire him much).

Will you observe dear before paying Sharpers if the Bill deli^d you have is dated? He never has sent a bill, but I suppose if the Bill Deli^d is dated Christmas 1853 that is sufficient. Will you tell Haji on his birthday (21) that I asked you to wish him many happy returns of it for me. The garden will soon want crops put in but I will write about it next time. I am very glad Kate continues satisfied and well conducted.

Adieu with all love to my Kindest and dearest.

Before he received this letter Mill wrote once more about the *Autobiography* in connexion with an intended meeting at Paris.

J. S. M. to H. M., 13 February 1854: I have not forgotten that I am to bring the biography with me. It *is* mentioned in the codicil, placed at your absolute disposal to publish or not. But if we are not to be together this summer it is doubly important to have as much of the life written as can be written before we meet—therefore will you my own love in one of your sweetest letters give me your general notion of what we should say or imply concerning our private concerns. As it is it shows confidential friendship & strong attachment ending in marriage when you were free & ignores there having ever been any scandalous suspicions about us.

Eight days later Mrs. Mill's letter on the subject had at last reached him.

J. S. M. to H. M., 20 February 1854: Your program of an essay on religion is beautiful, but it requires you to fill it up —I can try but a few paragraphs will bring me to the end of all I have got to say on the subject. What would be the use of my outliving you! I could write nothing worth keeping alive for except with your prompting. As to the Life—which I have been revising & correcting—the greater part, in bulk, of what is written consists in the history of my mind *up to* the time when your influence over it began—& I do not think there can be much objectionable in that part, even including as it does, sketches of the character of most of the people I was intimate with—if I could be said to be so with anyone. I quite agree in the sort of résumé of our relationship which you suggest—but if it is to be only as you say a dozen lines, or even three or four dozen, could you not my own love write it out your darling self & send it in one of your precious letters. It is one of the many things on which the *fond* would be much better laid by you & we can add to it afterwards if we see occasion. I sent the Examiner today I am sorry & ashamed of the spots of grease on it. The chapter of the P[olitical] E[conomy] I shall send by the post which takes this letter . . . I will give your 'happy returns' to Haji tomorrow. The last Sunday but one I took occasion in talking with him to say that you were the profoundest thinker & most consumate reasoner I had ever known—he made no remark to the point but ejaculated a strong wish that you were back here.

Two of the entries made by Mill in his 'little book' at about this time may find a place here.

Diary, 16 February, 1854: Niebuhr said that he wrote only for Savigny; so I write only for her when I do not write entirely *from* her. But in my case, as in his, what is written for only one reader, that one being the most competent intellect, is likeliest to be of use to the many, readers or not, whose benefit is the object of the writing, though not the principal incentive to it.

Diary, 20 February, 1854: Whenever I look back at any of my own writing of two or three years previous, they seem to me like the writing of some stranger whom I have seen and known long ago. I wish that my acquisition of power to do better had kept pace with the continual elevation of my standing point and change of my bearings towards all the great subjects of thought. But the explanation is that I owe the enlargement of my ideas and feelings to *her* influence, and that she could not in the same degree give me powers of execution.

In the letters of these weeks various problems arising from the probable necessity of Mill's retirement from India House and of possibly having to live permanently on the Continent come up repeatedly. He hoped, if his health should make this necessary, to be able to retire on two-thirds of his salary, but was on the whole inclined to try to hold on for another year or so, with the help of six month's leave during the following winter on a medical certificate which he thought ought to be readily granted, considering that he had just finished all the arrears and thus 'done in two months the work of $5\frac{1}{2}$'.[28] In the same connexion he explains to his wife about their income from investments that 'we are not yet at the £500 which you mention but we are past £400'.[29] The same thought had evidently been in his mind when a little earlier he had expressed much pleasure about the continued favourable receipts from his books.

J. S. M. to H. M., *29 January 1854:* The Logic has sold 260 copies in 1853—in 1852 it sold only 206. This steady sale must proceed I think from a regular annual demand from colleges & other places of education. What is strange is that the Pol. Ec. Essays sell from 20 to 50 copies each year and bring in three or four pounds annually. This is encouraging, since if that sells, I think anything we put our name to would sell. P[arker] brought a cheque for £102.2.5 which with the £250, & £25 which Lewis has sent for the Grote, is pretty well to have come in one year from writings of which money was not at all the object.

But doubts whether they will live to complete any of their plans creep in more and more frequently as the weeks pass on.

J. S. M. to H. M., *24 February 1854:* Altogether I hope the best for both of us, & see nothing in the state of either to discourage the hope. I hope we shall live to write together 'all we wish to leave written' to most of which your living is quite as essential than mine, for even if the wreck I should be could work on with undiminished faculties, my faculties at the best are not adequate to the highest subjects & have already done almost the best they are adequate to. Do not think darling that I should ever make this an excuse to myself for not doing my very best—if I survived you, & anything we much care about was not already fixed in writing you might depend on my attempting all of it & doing my very best to make it such as you would wish, for my only rule of life *then* would be what I thought you would wish as it now is what you tell me you wish. But I *am not fit* to write on anything but the outskirts of the great questions of feeling & life without you to prompt me as well as to keep me right.

So we must do what we can while we are alive—the Life being the first thing—which independent of the personal matters which it will set right when we have made it what we intend, is even now an unreserved proclamation of our opinions on religion, nature, & much else.

Apart from the suggested essay on religion on which Mill started work early in March, the main subjects discussed in the letters of the next few weeks are the proposed plans for parliamentary reform, the reconstruction of the Civil Service, and the revisions of a chapter of the *Political Economy*.

J. S. M. to H. M., 3 March 1854: The Civil Service examination plan I am afraid is too good to pass. The report proposing it, by Trevelyan & Northcote (written no doubt by Trevelyan) has been printed in the Chronicle—it is as direct, uncompromising & to the point, without reservation, as if we had written it. But even the Chronicle attacks the plan. The grand complaint is that it will bring low people into the offices! as, of course, gentlemen's sons cannot be expected to be as clever as low people. It is ominous too that the Times has said nothing on the subject lately. I should like to know who wrote the articles in the Times in support of the plan—possibly Trevelyan himself. It was somebody who saw his way to the moral & social ultimate effects of such a change. How truly you judge people—how true is what you always say that this ministry are *before* the public.

J. S. M. to H. M., 9 March 1854: The other note is from Trevelyan[30] and is an appeal that I ought to respond to, but it will be difficult, & without you impossible, to write the opinion he asks for, so as to be fit to print. But he ought to be helped, for the scheme is the greatest thing yet proposed in the way of *real* reform & his report is as I said before, almost as if we had written it. I wish it were possible to delay even answering his note till I could send a draft to you & receive it back but I fear that would not do.

J. S. M. to H. M., *14 March 1854:* I need hardly say how heartily I feel all you say about the civil service plan & the contempt I feel for the little feeling shewn for it, not to speak of actual hostility. I give the ministers infinite credit for it, that is if they really adopt the whole plan, for as their bill is not yet brought in (it is not as you seem to think, part of the Reform Bill) we do not yet know how far they will really go; but the least they can do consistently with their speeches, will be such a sacrifice of power of jobbing as hardly a politician who ever lived, ever yet made to the *sense* of right, without any public demand—it stamps them as quite remarkable men for their class & country. Of course all the jobbers are hard against them, especially newspaper editors who all now look out for places. Yet I so share your misgiving that they cannot know how great a thing they are doing, that I am really afraid to say all I feel about it till they are fully committed, lest it should do more harm than good. This was my answer to Trevelyan. 'I have not waited till now to make myself acquainted with the Report which you have done me the favour of sending to me, & to hail (?) the plan of throwing open the civil service to competition as one of the greatest improvements in public affairs ever proposed by a government. If the examination be so contrived as to be a real test of mental superiority, it is difficult to set limits to the effect which will be produced in raising the character not only of the public service but of Society itself. I shall be most happy to express this opinion in any way in which you think it can be of the smallest use towards helping forward so noble a scheme, but as the successful working of the plan will depend principally on details into which very properly your Report does not enter, I should be unable without some time for consideration, to write anything which could have a chance of being of any service in the way of suggestion.

'I am sorry to say you are mistaken in supposing that anything bearing the remotest resemblance to what you propose, exists at the I.H. It will exist in the India Civil Service by the Act of last year.'

Trevelyan's answer: 'You have done us a great service by the expression of your decided approbation of our plan for the reform of the English Civil Establishments; & as it is well known that you do not form your opinions lightly, I do not wish to trouble you to enter upon details of the subject at present. If you can suggest any improvement in the more advanced stages, we shall hope to hear from you again.' This looks as if he desired support more than criticism, but it is useful as it opens a channel by which, without obstrusiveness, we may write anything we like in the way of comment on the bill hereafter & be sure of its being read by the government. They have already quoted me in favour of the plan.

Fortunately it was not until early in May, some time after Mrs. Mill's return, that Trevelyan asked for the substitution of another enlarged letter for the one written at first, and it was no doubt with her assistance that the Paper on the Reorganization of the Civil Service, dated 22 May, was written.[31]

The concern with the revision of the chapter on the Futurity of the Labouring Classes was caused by an application of F. J. Furnival, 'one of the Kingsley set',[32] to reprint it: 'I did not expect the Xtian Socialists would wish to circulate the chapter as it is in the 3d edit. since it stands up for Competition against their one eyed attacks & denounciations of it."[33] Mrs. Mill approved of the plan and Mill undertook not only to revise the chapter but also to translate all the French passages in it. Sheets of the chapter went to Mrs. Mill for her comment.

J. S. M. to H. M., 6 March 1854: I quite agree with you about the inexpediency of adding anything like practical advice, or anything at all which alters the character of the chapter. The working men ought to see that it was not written *for* them—any attempt to mingle the two characters would be sure to be a failure & is not the way in which we should do the thing even if we had plenty of time & were together.—This morning has come from Chapman a pro-

posal for reprinting the article Enfranchisement of Women
or as he vulgarly calls it the article on Woman. How *very*
vulgar all his notes are. I am glad however that it is your
permission he asks. I hope the 'lady friend' is not H. Martineau. Mrs. Gaskell perhaps? You will tell me what to say.

When Mrs. Mill's comments arrived Mill wrote 'I think I agree in
all your remarks & have adopted them almost all' and transcribed in the
letter all the additions he had made to the chapter.[34] A 'saving clause'
on piece work which Mrs. Mill suggests was promptly inserted before
the chapter was sent to Furnival.[35]

Early in March Mill got seriously alarmed by the progressive
deterioration of his health, especially when a new symptom, night
perspiration, appeared. But his doctor, Sir James Clark, at first still
reassured him and Mill went away with the impression that his lungs
were not even threatened.

J. S. M. to H. M., 11 March 1854: This being one of the
great indications of consumption (though also of other ailments) it was well to find out what it meant. Clark thought it
was cheifly from the sudden change of weather & said that
almost everybody is complaining of night perspiration, the
queen among others. Whatever he may say, it is clear to me
that no weather could produce any such effects on me if
there were not a strong predisposition to it.

Only a few days later the doctor had however to admit 'that there
is organic disease in the lungs & and that he had known this all along'.[36]
Mill at first tried to keep from his wife this news, which to him
seemed a fairly certain sentence of death, till he could tell it to her by
word of mouth. His state of mind during the next few weeks is best
shown by some of the entries in the 'little book'.

Diary, 16 March 1854: It is part of the irony of life, and a
part which never becomes the less affecting because it is so
trite, that the fields, hills, and trees, the houses, really the
very rooms and furniture, will look exactly the same the day
after we or those we most love have died.

17 March: When we see and feel that human beings can take the deepest interest in what will befall their country or mankind long after they are dead, and in what they can themselves do while they are alive to influence that distant prospect which they are never destined to behold, we cannot doubt that if this and similar feelings were cultivated in the the same manner and degree as religion they would become a religion.

25 March: The only change I find in myself from a near view of probable death is that it makes me instinctively conservative. It makes me feel, not as I am accustomed—oh, for something better!—but oh, that we could be going on as we were before. Oh, that those I love could be spared the shock of a great change! And this feeling goes with me into politics and all other human affairs, when my reason does not studiously contend against and repress it.

31 March: Apart from bodily pain, and the grief for the grief of those who love us, the most disagreeable thing about dying is the intolerable ennui of it. There ought to be no slow deaths.

3 April: The effect of the bright and sunny aspects of Nature in soothing and giving cheerfullness is never more remarkable than in declining health. I look upon it as a piece of excellent good fortune to have the whole summer before one to die in.

4 April: Perhaps even the happiest of mankind would not, if it were offered, accept the privilege of being immortal. What he would ask in lieu of it is not to die until he chose.

12 April: In quitting forever any place where one has dwelt as in a home, all the incidents and circumstances, even those which were worse than indifferent to us, appear like old friends that one is reluctant to lose. So it is in taking leave of life: even the tiresome and vexatious parts of it look pleasant and friendly, and one feels how agreeable it would be to remain among them.

As the meeting with Mrs. Mill was delayed longer than expected and she got alarmed by the partial reports, Mill has at last to break the news to her, telling her at the same time that he had placed himself in the hands of another doctor, Ramadge,[37] whose book on a new treatment of consumption had inspired him with confidence, and that he was already slightly better.[38] Two days later he has already his wife's reply from Paris.

J. S. M. to H. M., *10 April 1854:* You will soon, darling, I know, feel calm again, for what is there that can happen to us in such a world as this that is worth being disturbed about when one is prepared for it? except intense physical pain, but that there is no fear of in this case. I am sometimes surprised at my own perfect tranquility when I consider how much reason I have to wish to live—but I am in my best spirits, & what I wrote even in the week after Clark's announcement before I had seen Ramadge, is written with as much spirit & I had as much pleasure in writing it as anything I ever wrote.

Indeed only a few days before he had written to her :

I want my angel to tell me what should be the next essay written. I have done all I can for the subject she last gave me.[39]

About the same time news had reached Mill that his mother was dangerously ill. He had apparently not seen her since his return, but early exchanged some notes with her and now he learnt that she was getting worse.

J. S. M. to H. M., *3 April 1854:* My poor mother I am afraid is not in a good way—as to health I mean. In her usual letter about receiving her pension she said 'I have been a sufferer for nearly three months—I have only been out of doors twice' &c. 'I have suffered and am still suffering great pain. I supposed the pain in my back was rheumatism, but it is not—it proceeds from the stomach, from which I suffer intense pain as well as from the back. Mr. Quain has been attending me during the time, and he and Sir Jas Clark have had a consultation and I am taking what they prescribe— I can do no more.' And again in answer to my answer 'I am just the same, but it is not rheumatism that I am suffering from, but my liver. I thought it was odd that my stomach should be so much affected from rheumatism. Sir J. Clark is coming here at the end of the week to have another consultation. I cannot write much as I am so very weak.'[40] This looks very ill I fear—very like some organic disease. Mrs. King she says is a little better & is probably coming to England.[41] I told her what you said a propos of Mrs. King's illness. She wrote 'I hope Mrs. Mill is still going on well.'

In the last letter to his wife before her return the news about his mother is still more grave.

J. S. M. to H. M., *11 April 1854:* I am sorry to say darling I had two notes from Clara & Mary[42] both saying that my mother is very ill—one says that Clark & the other medical man Quain call her disease enlargement of the liver, the other tumour in the liver & they think very seriously of it though not expecting immediate danger. I need not send the notes as you will see them so soon.

It had been intended that Mill should meet his wife in Paris where she had arrived about the first of April and was stopping for some days, awaiting better weather for the crossing and in order to give her daughter an opportunity to see the *semaine sainte*. At first it seemed uncertain whether Mrs. Mill would be strong enough to continue the journey to England, but in the end it proved that it was Mill who was unable to come to Paris to meet her, because he had, in addition to his illness, developed a bad carbuncle, and about the middle of April the two ladies joined him at Blackheath Park.

During the next six weeks Mill's health continued to get worse so that, as he wrote a little later,[43] 'the great and rapid wasting of flesh' made him fear that he would soon be 'incapable of any bodily exertion whatever'. His doctors were urging him to go away but he delayed until the beginning of June when at last, with little hope of recovery, he set out for a tour of Brittany. But before he left it was necessary to say good-bye to his mother, who was clearly dying. Warned of the approaching end in a very formal letter of his sister Harriet,[44] he went to see his mother, and a few days later, wrote to her once more. The letter was evidently intended to convey some information to his sisters rather than for his mother, who, as he must have known, was no longer in a state to read it.

J. S. M. to Mrs. James Mill:[45] Blackheath Park, June 9, 1854/My dear Mother—I hope that you are feeling better than when I saw you last week & that you continue free from pain. I write to say that I am going immediately to the Continent by the urgent recommendation of Clark who has been pressing me to do so for some time past & though I expect to return in a few weeks it will probably be to leave again soon after. I wish again to remind you in case it has not already been done how desirable it is that someone who is fixed in England should be named executor to your will, either instead of me, which I sh^d prefer, or as well as myself.

My wife sends her kindest wishes & regrets that her weak health makes it difficult for her to come to see you as she would otherwise have done. Ever my dear mother

affectionately yours

J. S. M.

Mrs. James Mill died six days later, on 15 June. The news, conveyed in a letter by his brother-in-law Charles Colman, however, did not reach Mill until the 26th in Brittany. He had left on the day he had written to his mother and remained away for a little over six weeks. Again all but one of the sixteen letters he wrote to his wife during this tour have been preserved[46] and allow us to follow his daily moods and movements. After spending three days at St. Helier on the island of Jersey, he crossed to St. Malo, where he was held up by rain for a day and started writing an essay on Justice,[47] the plan of which had formed itself in his mind on the boat. But, as soon as the weather improved, he set out on his tour around the coast of Brittany, spending all day in the open, travelling only short distances by various means of conveyance but walking an astounding and, as his strength increased, rapidly increasing amount. All the time he was looking at the various towns

with an eye to their suitability as places for permanent residence and
reporting to his wife on the prices of food and similar items. At Morlaix he found a companion for a few excursions who, like himself,
was seeking a cure for consumption.

J. S. M. to H. M., Brest, 24 June 1854: I went there [from
Morlaix to the central country of Brittany] as I said I was
going to, with an Englishman who it seems is a barrister &
is named Pope. He turned out a pleasant person to meet, as,
though he does not seem to me to have any talent, he is
better informed than common Englishmen—knows a good
deal of French history for example, especially that of the
Revolution—& seems either to have already got to or to be
quite ready to receive, all our opinions. I tried him on
religion, where I found him quite what we think right—on
politics, on which he was somewhat more than a radical—
on the equality of women which he seemed not to have quite
dared to think of himself but seemed to adopt it at once—
& to be ready for all reasonable socialism—he boggled a
little at limiting the power of bequest which I was glad of
as it shewed that the other agreements were not mere following a lead taken. He was therefore worth talking to & I
think he will have taken away a good many ideas from me.
. . . From that [the French newspapers] I saw that there had
been a debate on the ballot & that Palmerston had made *the*
speech against it but that was all. I reckon on leaving our
opinion on that question to form part of the volume of essays,
but I am more anxious to get on with other things first, since
what is already written (when detached from the political
pamphlet that was to have been[48]) will in the case of the
worst suffice, being the essentials of what we have to say,
& perhaps might serve to float the volume as the opinion on
the ballot would be liked by the powerful classes, and being
from a radical would be sure to be quoted by their writers,
while they would detest most of the other opinions.

Six days later his wife's reply to the last passage makes him return
to the subject.

J. S. M. to H. M., Lorient, 30 June 1854: I wish I had seen
a full report of Palmerston's speech—what was given of it
in the Spectator did not at all account for your high opinion
of it, containing only the commonplaces I have been familiar
with all my life—while the speeches *for* the ballot were
below even the commonplaces. The ballot has sunk to far
inferior men, the Brights etc. When it was in my father's
hands or even Grote's such trash was not spoken as that the
suffrage is a *right* &c. &c. But Palmerston's saying that a
person who will not sacrifice something to his opinion is not
fit to have a vote seems to me to involve the same fallacy. It is
not for his own sake that one wishes him to have a vote. It is
we who suffer because those who would vote with us are
afraid to do so. As for the suffrage being a trust it has always
been so said by the Whig & Tory opponents of the ballot
& used to be agreed in by its radical supporters. I have not
seen a single new argument respecting the ballot for many
years except one or two of yours. I do not feel in the way
you do the desirableness of writing an article for the Ed[in
burgh] on it. There will be plenty of people to say all that is
to be said against the ballot—all it wants from us is the
authority of an ancient radical & that it will have by what is
already written & fit to be published as it is: but I now feel
so strongly the necessity of giving the little time we are
sure of to writing things which nobody could write but
ourselves, that I do not like turning aside to anything else.
I do not find the essay on Justice goes on well. I wrote a good
long piece of it at Quimper, but it is too metaphysical, & not
what is most wanted—but I must finish it now in that vein
& then strike into another.

In the interval between these two letters the news of his mother's
death had reached him.

J. S. M. to H. M., Quimper, 26 June 1854: It is a comfort
that my poor mother suffered no pain—& since it was to be,
I am glad that I was not in England when it happened, since

what I must have done & gone through would have been very painful & wearing & would have done no good to any one. It is on every account fortunate that another executor has been appointed. There is a matter connected with the subject which I several times intended speaking to you about, but each time I forgot. Unless my memory deceives me, the property my mother inherited from her mother was not left to her out & out, but was settled equally on her children. If so, a seventh part of it, being something between £400 & £500, will come to me, & I do not think we ought to take it—what do you think? Considering how they have behaved, it is a matter of pride more than of anything else—but I have a very strong feeling about it.

J. S. M. to H. M., *Nantes, 4 July 1854:* About the matter of my mother's inheritance, of course as your feeling is so directly contrary, mine is wrong, & I give it up entirely, but it was not the vanity of 'acting on the supposition of being a man of fortune'—it was something totally different —it was wishing that they should not be able to say that I had taken anything from their resources. However that is ended, & I need say no more about it.

From Nantes Mill went for a fortnight to the Vendée, again in the company of his new acquaintance, Mr. Pope, and from the southernmost point of his journey he reports continued improvement of his health.

J. S. M. to H. M., *Rochefort, 16 July 1854:* You may know by my taking it so leisurely that the journey continues to do me good; indeed it seems to do me more & more—I was weighed at La Rochelle & had gained two pounds more, making six pounds since St. Malo—it shews how much weight I must have lost before, these six pounds make not the smallest perceptible difference to the eye—I have gained still more in strength; yesterday at Rochelle I was out from eight in the morning till nine at night *literally* with only the exceptions of breakfast & dinner—& walking all the time, except an occasional sitting on a bank.

On his return to Nantes he found another letter from his brother-in-law, enclosing a letter from his mother found after her death, and asking for instructions concerning the disposal of her furniture, which she had described as belonging to Mill. He copied both letters out in full for his wife and commented:

J. S. M. to H. M., Nantes, 19 July 1854: Of course we can only say that the furniture was my mother's & must be dealt with as such—but I cannot write the note without consultation so unless you think it can wait for my return (as I shall be home now in little more than a week) perhaps darling you will write to Rouen what you think should be said & in what manner, both about that & the plate.

The instructions asked for promptly reached Mill and in his last letter (Rouen, 24 July) he replies that he will write 'the letter to Colman exactly according to your pencil which seems to me perfectly right' and the following letter is accordingly dispatched:

J. S. M. to Charles Colman, Rouen, 24 July 1854:[49] Dear Colman, Owing to a change in my route, I did not get to Nantes till later than I originally intended. With regard to my mother's furniture, I always considered it hers, & have often told her so. I think it or its proceeds should be equally distributed among all her daughters. The plate which my mother had also to be distributed equally in the same manner I am,

yʳˢ faithfully,

J. S. Mill

Chapter Ten

ITALY AND SICILY
1854–1855

MILL's expectation that he would have no difficulty in obtaining a medical certificate saying that he ought to go to the south for six months during the winter of 1854–5 proved only too true. About the middle of November his doctor peremptorily ordered him away for eight months. But it was not to be the joint holiday to which he and his wife had been looking forward. Apparently Mrs. Mill was not strong enough for a long journey[1] and after taking her to Torquay he left Blackheath Park on 8 December for an extensive tour of France, Italy and Greece. During his absence he wrote to her almost daily, though he could often post his letters only once a week and some of them in consequence run to very great length. All of the 49 letters written during the journey have been preserved[2] and if printed in full would make a fairly thick volume. For their detailed description of the places visited these letters, particularly those from Sicily and Greece, might deserve some day to be printed in full. In the course of the present narrative we must, however, confine ourselves to a few extracts which throw further light on Mill's intellectual and emotional state.

The journey began inauspiciously. A miserable crossing of the channel, during which Mill, always a sufferer from sea-sickness, was really ill, brought him to Boulogne hardly able 'to totter up the steps', and further upsetting his digestion, from which he suffered throughout the journey as much if not more than from the symptoms of his pulmonary disease. After a night in Paris he commenced his roundabout journey to Marseilles *via* Bordeaux and the valley of the Garonne across the whole South of France.

Orleans, 9 December 1854: Yesterday in the railway I was afraid that I was getting into that half mad state which always makes me say that imprisonment would kill me—& which makes me conscious that if I let myself dwell on the idea I could get into the state of being unable to bear the impossibility of flying to the moon—it is a part of human nature I never saw described but have long known by experience—this time the occasion of it was, not being able to get to you—when I reflected that for more than six months I was to be where I could not possibly go to you in less than many days, I felt as if I *must* instantly turn back & return to you. It will require a good deal of management of myself to keep this sensation out of my nerves.

On the way to Bordeaux he stopped at Libourne, and after two days at Bordeaux he started out by diligence in slow stages up the valley of the Garonne to Toulouse, Carcassone, Narbonne and Beziers to Montpelier. Here he stopped for five days, reviving memories of the time, thirty-four years earlier, when, as a boy of fourteen, he had spent there with Sir Samuel Bentham and his family 'the six happiest months of his youth'.[3] He continued via Nimes to Avignon where he remained for the two Christmas holidays, and where for the first time, and the only time for a long while, he felt perfectly well—as it was indeed the climate of Avignon which years later, after the sad event of his wife dying there led him to choose it as his permanent home, should at last restore to him the health which he had been vainly seeking for so long. After another miserable sea journey from Marseilles to Genoa he felt for the first time really in a foreign country.

Genoa, 30 December 1854: I seem much further from my dear one than in France—any place in France if it be ever so far off seems so much a home to us. I do not get on well with the Italians here not only from the badness of my Italian but of theirs, for it is a horrible patois almost as unItalian as the Venetian but without its softness. Adieu darling—love me always—a thousand dearest loves.

In another letter, begun on the same evening but continued on the following two days, he commenced his more detailed descriptions of the country mixed with more general reflections. He started on his further journey in a *voiture* taken together with a number of Italians to Sestri and Spezia, and according to his usual habit walked large parts of the way.

Sestri, 31 December 1854: There is great complaint of the distress of the people here—my fellow traveller said everything had failed except olives—not only the vines but all the grain & that the propriétaires are dying of hunger. A propos I have been reading of a great & rapidly extending disease among silkworms, propagated by the eggs—it seems as if there was a conspiracy among the powers of nature to thwart human industry—if it once reaches the real necessaries of life the human race may starve. The potato disease was a specimen & that was but one root: if it should reach corn? I think that should be a signal for the universal & simultaneous suicide of the whole human race, suggested by Novalis. What a number of sensible things are not done, faut de s'entendre! In the meantime let us make what we can of what human life we have got, which I am hardly doing by being away from you. I think I should feel the whole thing worthier if I were writing something—but I cannot make up my mind what to write. Nothing that is not large will meet the circumstances.

Spezia, 1 January 1855: Every possible good that the new year can possibly bring to the only person living who is worthy to live, and may she have the happiest & maniest new years that the inexorable powers allow to any of us poor living creatures.

In Spezia he stopped for a day and, as everywhere, was inquiring about the suitability of the place as a permanent domicile; but better news from his wife, with whom the climate of Torquay seemed to agree at the time, made him again more doubtful whether he wanted to live abroad.

Spezia, 2 January: The nuisance of England is the English: on every other account I would rather live in England passing a winter now & then abroad than live altogether anywhere else. The effect of the beauty here on me, great as it is, makes me like the beauty of English country more than I ever did before—there is such a profusion of beauty of *detail* in English country when it *is* beautiful & such a deficiency of it here & on the Continent generally & I am convinced that a week's summer tour about Dartmoor would give me as much pleasure as a week about Spezia.

In Pisa he stopped for six days, because his condition for a while got seriously worse, but on the 9th he proceeded by train to Sienna and thence started on the following day a long journey by diligence to Rome, where he at last arrived on the 14th. After a short note added to the letter written during the journey and posted on arrival follows a first long letter.

Rome, 15 January: I have read up the Times at the old place, Monaldini's—there is another place of the same kind now, Piali's, also in the Piazza di Spagna, which seems more frequented, especially by English. The only thing I found noticeable was the Queen's letter[4]—was there ever such a chef d' œuvre of feebleness—O those grandes dames how all vestige of the very conception of strength or spirit has gone out of them. Every word was evidently her own—the great baby! & it is not only the weakness but the *decousir*, the incoherence of the phrases—sentences they are not. No wonder such people are awed by the Times, which by the side of them looks like rude strength.—Whom should I find here, in the same inn, but Lucas[5]—not a bad rencontre to make at Rome. I left my card for him & shall no doubt see him tomorrow. Au reste, nobody else here whom I know, judging from the lists at the libraries. Hayward[6] appears to have been here in the autumn but no doubt has left. There is a Lady Duff Gordon but I suppose & hope it is the *mother* of the baronet.[7] And there are a few people whom I have just seen—Lady Langdale—some of the Lyalls—& others whom I forgot. If Naples is like Rome I have no chance of a companion. I have found the address of Dr. Deakin & shall call on him tomorrow. I have been considerably better today but think it is best to consult somebody about my stomach & my strength—I am anxious to get back the last, since at present long walks which have done me so much good hitherto, are impossible. I have not ventured to take quinine while my stomach was disordered, which it is still, a little. I see a great many English priests all about, as well as many other English. On Thursday I believe there will be fine music at St. Peter's which I will certainly hear.—There is so much to do & to see here, that it has taken off my nascent velleity of writing. On my way here cogitating thereon I came back to an idea we have talked about, & thought that the best thing to write & publish at present would be a volume on Liberty.[8] So many things might be brought into it & nothing seems more to be needed—it is a growing need too, for opinion tends to encroach more & more on liberty, & almost all the projects of social reformers of these days are really *liberticide* —Comte's particularly so. I wish I had brought with me here the paper on Liberty that I wrote for our volume of Essays—perhaps my dearest will kindly read it through & tell me whether it will do as the foundation of one part of the volume in question. If she thinks so I will try to write & publish it in 1856 if my health permits as I hope it will.

Most of his letters from Rome are filled with accounts of his sightseeing. He seems at first mainly to have been attracted by the sculptures.

Rome, 16 January: I went through the [Vatican] Museum, catalogue in hand, to-day, & knowing the whole, shall return often to see those I most like. It gave me quite as much & more pleasure than I expected. The celebrated Meleager I do not care a rush for—I should never have guessed it to be ancient. The Apollo is fine but there is a Mercury (formerly mistaken for an Antinous) which seems to me finer & a gigantic sitting Jupiter who is magnificent. The Ariadne if such she be is most beautiful & so are many others. The Laocoon I can see deserves its reputation but it is not the sort of thing I care about. I see with very great interest the really authentic statues & busts of Roman emperors & eminent Greeks—although as you know, not only no physiognomist but totally incapable of becoming one. But I find the pleasure which pictures & statues give me, increase with every experience, & I am acquiring strong preferences & discriminations which *with me* I think is a sign of progress.

Rome, 22 January: The picture gallery at the Capitol is about equal to the Borghese. I liked best a Fra Bartolomeo & some Venetian portraits. The ancient sculptures are fully equal, for their number, to those at the Vatican; the dying Gladiator perhaps superior to any. There are some reliefs of scenes in which Marcus Aurelius is introduced which appear to me wonderful & are very delightful to me from my extreme admiration of the man. The place is full too of curiosities: the brazen she wolf of Romulus which was struck by lightning at the time of Julius Cæsar's death, the fragments of a most curious plan of old Rome, unfortunately dug up in many small pieces: the original Fasti Consulares also fragmentary but in large fragments, going back to some of the consulships preceding the Decemvirate. All these are believed genuine by Niebuhr & the most critical judges who have fully examined the evidence. These are much more interesting to me than the remains of Roman buildings which with two or three exceptions are very ugly & all very much alike. Lucas says his business at Rome is coming to a crisis: he came to prevail on the Pope to take off the interdict lately laid on priests against interfering in politics: if he cannot proceed in this, he & others mean to give up politics for the present. Cullen, the Archbishop, is the head of the party opposed to him & he & Cullen are to meet this week by desire of the Pope, to try if they cannot arrange matters amicably: if not, the Pope will have to decide between them. I conjecture that the interdict, so absurd in a Catholic point of view, was procured by Louis Napoleon to prevent the English government from being embarrassed by Ireland during this war. Lucas thinks it is not this, but Cullen's Whiggish inclinations, & it is curious that while Cullen was supported in getting the Archbishopric on the one hand by MacHale on the other if Lucas says true Lord Clarendon was writing the strongest letters in his support on the ground of his being a perfectly safe man: *three* people known to Lucas have he says seen a letter from Ld Clarendon to the brother of More O'Ferrall to that effect. This shews skilful duplicity in Cullen at all events.

Rome, 24 January: Lucas has just been here. He has had his meeting with Cullen today, finds him very hostile—no chance of an amicable arrangement—means to stay here & fight it out—but can do nothing just at present, therefore thinks he shall be able to go to Naples—& if so Mr. Kyan[9] proposes to go too. So we shall be a party of three. I should have liked Lucas better without Kyan but he is not disagreeable nor much in the way. We shall see. Meanwhile they are going with me to some more pictures tomorrow.

Mill's health, which had been very bad during the early part of his stay in Rome—he had lost fifteen pounds since the temporary high at Avignon, was improving sufficiently towards the end of January for him to think of further travel and finally he agreed to start for Naples on the 29th. During the last three days he made another round of galleries and churches.

Rome, 26 January: No letter today—& I rather fear she did not get mine in time to write on the 16th in which case I fear I shall not hear till I get to Naples. That will be on the 31st the places being taken for Monday, two banquettes & one coupé being the best we could do. I saw the Doria gallery today (a wet day) with Lucas & Kyne, & the Colonna

& Braschi palaces by myself. The Doria disappointed me—
it is a very large collection & would make a sufficient national
gallery for a second rate kingdom, but most of the pictures
seemed to me third rate. There is however one long corridor
full of portraits by Titian, Giorgione, & Rubens—in this
was also a fine Francia, & (very like Francia) a Giovanni
Bellini—these two & Perugino have a complete family like-
ness—a Leonardo which though called a portrait of the
second Giovanna of Naples is vastly like his one always recurring face—& finally the Magdalen of Titian, a splendid
picture, perfectly satisfactory & pleasurable in execution
(conception apart) but as a Magdalen ridiculous. I have seen
many Titians at Rome & they all strengthen my old feeling
about him—he is of the earth earthy. At the other two
palaces there were some fine pictures, the majority portraits
by the Venetians—at the Braschi the so called Bella of Titian
which I don't like, & what is reckoned a chef d'œuvre of
Corregio of whom there are few good specimens here which
I don't like either though I can see that it may have strong
points of colouring. Lots of Gaspar Poussins at all three,
deadly cold, & several ambitious Salvators to my feeling
quite poor: a St. John & his famous Belisarius, which seems
to me inferior to the poorest even of the Bolognese painters.
Evidently the culmination of painting was in the three
generations of which Raphael forms the last, Titian belonging to it also though as he lived nearly 60 years longer than
Raphael one fancies him of a later date. The worship of the
still earlier painters is a dandyism which will not last, even I
hope in Germany: the contempt of the Bolognese eclectics
who came a century after has a foundation of reason but is
grossly exagerated. Guido especially has risen greatly with
me from what I have seen at Rome & so has even Domeni-
chino whose finest pictures are here: him however I do not,
as a matter of taste, care the least about. But I begin to think
Ruskin right about Gaspard & Salvator, perhaps even
Claude, & to think the modern English landscape painting

better than theirs. If I did not write my impressions every day I should not write them at all, for seeing so many pictures one remembrance drives out another—but they leave a total impression extremely agreeable. I never was *immersed* in pictures before, & probably never shall be again to the same degree, for at any place but Rome one hardly can be, & even at Rome with her, there would be so much greater activity of other parts of the mind that the atmosphere would be different. Even the season & the bad weather contribute by throwing me upon the indoor pleasures of the place. My dearest may well smile at my pretension of giving opinions about pictures, but as all I say about them is the expression of real feelings which they give or which they fail to give me, what I say though superficial is genuine & may go for what it is worth—it does not come from books or from other people—& I write it to her because it shews her that I have real pleasure here & have made really the most of Rome in that respects & in others.

Rome, 28 January: When I have paid my bill here, my journey will have cost me up to this time (deducting the fees to Deakin medecine & everything else not properly chargeable to travelling & living) as nearly as possible £50. That is for about seven weeks and a half of time, but the distance travelled is considerable. I shall post this at the moment of leaving, (seven tomorrow morning) for the diligences start from the very court yard of the post office.

After a night in Terracina Mill and his two companions Lucas and Kyne arrived in Naples on 30 January. For ten days Mill, who knew Naples from his visit with Mrs. Taylor sixteen years earlier, acted mainly as cicerone to his friends, confined by bad weather mainly to the town itself except for a visit to Paestium.

Naples, 9 February 1855: The papers bring up the news to the large divisions again at the ministry & their resignation[10] —a real misfortune for it is a chance if the next is as good.

I think it was foolish of them to oppose an enquiry. When such accusations are made & believed, no matter how insufficient the authority, they *ought* to be enquired into. And everything practical which is under the management of the English higher classes is always so grossly mismanaged that one can quite believe things to be very bad, though not a jot the more because it is asserted by the Times & its correspondent. How very Times like to cry out now for Lord Grey as war minister after all their attacks on him in & out of office for incapacity & conceit. I shall think seriously about the book on Liberty since my darling approves of the subject. Lucas & his friends left early this morning, much delighted with his visit & said repeatedly that he had seldom enjoyed three weeks as much as since he had met me at Rome. He is really for an Englishman a well informed man —for every historical fact or Latin quotation I brought out he had one as good. And he has some will & energy which distinguish him from nearly everybody now—talks really intelligently on politics on which he & I generally agree.[11] Of course a professed Catholic could not agree with me on much else & I should have talked much more controversially with him but for the presence of his friend Kyne latterly whose priesthood imposed a restraint on us both. . . . Nothing can be more beautiful than this place. You can I dare say imagine how I enjoy the beauty when I am *not* looking at it—now in this bedroom by candlelight I am in a complete nervous state from the sensation of the beauty I am living among—while I look at it I only seem to be gathering honey which I savour (?) the whole time afterwards. I wonder if anything in Sicily or Greece is finer.

Gradually during the three weeks which Mill spent in and around Naples his health and strength increased and he became again able to enjoy his accustomed long walks and climbs.

Sorrento, 12 February: Here I am darling & at the same inn, La Sirena which looks as pretty as possible; only I think we were not on the ground floor which I am now. By the bye I only ascertained today, by finding the number of the house in Mrs. Starke, that my inn at Naples, the Hotel des Etrangers, is the very casa Brizzi which we were in, though not then *called* a hotel.

Sorrento, 13 February: Out today from half past nine till five. I have recovered all my strength. How pleasant, once more, after $3\frac{1}{2}$ hours walking, much of it climbing, to find myself at the foot of a very steep & rather high mountain and not feel that I had rather not climb it. I did so, & when I had got to the top was not at all tired—& scarcely tired when I got back to the inn, three hours after. The mountain in question was the Punta della Campanella, or promontory of Minerva, occupying the extreme end of the Peninsula of Sorrento.

Naples, 17 February: There is a fresh arrival of newspapers today, the only one for nearly a week: containing the new ministry. Palmerston will now either make or mar his reputation—which will be expected from him & he will be ambitious of being remembered as the Lord Chatham of this war, I was glad to see Ld J. Russell, even at this late hour, hoping that Lord Raglan would disregard the 'ribald press' —pity he never said so till he felt the ribaldry of the Times against himself in its grossest form. I perceive by incidental mention that the newspaper stamp is to be given up—also that the government are to bring in a bill for limited liability in partnerships. My dearest one knows that I am not prone to crying out 'I did it', but I really think my evidence[12] did this—for although there are many others on the same side, yet there would but for me have been a great overbalance of political economy authority against it—besides I have nowhere seen the objections effectually answered except in that evidence. We have got a power of which we must try to make a good use during the few years of life we have left. The more I think of the plan of a volume on Liberty, the more likely it seems to me that it will be read & will make a sensation. The title itself with any known name to it would sell an edition. We must cram into it as much as possible of what we wish not to leave unsaid.—I have been reading here, for want of another book, Macaulay's Essays. He is quite a strange specimen of a man of abilities who has not even one of the ideas or impressions characteristic of this century & which will be identified with it by history—except, strangely enough, in mere literature. In poetry he belongs to the new school, & the best passage I have met with in the book is one of wonderful (for him) admiring appreciation of Shelley. But in politics, ethics, philosophy, even history, of which he knows superficially very much—he has not a single thought of either German or French origin, & that is saying enough. He is what all cockneys are, an intellectual dwarf—rounded off & stunted, full grown broad & short, without a germ of principle of further growth in his whole being. Nevertheless I think he feels rightly (what little he does feel, as my father would say) & I feel in more charity with him than I have sometimes done, & I do so the more, since Lucas told me that he has heart disease, & is told by his physician that whenever he speaks in the H. of Commons, it is at the hazard of falling dead.

Mill's spirits revived further after reaching Palermo. The dreaded crossing from Naples, on an exceptionally fine and calm day, was accomplished without the after-effect of the earlier sea-passages, and after a few days in Palermo he felt himself fitter and more energetic than he had done for a long time. Indeed his feats of walking would be remarkable in a man of perfect health and a little later (March 5) he himself observes:

it is curious that when I am too tired or weak to do anything else I can climb mountains: that is if they are steep enough, for a long ascending slope fatigues me greatly.

The first long letter from Sicily gives a full description of a tour on Monte Pelerino in which Mill grows unusually enthusiastic.

Palermo, 24 February: The view all the way up had been very fine but from the top was one of the most glorious I should think in the world. The whole north coast of Sicily (all mountain & bay) as far as the eye could reach, the sea studded with the little round Lipari islands, the larger island of Ustica farther west, the exquisite Vega of Palermo & the town itself spread out as in one of the bird's eye Panoramas, the amphitheatre of mountains around it. Before I had reached the top I had caught the first view of Etna, which I thought I recognized in a white dome like object that rose through & above the white clouds—& when I reached the top, the soldiers confirmed this. The day was the most perfect of summer days—the wind light & easterly, just sufficient to temper the sun's heat—the soldiers called it scirocco di levante, to distinguish it I suppose from the real African scirocco—Goodwin[13] calls it the vento Greco. After enjoying the view for some time I started down the mountain. It was 12 when I was at the top & it took an hour & a half to reach the foot. I certainly never at any time of my life could have first climbed & then descended this mountain more vigorous & fresh. I feel equal to climbing Etna itself if this were the season for it. When I got to the inn I was not even tired, except indeed my arms with the weight of plants I carried, to the edification & amidst the apostrophes of the public—who were full of questions & remarks—the most complimentary of which was one I overheard, one woman having given a shout of astonishment (all speaking here by common people is shouting) when another quietly remarked to her that it was for my bella, & was a galanterra. I wish, indeed, it had been for my bella, & a day never passes when I do not wish to bring flowers home to her.

A little earlier in the same letter he reports how through the lack of a library or reading room :

I am thrown on my own books & have begun reading Goethe's Italian travels which I had in Italy formerly & read—I like them much better now—he relates impressions in so very lively a manner & they seem to me to be all true impressions —he went, too, a learner in art, & I find many of his feelings at first very like mine. I forgot, though bringing German books, to bring a German dictionary, but I get on tolerably without one. I have also Theocritus, a proper book for Sicily.

Palermo, 24 February: These travels of Goethe give me a number of curious feelings. I had no idea that he was so young[14] & unformed on matters of art when he went to Italy. But what strikes me most in this & in him is the grand effort of his life to make himself a Greek. He laboured at it with all his might, & seemed to have a chance of succeeding—all his standards of taste & judgement were Greek—his idol was symmetry: anything either in outward objects or in characters which was great & incomplete (*exorbitant* as Balzac says of a visage d'artiste) gave him a cold shudder—he had a sort of contemptuous dislike for the northern church architecture, but I was amused (& amazed too) at his most characteristic touch—that even Greek, when it is the Greek of Palmyra, is on too gigantic a scale for him: he must have something little & perfect, & is delighted that a Greek temple he saw at Assisi was of that & not the other *monstrous* kind. He judged human character in exactly the same way. With all this he never could succeed in putting symmetry into any of his own writings, except very short ones—shewing the utter impossibility for a modern with all the good will in the world, to tightlace himself into the dimensions of an ancient. Every modern thinker has so much wider a horizon, & there is so much deeper a soil accumulated on the surface of human nature by the ploughings it has undergone & the growths it has produced of which soil every writer or artist of any talent turns up more or less even in spite of himself—in short the moderns have vastly more material to reduce to order than the ancients dreamt of & the secret of harmonizing it all has not yet been discovered—it is too soon by a century or two to attempt either symmetrical productions in art or symmetrical characters. We all need to be blacksmiths or ballet dancers with good stout arms or legs, useful to do what we have got to do, and useful to fight with at times—we cannot be Apollos and Venuses just yet.

Continuing the same letter on the next day Mill begins to develop plans for work to be done after his return home.

Palermo, 25 February: I have been thinking darling that when I get back I should like to reprint a selection from the review articles &c. It seems desirable to do it in our lifetime, for I fancy we cannot prevent other people doing it when we are dead, & if anybody did so they would print a heap of trash which one would disown: now if *we* do it, we can exclude what we should not choose to republish, & nobody would think of reprinting what the writer had purposely rejected. Then the chance of the name selling them is as great as it is ever likely to be—the collection would probably be a good deal reviewed for anybody thinks he can review a miscellaneous collection but few treatises on logic to political economy—above all it is not at all desirable to come before the public with two books nearly together, so if not done now it cannot be done till after some time after the volume on Liberty—but by that time, I hope there will be a volume ready of much better Essays, or something as good. In fact I hope to publish some volume almost annually for the next few years if I live as long—& I should like to get this reprint, if it is to be done at all, off my hands during the few months after I return in which India house business being in arrear will prevent me from settling properly on the new book. Will my dearest one think about this & tell me what her judgment & also what her feeling is.

After ten days in Palermo Mill set out on March 2nd with a muleteer and two mules for a tour round Sicily from which he expects:

such a fortnight's journey for beauty & interest as I never had in my life before & as much pleasure as I can have separated from her (March 1). [He finds his] muleteer pretty much of the same politics as myself (but in his case) turning chiefly on taxation, the excess of which is certainly one of the great evils of this government (March 2).

But riding a mule proved at first much more exhausting than he expected and even seemed to make it doubtful whether he would be able to carry out his plan of going in this way all round the West and South of Sicily. He visited the ruins of Segesta and Selinus and gradually adjusted himself to the new mode of conveyance by walking great parts of the way and sitting the rest of the time on the pack-mule on the top of his luggage rather than in the saddle. But after a little more than a week of this sort of travel he was inured to the hardships and had acquired a new although, as it proved, unjustified confidence in the state of his health.

Scicca, 11 March: As we had 35 Sicilian, about 40 English, miles to go today, the guide very reasonably proposed to start at seven [from Caotel Vitrano]: but after I was up & ready, it was raining steadily & the sky was one mass of unbroken cloud, seeming to preclude our going any further today. However after I had breakfasted & read the idyls of Theocritus & a canto of the Purgatorio of Dante (I finished the Inferno, as well as Tasso, long since) there seemed some signs of clearing, the rain ceased, & we started at half past nine, the mules receiving an extra feed to enable them to do the whole distance without stopping: & they arrived here, apparently not fatigued, at half past six. Of course I had to do a considerable part of this on the mule, but I certainly walked a good deal more than half, & under such difficulties as you may suppose. I never knew before what a country without roads is. I fancied there were mule paths like those at Nice or Sorrento: but those are *made* roads as much as turnpike roads are, & as well suited for the kind of traffic they are meant for as the ground admits. Not above five miles of the forty today were made road, & that was where the soil was so dense a clay that it would have been totally impassable unless paved in the middle. Taught by experience I now know that in so long a day's journey there was nothing to do except to splash, not exactly through thick & thin, but through thin, reserving my efforts to avoid the thick when possible. When you consider that I had to ride on the mule for long distances with my feet in the state implied, you will see that this mode of travelling would have been madness if I had been at all in the condition of a pulmonary patient. Evidently the pulmonary disease has long been arrested, & my digestion & general health are the things to be now considered, & the walk to-day with all its difficulties was not at all too much. I always got off the mule when my feet began to get cold.

Bad weather continued to dog his way for another three days when he reached Girgenti. From there a week or more of this sort of journey in fine weather and, apart from severe attacks of indigestion and occasional struggles with fleas at the ınns, tolerable comfort brought him to Syracuse and the end of the mule ride.

Syracuse, 21 March: I had the good luck to approach the town in a bright afternoon feeling & looking like the finest July day. The approach was from the side of the greater harbour, which was calm & glassy, & across it the large white buildings of the town shone brightly in the sun. You know the town is at present confined to the island, which was only one of the five large quarters in the time of Syracusan greatness: but even now it looks, & is, one of the largest towns of Sicily. I do not think there is any town, not even Athens, which I have so much feeling about as Syracuse: it is the only ancient town of which I have studied, & know & understand, the locality: so nothing was new or dark to me. I cannot look at that greater harbour which my window in the Albergo del Sole looks directly upon, without thinking of the many despairing looks which were cast upon the shores all round (as familiar to me as if I had known them all my life) by the armament of Nicias & Demosthenes. That event decided the fate of the world, most calamitously. If the Athenians had succeeded they would have added to their maritime supremacy all the Greek cities of Sicily & Italy, Greece must soon have become subordinate to them & the empire they formed in the only way which could have united all Greece, might have been too strong for the Romans and Carthaginians. Even if they had failed & got away safe, Athens could never have been subdued by the Peloponesians but would have remained powerful enough to prevent Macedonia from emerging from obscurity, or at all events to be a sufficient check on Phillip & Alexander. Perhaps the world would have been now a thousand years further advanced if freedom had thus been kept standing in the only place where it ever was or could then be powerful. I thought & felt this as I approached the town till I could have cried with regret & sympathy. . . . O the splendor of the evening view from my window. Down immediately on the greater harbor over which boats, apparently pleasure boats, were moving—the softest light over the plain & highlands, &, to the right, Etna, which can be seen from nearly all Sicily. On enquiry finding there was a diligence (the mail) to Catania in ten hours, & that it would take my diminished luggage, I resolved to go by it & to stay in these comfortable quarters long enough thoroughly to enjoy the place. So I parted from my muleteer with great good will on my side & apparently on his. If I go round Etna I shall miss him very much, but it would be too expensive to keep him on till then. The last six days, the fine weather part of this mule journey, have been delightful, but I am not sorry to exchange it now for going from place to place by diligence & taking walks from the places I stop at.

After three more days in Syracuse which Mill thoroughly enjoyed and on which he reported in great detail, he continued on the 25th to Catania, where he arrived somewhat exhausted and with a new attack of indigestion which, although he did not allow it seriously to interfere with his sightseeing and excursions during the next three days, somewhat diminished the pleasure of it. But continued weakness in no way diminished his enthusiasm over the beauty of the two-day journey to Messina where, after visiting Taormina, he arrived on the 30th. He found that a steamer to Corfu was due to leave on the 1st and decided to risk the long sea passage, but a delay in the arrival of the steamer kept him waiting at Messina for another three days.

Messina, 1 April: I passed the rest of the day in putting in order my great accumulation of plants, & in reading Dante & the handbook for Greece. Nothing is more likely to keep off sea sickness than filling my brain with an exciting conception of what I am going to do. I think I shall do in Greece the contrary of what I have done in Italy, that is, I shall take what opportunities I may have & even seek opportunities of conversing with the educated class of natives. I am curious about the mind of the leading people of Greece & feel that I have almost everything to learn about them. Doubtless my introductions to Finlay[15] & Wyse[16] will give me opportunities, & going in the first week in April I shall have a good deal of time. I am obliged to ménager the books I have with me to make them hold out. I am keeping Sophocles for Greece, Theocritus & the two Sicilian pastoral poets, Bion & Moschus, I have finished, & like the two last much better than the first, whom I think greatly overrated, & quite inferior to his imitator, Virgil.

Messina, 2 April: Messina would be on some accounts the best place in Sicily for us to live in: it is I think still more beautiful than Palermo; & there is more life in the place, more foreigners come there & it is practically much nearer to England & France owing to the English & French steamers to Malta & the Levant which do not go near Palermo: it is strange therefore that there should be but one post in a week & I suspect there must be ways of sending *via* this or that in the intervals. Oates says the Galignani reaches him, sometimes, very quickly, by the French steamers. But I do not think we should like to live in so stagnant a place as Sicily where one falls a month behind in news if one has not one's own newspaper & meets no one who knows a single European fact.

Chapter Eleven

GREECE
1855

AFTER forty-eight hours spent foodless on his back in his cabin, Mill arrived at Corfu in tolerably good shape on 6 April—in 1855 Good Friday, both according to the Western and to the Greek calender. The Ionian Islands were then still a British possession and Mill soon found agreeable company and, with an Irish botanist and a young man from Oxford, for eight days explored Corfu and finds it 'decidly the most beautiful & agreeable little bit of our planet that I have yet seen & I do not at all expect to find anything better in Greece'.[1] He soon came to envy the post of High Commissioner there when an unexpected offer from the Colonial Secretary, Bowen, seemed almost to provide the perfect answer to his search for a place at which to live.

Corfu, 8 April 1855: I breakfasted with him [Bowen] in his very nice rooms & took the opportunity of asking him about the eligibility of the place for living in, telling him my reason for being interested about it—that either my wife's health or my own, or both, might very possibly make it desirable for me to fix in a southern climate. He gave the greatest encouragement—said it had often surprised him that so few English settle here, that it can only be because the advantages of the place are not known. He said the common idea of the English here is that you can live as well on £600 a year here as on £1200 in England, but that quiet & economical people

can do much better: for instance his predecessor as Colonial
Secretary told him he never spent more than £500 though he
had several children & kept a carriage & two or three horses.
He asked me if I should like to be Resident of one of the
islands—saying that the work does not take above two hours
a day to an energetic person as he has not to govern but to
review the acts of the native government all of which must be
submitted to him in writing for his sanction—that the pay is
£500 & a house, or rather *two* houses, in town & country,
that the appointment is not with the Colonial Office but with
the Lord High Commissioner who is always eager to get
better men than the officers accidentally in command of the
troops, whom he is generally obliged to appoint for want of
better & whose incompetence & rashness sometimes go near
to drive him mad—that either Cephalonia or Zante will be
vacant within a year; that they are not bound to any representation except that they give a ball to the cheif people of
the island once a year on the queen's birthday & a dinner to
the members of the native government about twice a year.
This is tempting, now when I see how much pleasanter at
least Corfu is than most of the places we could think of going
to: & if Ward[2] had been going to remain I could probably
have had the place for asking. The new man[3] is the son of an
India director but my having known him, as he died under a
cloud, would not I suspect be much of a recommendation to
the son. Bowen introduced me at the garrison library, the
only place where one can see English newspapers & periodicals—there I learnt for the first time Hume's death:[4] if all
did as much good in proportion to their talents as he, what a
world it would be! also that Lewis is Chancellor of the
Exchequer & Vernon Smith at the India Board:[5] this last I
suspect will give me a good deal of influence there.

Towards the end of his stay in Corfu, and after a long and anxious
pause, Mill at last received news from his wife. Apparently her health
had been badly affected by the severe winter.

Corfu, 14 April: Thank heaven it is over—the illness &
the winter too—& though the last letter does not say how
you are the handwriting & its being in ink are encouraging.
Respecting the danger of travelling in Greece my precious
one will have seen by my last letter that I am quite attentive
to the subject, & shall not run any serious risks. I shall be
guided by Wyse who must know the state of the country.
You might well say that some other person's savoir faire was
wanted 'in addition' to mine—I could not help laughing
when I read those words, as if I had any savoir faire at all. . . .

Bowen afterwards renewed the subject of the Residentship, said that Zante will be vacant this year, that it will be
offered to Wodehouse[6] & if he takes it Cefalonia will be
vacant & that he is almost sure Sir J. Young has no one to
whom he wishes to give it & seemed very desirous that I
should think seriously about it. I told him that I had not
made up my mind to leave the India house but might very
possibly be obliged to do so & that this opening would be a
strong additional inducement. As one dinnering leads to
another I found myself in for another dinner with Sir J.
Young, yesterday: the only persons present were the Regent
of Corfu (a Count something) & Col. Butler.[7] I learnt a good
deal & so did the Governor from the Regent, about the stat-
istics of the island & had some talk with Sir J. Y. about the
taxes. I was glad to see so much of him in case we should
think in earnest about coming here—I do not believe there
is a more beautiful place in the world & few more agreeable
—the burthen of it to us would be that we could not (with
the Residentship) have the perfectly quiet life, with ourselves
& our own thoughts which we prefer to any other, but if we
have tolerable health there is not more of societyizing than
would be endurable & if we have not, that would excuse us.
This morning is the day for going to Athens, but the steamer
has not arrived & I cannot tell when we shall get off . . . I
am impatient to get to Greece now, having seen this island
thoroughly & so as never to forget it: & it has seemed to me

always more & more charming. All however say that the climate is extremely variable, much rain, a good deal of cold, & intense heat for three months. . . . Bowen tells me that Reeve[8] is editor of the Edinburgh! it is indeed fallen. Who will consent to have his writings judged of, & cut & carved by Reeve? For us it is again a complete exclusion.

There is no further mention of the Residentship in Mill's letters, but from a letter written about this time by Mrs. Mill to her brother in Australia it would seem that it was probably at her wish that he did not accept the offer.

Mrs. Mill to Arthur Hardy, about April 1855:[9] Mr. Mill has the offer of a very nice place under government in one of the Greek islands, it being supposed that the climate might suit both his and my health, but tho' much tempted I do not think we shall accept it, we both dread the heat which is said to be excessive in the summer.

Leaving Corfu on the morning of 15 April, and after first slowly steaming along the Ionian Islands and up the Gulf of Corinth, and after a carriage drive across the Isthmus, Mill reached Athens on the evening of the 17th.

Athens, 19 April: I have made good use of the two days I have been here: yesterday I saw almost all the antiquities & went today to Eleusis. I have already got quite into the feeling of the place—with regard to scenery it is hitherto rather below my expectation, very inferior to Corfu & the Corinthian Gulf, the mountains though otherwise fine being arid & bare, & very like those of the South of France, while the peculiar beauty of this place, the bright & pure atmosphere, I have not had—both these days though sunny having been extremely hazy, so that I did not see the mountains half as well as on the rainy day of my arrival. Wyse says that Lord Carlisle had the same ill luck, & only had before his departure a few days of brilliant weather. Nevertheless the view from the Acropolis was splendid. The temples surpassed my expectation rather than fell short of it though I had not fancied that so much of the Parthenon had perished. The beauty of it however is what no engravings can give any proper idea of even independent of what all the buildings here owe to the excessive beauty of the Pentelican marble they are made of. The temple of Theseus I have from my childhood been familiar with a print of: I should never be tired of looking at it. The interior has been made a museum for the sculptures they occasionally dig up & I was not at all prepared for their extreme beauty; there is one statue very like, & I think equal to, the Mercury of Antinous of the Vatican, & a number of sepulchral groups in which grace & dignity of attitude & the expression of composed grief in the faces & gestures are carried as far as I think mortal art has ever reached.

20 April: The Acropolis with its four temples, (though the Propylaea is not really a temple) combines magnificently with the hills about—& of the distant mountains Pentelicus & the island of Aegina [?] are the finest, except the group at the Isthmus which are glorious. What light it throws on Greek history to know that the AcroCorinth is seen as a great object from all these heights—much larger & nearer looking than the Knockholt beeches from home. I think that corner of the Morea must be perfectly divine. The gulf or narrow channel between Salamis & the main land in which the battle was fought is just under our feet but I can*not* realize the history of the place while I am looking at it—all the alentours are so different. I shall do that better in our drive at dear Blackheath.

On the following, perfectly cloudless but still somewhat hazy day Mill climbed Pentelicus and was rewarded with a perfect view.

21 April: I never saw any combination of scenery so perfectly beautiful & so magnificent—& the sunset & evening lights on the innumerable mountains in front of us returning were exquisite. The haze does not so much affect the beauty of the lights when the sun is low. The more than earthly beauty of this country quite takes away from me all care or feeling about historical associations, which I had so strongly at Syracuse. *That* I shall have when I read Greek history again after becoming acquainted with the localities. I was not at all tired, except the hand which carried the plants, for the load which Perry[10] & I brought in was quite painful to mind & body. I never felt so much the embarras des richesses. Determining them with imperfect books takes several hours in every 24: it is now past 12 & I have only determined about a third, the rest must remain in water & in the tin case till tomorrow—to be determined by day light—nor have I been able to change a single paper. I am here in the season of flowers as well as of all other beauty. It is quite true that nothing, not even Switzerland, is comparable in beauty to this—but as in all other cases, other inferior beauty will be more, not less, enjoyable in consequence. If *my* darling beauty could but see it! it is the only scenery which seems worthy of her. Even Sicily recedes quite into the background. And it is but a fortnight since I thought nothing could be finer than Messina!

After ten days in Athens Mill started on 28 April with three companions for the first of his longer excursions, to Nauplia, Argos and Corinth, which, however, he had scarcely time to describe since after only one night at Athens he starts on 2 May for a much longer excursion to the north. With one companion, a young Englishman he had met at Athens, and a guide, Mill travelled for thirteen days through Attica, Euboea and Central Greece and with his detailed daily accounts filled a letter of 22 closely written pages which he posted after his return to Athens.

Tatoe (the ancient Deceleia), 2 May: I have got thus far, my angel, & am now writing in a nice room of a very pretty maison de campagne in I should think the finest situation in Attica, belonging to somebody who was minister of war during part of the revolutionary period. It stands a little way up Parnes, on the side next to Pentelicus, at a short distance from the place which the Lacedaemonians fortified in the latter part of the Peloponesian war to take military possession of Attica. Where there are no inns, travellers are of course entertained in private houses—the owner of this is now absent. We form quite a caravan, having four horses & two mules, three for ourselves and the guide, three for luggage & utensils, beds, provisions &c. also three muleteers & a cook: all this being provided for the 25 francs a day we each pay, which also includes the remuneration of the guide. . . The commencement of the journey is auspicious. I am writing this while waiting for dinner, on a table spread as neatly as at home & I have no doubt we shall dine as well & as pleasantly as at the hotel at Athens. Our guide George Macropoulos, evidently understands this part of the business, though he does not know the mountains from a distance & misleads us in the most absurd manner. I have hitherto found, much to my surprise, the Greeks a remarkably stupid people—the stupidest I know, without even excepting the English. I make every allowance for the fact that they & we communicate in languages which are foreign to both & which they know very imperfectly—but they do not shew the cleverness that French, Italians & even Germans do in making out one's meaning, & they never seem able to find out what one wants. Invariably they do the very opposite of what one tells them, being much too conceited to say they do not understand. . . . My travelling companion Dawson is pleasant mannered & seems desirous of information but very little educated & even leaves out many an *h*—which one would not have expected from his appearance or the tones of his voice, or his general manner of expressing himself.

On the next day the party, after crossing the range of the Parnassus, descended through the valley of Tanagra, continued along the coast of the channel of Euripus, over which they finally passed to Euboea over the bridge at Chalcis, where they spent a night in the house of a local merchant. Proceeding north through the mountains in the interior of the island they made their next stop at Achmet Aga.

Achmet Aga, 4 May: a village *made* entirely by an Englishman named Noel who for his reward has lately had his house
actually gutted of everything worth removing, & the whole
village plundered by a set of brigands. It is in his house we
are lodged quite unexpectedly, for the guide told us he had
asked hospitality of a *German* named *Emile*. This is exactly
like the ignorance & gross inaccuracy of these guides (this
man is thought one of the best, & I have tried two others.)

Continuing their way further north in the company of their host for
the night, Mill's enjoyment of the beauty of the landscape steadily
increased. Writing from 'a village in the north of Euboea where we
are lodged very comfortably' he wrote on

5 May: It is useless attempting to describe it. Whatever
one picks out as the choice bits in any other southern country
compose the whole of Greece, & here we have it mixed with
much of what is finest in the northern countries. We often
overlook the Aegean on the Eastern side of the island, with
Scyros apparently quite near— a long mountain ridge: & at
last came in sight of the Gulf of Nolo in front with Othrys &
Pelion behind it & the islands of Peparethis Sciathos &
others over against its entrance—(on a clearer day we should
also have seen Ossa & Olympus) making the divinest view I
ever beheld. About the middle of the day we came to a large
rich village where the people were assembled for the fête of
their patron St. George & we saw dancing—of the most bar-
baric kind to truly Turkish music, a drum going like strokes
of a blacksmith's hammer & a sort of flute sounding like a
bagpipe. There was general personal cleanliness & much fine
dressing—they are an odd people, like South Sea islanders I
should think. Noel showed us several of the cottages of his
peasants—one large room with an earthen floor, the fire in
the middle & a hole in the roof above it for the smoke—one
end of the room sometimes partitioned off, for all the animals
cows, oxen & all. In the midst of one of these stood the pay-
sanne, a neat, still handsome woman, quite finely dressed for

the fête, making the oddest contrast with all that surrounded her. At the dancing nothing could exceed the polite attention we received from all the people. It is impossible to dislike such universally good humoured & courteous people but they are almost savages. They always consider & speak of themselves as Orientals not Europeans.

On the following day they reached through 'Yerochori' (Xirochorion) the channel which separates Euboea from what was then the northernmost strip of Greek mainland at Oreos and after long negotiations succeeded in hiring the only boat in the roads large enough to take horses up the gulf of Zeitun. Unfavourable winds prolonged what need have been no more than a three-hour crossing to more than twenty, including a whole night which Mill, without damage to his health, spent on the deck, landing at last at

Stylidha (*Stylis*), *7 May:* Our guide wanted us to land at Molos on the south side, very near Thermopylae, & not go to Lamia at all, & by this we should have saved a day, but as the dangerous part of the journey, if any, begins here, & we were told that there were only national guards at Molo, in whom we felt no confidence, we decided (as the Eparchos[11] had advised) to land at Stylidha, the port of Lamia on the north side. There we waited on the civil & military authorities, presented our ministerial order, & are to have a guard of six regular soldiers & mounted gendarmes tomorrow. To this we are legally entitled: what we give to them is backshish —a word in much use here—in which form they will cost us about a dollar a day.

Topolia, *9 May:* We started from Stylidha with our six guards who however were not regular soldiers: but they only went with us to Lamia, three hours off, past the head of the gulf. Here the commandant gave us two non-commissioned officers & eight privates, to whom the commandant of the following station of his own accord added two more; so we are well protected. The number makes no difference in what we pay. Some of them go before us & some behind, & at the commencement they threw out vedettes to right & left but they left off this when they got into the narrow ways. At the head of the gulf there is a considerable plain & the part near Lamia is better cultivated than any other part of Greece I have seen. There is however a great deal of marsh round the head, as with the Lake of Como. After crossing this place we entered the pass of Thermopylae, between Oeta & the gulf; first crossing the Spercheius, a river of some size, the first real river I have seen in Greece. But Leonidas would not know the place again, for in the 2350 years which have since passed, the Spercheius has brought down so much soil that it has converted the narrow pass into a broad flat partly marsh, partly covered with scrub, through which the river winds its course in a very slanting direction & at last falls into the gulf. The side of Oeta rises very steep, but covered with copse. The place of the ancient pass is fixed by some hot sulphureous spring which now as then gush out from the foot of the mountain, & also by the tumulus which was raised to contain the slain.

After a night spent at the village of Boudonitza they crossed the mountain range towards the south. The same day's entry then continues:

We were now completely in Swiss scenery. When we reached the top of the pass we looked down suddenly upon the great valley of Phocis, larger and broader than the Valais, & reaching from Boeotia to Thessaly—it lies between the range of Parnassus & that of Oeta, the former of which was now spread out before us, & the groups of summits more particularly known by the name of Parnassus was exactly opposite. Clouds however being on most of the tops & it soon began to rain, & it rained at intervals all the rest of the day. The valley is very green at this season—the centre alone is cultivated, though the whole is evidently very fertile—the rest is waste or beautiful woods of oak & plane: several beautiful streams run down it towards Boeotia & I suppose all join it lower down. But a village or two of few houses, just visible in nooks of the mountain, are all that remains to represent the twenty cities of Phocis. People talk of coming to Greece to see ruins, but the whole country is one great ruin.

From Topolia a very short day's journey of only four hours took them to Delphi.

Delphi, 10 May: Delphi is one of the very few places in Greece of which the views in Wordsworth's Greece[12] give a more favourable idea than the truth: it is however fine; backed by a very precipitous cleft portion of Parnasses & looking down into the broad valley with a narrow gorge at the bottom of it, rapidly ascending from right to left. I dare say it was very imposing when it was a fine town with a magnificent temple: it seems to have been at that time built on artificial ground supported by a solid wall along the mountain side, much of which (most splendid masonry) still remains. The Castalian spring is a humbug. The only bit of ground approaching to a level to be found near the town was also propped up by a wall & formed the stadium or race-course for the Pythian games, the most important & celebrated in Greece next to the Olympic.

After a partial ascent of Parnassus the party almost completed their circuit of the mountain by descending to the plains of Boeotia and Lake Copias, Mill as usual noting all the places with classic associations, from the exact spot where Oedipus met his father to the scene of the tragic adventure of Philomela and of the battle of Chaeronea. The last two stages of this tour, via Livadia and Plateae, were somewhat spoiled for Mill by a more than usually severe attack of indigestion. Arriving back at Athens on 15 May, he was further disquieted by unfavourable news about his wife's health. But as a second letter gave a somewhat more reassuring account he decided to go on with his original plans, and after a short rest, he proceeded on his tour of the Pelopennesus.

Athens, 15 May: I shall now take three clear days of rest before starting again, for which I shall be much the better, although I am not at all done up by the journey. I have been more fatigued some days than others, but not *increasingly* fatigued: when I have been able to take a long walk before riding at all, I have hardly been tired at all—& so when the country has admitted of much trotting & galloping. It is the sitting on horseback with my feet dangling that fatigues me when long continued: but I now recover myself by walking, which I could not so well do in Sicily. My digestion is not quite so bad & I hope by degrees to bring it round. Probably *now* a perfectly regular life such as we have at home will agree better with it than travelling. But to all appearance the pulmonary complaint has derived the greatest benefit from this holiday. I called on Wyse this morning & saw him: he agreed in all I said about the Greeks, & told me many things shewing the same brainless stupidity, & incapacity of adapting means to ends, in the acts of their government which I had observed in the common people. I now perfectly understand all I see in Greece, but I must say I now feel little or no interest in the people. Still if they get education they may improve. Wyse thinks the stupidity is in a great measure laziness but he admits them to be stupid.

At Athens Mill parted from his companion and on 18 May started alone on his Peloponnesian journey, which on the first two days took him merely to Megara and Corinth respectively. Only the third day, his forty-ninth birthday, brings him to really new fields.

Valley of the Lake Stymphalus, 20 May: This day last year I did not think I should be alive now, much less that I should pass my next birthday in Arcadia, & walk & ride nearly 14 hours of it. . . . I am glad I have not missed this as it is not only of a totally different character from all else in Greece, but the mountains finer. They run into so many intersecting ranges that I have not yet got to understand them, but we do seem to have now come up to a high barrier range running east & west. We are in a village at the end of the valley of the Lake Stymphalus.

In two further long stages Mill continued south, almost the whole length of the peninsula, towards Sparta. Although he feels he is thinner than he has been before in his life, he stood the strain well.

Vurlia, 22 May: [Laconia] however though it would be admired anywhere else, is altogether the least striking part of Greece, the forms of the mountains being more rounded than usual, & the whole being a complete wild with a barren arrid appearance—only fine when a glimpse is caught of the Taygetus: but I was well rewarded at the last by the very finest view in Greece, at least made so by the lights of the sunset, but it must always be one of the finest. This was in the descent to this village of Vurlia (near the site of Sellasia) which is itself very high up in the mountains on the east side of the magnificent green valley of Sparta. The opposite boundary is all formed by the range of Taygetus on which this house directly looks—& which is as fine as any part of the Alps & much finer than Parnassus or any other mountain I have seen in Greece. The highest part is something like the Dent du Midi at the head of the Lake of Geneva & at present brilliant with snow like that, but from that highest part it extends in a jagged ridge or series of peaks to right & left, fully to the length of the Mont Blanc group of mountains. Below it glitters the Eurotus—the valley immediately under the village is hid, but above & below it glitters like an emerald, as do also the sides of the mountains, & the view northward to the mountains of Western Arcadia by the sunset lights was glorious—the mountains themselves very fine —especially one like an enormous dome with smaller domes to right & left for shoulders. I shall see this valley to-morrow —unhappily time does not admit of my passing a night at Sparta & seeing the country in the way I should wish.

Khan of Georgitzi in Laconia, 23 May: I walked to Sparta after breakfast, a three hours walk. The valley, like all other scenery, loses much by the glare of the sunshine, but it does not disappoint the expectations that it raised, except that the

mountains on the opposite side to Taygetus are comparatively tame. The scale of the scenery is so great, that what
seemed from above one great though uneven valley is partly
made up of the buttresses of Taygetus—a range of green
mountains projecting forward from the great range—behind
and above these is a region of firs, & above that is the region
of snow. There are besides lower hills along the middle of
the valley so that the really level ground is narrow—until we
reach Sparta where these intermediate hills appear to cease,
& we see the mountains on both sides gradually decline into
the long low ridges which form the two great southern
promontories of Malea & Matapan.

Sparta itself, a new village, proved comparatively disappointing and
the only impression worth recording was a visit to the local and somewhat westernized judge. Turning northward again up the valley
Eurotas into the interior, the plague of vermin became serious:

Constantinos in Messenia, 25 *May:* I am writing in the usual
great hayloft, devoured by fleas—those in Sicily were
nothing to them, these are so numerous & bite so hard.
The people alas keep their rugs etc. here, which ensures
what I am suffering. Since I began the last sentence I caught
one in the act of getting into my nostril. They make their
way up from the floor much faster than I could catch them if
I did nothing else. I have two days to relate. The ways from
Laconia into Messenia are two: one up a gorge of Taygetus,
& through a very conspicuous gap in the ridge, to Calamata:
the English at Athens all recommend this route, which is the
shortest but the most difficult. The guide however said horses
could not go—mules must be taken at Sparta & the horses
send round—which would cause expense & delay, & though
I suspect the difficulty is of the guide's own making, I gave
up the idea. (The fleas are now attacking in columns, &
firing into many parts of my body at once.) The other way is
by rounding the extreme north end of Taygetus, & this we
began on the 23rd & completed on the 24th.

The excursion into Messenia by this second somewhat roundabout route took Mill altogether four days, with the flea plague getting worse every night: proceeding hence north through Laconia he was gradually getting tired of travelling, and even his final visit to Olympia on the day before reaching the port of Pyrgos could do little to revive his flagging spirits. From Pyrgos he proceeded by boat to the British island of Zanti, his real port of embarkation.

Zanti, 29 May: Our boat was a decked one with two masts & four great oars, & a hole below where there was just room for me to lie, & I turned in at dark—& though the fleas in the boat or in my clothers, or both, kept running all over me & biting me, my sleepiness made me sleep very sound though conscious of often waking & doing battle with them. When I finally awaked at half past five this morning we seemed almost arrived but as there had been an almost complete calm they had had to row all night. We did not arrive till eight. The inn here though a poor one is a perfect luxury after my late lodgings. I made myself thoroughly clean & comfortable, then breakfasted heartily from which I have since suffered not the smallest inconvenience, but it is so hot here that I have been very little out except to the bankers. The air as usual was so hazy that the coast of Greece was invisible when I landed, but I shall perhaps see it from the castle hill which I propose climbing in the cool of the evening. People here say the summer has set in hot all at once. The banker here introduced me to the club where I saw the latest Galignani's: everything both in England & the Crimea as unsatisfactory as ever.

Zanti, 30 May: I had my climb in the evening to the castle & saw the sun set from it about 7 oclock, so much shorter are the summer days in this southern latitude. The view is very fine. The promontory of Castel Tornese in the Morea was very distinct, & seemed quite near: the mountains behind Mesolonghi & those of Arcadia looked dim in the hazy distance. So good bye beautiful Greece—more beautiful than I ever expected, but beautiful as you are I never wish to see you again—for I do not wish ever again to go so long a journey without my beloved one, & the country will not be fit for her to come to while we live.[13] What a pleasure it is to see again something looking like civilization.

On the following day Mill boarded the steamer from Athens to Ancona and during the stop at Corfu posted the long report of his tour of the Peloponnesus to Mrs. Mill at Paris, where, as letters waiting for him informed him, she was shortly proceeding to meet him. From Ancona, where he arrived on 3 June, he started on the following day for the journey to Paris, which he did not expect to complete in much under three weeks, since he felt that he could 'not venture to travel by diligence, i.e. day & night more than part of the way'. And although he is compelled to use right from the start the more comfortable mode of travelling by *voiture*, his apprehensions of the strain of the journey proved only too soon justified. At Florence, where reports of bandits on the direct road to Bologna led him to make a detour, renewed hæmorrhages of the lung proved how ill founded had been his hope of the disease being stopped and compelled him to consult a doctor. This and the dates of the diligences forced on him a three-day delay which he used for some sightseeing and one more long letter to Mrs. Mill.

Florence, 7 June: She will not have to wait very long for me at or near Paris & I shall see her in a fortnight at furthest. I look forward to it with delight—but ah darling I had a horrible dream lately—I had come back to her & she was sweet & loving like herself at first, but presently she took a complete dislike to me saying that I was changed much for the worse—I am terribly afraid sometimes lest she should think so, not that I see any cause for it, but because I know how deficient I am in self consciousness & self observation, & how often when she sees me again after I have been even a short time absent she is disappointed—but she shall not be, she will not be so I think this time—bless my own darling, she has been all the while without intermission present to my thoughts & I shall have been all the while mentally talking with her when I have not been doing so on paper.

Florence, 8 June: [I] sat a great while in the Tribune (?) full of admiration—not of the Venus de Medici for decidedly I do not like her: I never liked the casts of her, & I do not like the original a bit better. I think her the poorest of all the Venuses. She is neither the earthly Venus nor the Urania. Of course she is a beautifully formed woman, but the head is too *too* ridiculously small, as if to give the *idea* of having no room for brains—& they may well say she does not look immodest, for the expression of the face is complete old maidism. At least these are very strongly my impressions & I am sure they are quite spontaneous. But there is a host of most beautiful statues & pictures there though the statues not quite equal to the Vatican. There are enough to make me feel in an atmosphere of art—even to be among all those Roman emperors whom I have got to know like personal acquaintances. There are also so many fine statues & pictures all over Florence that I could soon get into the kind of feeling I had at Rome of being bathed in art. It is strange that the Florentines should have had so many great painters & sculptors—I suppose they are like the English, who though so unpoetical a people have had more great poets than any other country. I am convinced that the Florentines are a most un-artistic, tasteless people. Who but such a people would let all the churches be masses of deformity which are positive eye-sore, and disgrace the city—like houses half built, of half burnt bricks—things in which no private person could bear to live—the only material exceptions being the Cathedral which has no front, & Santa Maria Novella which has nothing but a front. . . . The town itself is a good deal more lively now when the shops are open, & I sometimes for a moment forget that I am not in a French town. I feel more in Europe than I have done at any other town of Italy. I think I could feel quite at home here if our home *was* here—but according to Wilson[14] it is a place quite unfit for pulmonary invalids, both in winter & summer.

Florence, 9 June: What I left undone yesterday I have done today, & I have seen Florence itself pretty completely, though nothing of its environs. I passed a great part of the morning in the Pitti Gallery. . . . It is a very large collection, mostly of good pictures, and many chefs d'œuvre. Those which struck me most were two of Perugino which Murray in ten columns of notices does not even mention—one a descent from the Cross, which when I had only seen the print of it I thought one of the greatest pictures ever painted —all the disagreeable of the subject taken away & nothing but a beautiful dead body & the most beautiful feelings in the numerous gracefully grouped spectators. The other is an adoration of the infant Jesus by the Virgin & some children —a small thing compared to the other but quite admirable by the naturalness & natural grace of the children—the Virgin also very beautiful. There are many fine pictures by Fra Bartolomeo & Andrea del Sarto, masters whom I admire more & more.

Another two days' travel by diligence brought Mill to the railhead at Mantua and by rail to Verona and on the following day to Milan, where from some new Galiagni's he learnt about events in the world.

Milan, 12 June: I read Lord John Russell's disgusting speech on the impossibility of doing anything for Poland & the extreme desirableness of maintaining Austria in all her possessions—I felt a strong desire to kick the rascal—it is a perfect disgrace to England that he should be tolerated as a liberal (!) minister a day after such a speech. What with our sentimental affection for one despot & our truckling to the other great enemy, we are likely to have a precious character with all lovers of freedom on the Continent!

In spite of continuous spitting of blood and in spite of the warning that the road over the Gothard was not yet open for wheel carriages, and that the highest point of the pass must be crossed in sledges, Mill chose that route as the one likely to bring him quicker to his destination.

Lugano, 14 June: I had the mortification of finding that I had lost my botanical tin box—which has been most useful to me, holding an apparently impossible quantity of specimens & keeping them fresh in the hottest weather for 24 hours. It must have fallen or wriggled out of my great coat pocket in the diligence or railway carriage. I am much vexed at it. I have lost nothing else of consequence in this journey—nothing beyond a pocket handkerchief which I lost on Pentelicus & an old shirt which must have been kept by some blanchisseuse—though I hardly ever failed to count the things & compare them with the note.

Airolo, 16 June: Today it rained worse than ever, but I took my place for Fluelen on the Lake of Lucerne, & proceeded up the pass to the place where the sledging begins— & to my consternation found that the sledges, little things holding two persons each, were entirely open. Several passengers were as much surprised as I was, saying that on the Simplon & the Mont Cenis the sledges are covered, & that they should not have come if they had known—but to me it was out of the question going on, as I should have been thoroughly soaked & had a day in the diligence afterwards, which in my present state would have had a good chance of killing me. I had no choice, disagreeable as it was, but to get out bag & baggage & go back to Airolo by the return diligence about an hour & a half afterwards, here to wait till the rain ceases, which maybe by tomorrow morning, or in these mountains may not be for some time.

Fortunately the next day was fine, and Mill reached Fluelen without excessive discomfort but sufficiently tired to feel that he ought to devote the next morning to his 'real rest', a five-hour morning walk, before continuing by the steamer to Lucerne. Leaving there on the 19th for Basle and Strasbourg, he probably reached Paris and Mrs. Mill three days later.

Chapter Twelve

LAST YEARS AND DEATH OF
MRS. MILL
1856–1858

WE have no documents of the winter 1855–6, which Mill and his wife spent again in England. In July and early August 1855 they went with Haji and Lily to Switzerland, travelling slowly to Genova during the last week of July and visiting Chamonix later. At the end of this tour, while Mrs. Mill went on to Paris, Mill left her at Besançon to go for a week's walking tour to the French Jura. Two of his letters written from this tour[1] are extant and again testify of the prodigious feats of walking which the invalid found not only compatible with but conducive to his health.

J. S. M. to H. M.: Le Pont/on the Lac de Joux [Vaux],/ Wed^y, ev^g [August 13, 1855]/ I enjoy the place very much & you may suppose I am very well when I say that after climbing Mont Tendre, a most beautiful mountain, one of the highest in the Jura, which with a rest on the grass at the top & the return took six hours, I only staid half an hour to eat a crust of bread & drink a whole jug of milk, & set off again to climb another mountain & make a round which took another five hours—& I am now not more tired than is agreeable. The views of the Alps here are splendid, especially that from the Mont Tendre—in spite of a great deal of haze towards Berne & Savoy I saw the snowy range for a great distance, Mont Blanc tolerably & the Dent du Midi, the nearer Valais mountains & the whole lake of Geneva from end to end well: also the lake of Neuchatel, the whole Jura, & France I should think nearly to Dijon. The evening walk was still finer: the bit of Valorbe which I descended to get to the source of the Orbe (the place where the water of the two lakes is supposed to come out) equals anything I ever saw—a narrow gorge between precipices but itself full of the richest Jura verdure of pasture & wood so high as almost to hide the precipice: & the source with its exquisite clearness & great mass of water coming out from under an amphitheatre of precipice in the heart of a wood far surpasses Vaucluse. I also went over in the rocks above a really immense cave but without any stalactites. If my beloved one was with me I could stay here with pleasure the whole week —the inn would do—a *little* below the mark of St. Martin but larger rooms. As it is I shall leave tomorrow: for quiet enjoyment one requires to be two—by oneself there is nothing but activity.

Mill appears to have joined his wife at Boulogne about a week later and to have reached London after another ten days, about the last day of August.

In the autumn of 1856 Helen Taylor at last obtained her mother's consent to her trying her luck on the stage. Her passion for the theatre, which had already shown itself when she was quite a young girl, seems never to have left her, but her mother had for years opposed her wish to become an actress. At last it was arranged through the actress Fanny Stirling, who appears to have been an old acquaintance and perhaps had taught Helen Taylor, that the latter should try her powers with a provincial company which was looking for a person to act the chief parts in tragedy at their theatres in Newcastle and Sunderland. Great secrecy was to be observed and Helen Taylor not only assumed the name of 'Miss Trevor', under which alone she was known during the eighteen months or two years of her stage career, but all possible precautions were taken to prevent the reason for her absence from home becoming known or her correspondence with her mother giving any clue to her identity. Towards the end of November her brother Haji accompanied her to Newcastle and from her mother's first letter we gain some idea of the long struggle which must have preceded this decision.

H. M. to Helen Taylor, 24 November 1856 :[2] I wish you to be wholly uninfluenced by me in all your future proceedings. I would rather die than go through again your reproaches for spoiling your life. Whatever happens let your mode of life be your own free choice henceforth.

Helen Taylor's stage career, which we can follow closely in a long series of letters exchanged almost daily between mother and daughter,[3] is outside the scope of this book. It was from the beginning full of disappointments and one may well doubt whether the predominantly intellectual young woman was really suited for the stage. The letters are of course mainly concerned with Helen Taylor's practical problems, Mrs. Mill entering into the minutest details of her dresses, etc. But they also throw a good deal of light on the relation between the two hitherto inseparable women. They do not seem to have been entirely easy. Both highly strung and hyper-sensitive, the letters alternate between the most effusive professions of affection and a plaintive tone of misunderstood intentions, the mother in particular constantly feeling hurt by the apparent coolness of the daughter, who vacillates between assertion of her new independence and complete reliance on her mother's guidance.

After a joint Christmas holiday at Brighton Helen Taylor again went north to another theatre at Doncaster and later to Glasgow where her mother went to pay her a long deferred visit in February. Mill, who for a little while had again suffered from trouble with head and his eyesight, was on that account able to take a few days off and to accompany Mrs. Mill as far as Edinburgh. From the eight existing letters[4] which Mill wrote to his wife during the fortnight's absence only a few passages need be quoted.

J. S. M. to H. M., 17 February 1857 :[5] It was the strangest feeling yesterday & this morning to be here & at the same time fresh from all those places. I have hardly anything running in my mind's eye but innumerable large railway stations. On Saturday night at York I slept little & dreamt much—among the rest a long dream of some speculation on animal nature, ending with my either reading or writing, just before I awoke, this Richterish sentence: 'With what prospect then, until a cow is fed on broth, we can expect the truth, the whole truth & nothing but the truth to be unfolded concerning this part of nature, I leave to' &c. &c. I had a still droller dream the same night. I was seated at a table like a table d'hote, with a woman at my left hand & a young man opposite—the young man said, quoting somebody for the saying, 'there are two excellent & rare things to find in a woman, a sincere friend & a sincere Magdalen'. I answered 'the best would be to find both in one'—on which the woman said 'no, that would be *too* vain'—whereupon I broke out 'do you suppose when one speaks of what is good in itself, one must be thinking of one's own paltry self interest? no, I spoke of what is abstractedly good & admirable'—how queer to dream stupid mock mots, & of a kind totally unlike one's own ways or character. According to the usual oddity of dreams, when the man made the quotation I recognized it & thought that he had quoted it wrong & that the right words were 'an *innocent* magdalen' not perceiving the contradiction. I wonder if reading that Frenchman's book suggested the dream. These are ridiculous things to put in a letter, but perhaps they may amuse my darling.

In the following letters there are some references to his working on a revision of the *Political Economy* for the fourth edition.

J. S. M. to H. M., 19 February 1857:[6] I pass the evening always at the Pol. Economy, with now & then a little playing to rest my eyes & mind. There will be no great quantity to alter, but now & then a little thing is of importance. One page I keep for consideration when I can show it to you. It is about the qualities of English workpeople, & of the English generally. It is not at all as I would write it now, but I do not, in reality, know how to write it.[7]

After about ten days in Glasgow Mrs. Mill fell seriously ill, probably with another hæmorrhage from the lungs.

J. S. M. to H. M., 24 February 1857:[8] It was less of a shock the first moment than I should have thought it would have been—no doubt because the *same* letter said you were better & because the sight of your beloved handwriting gave me confidence—but I have been growing more anxious every hour since. Thank Heavens however we know by experience that this is not necessarily dangerous—though a warning of the danger there always is. It must have been much less bad than the former time, or you could not have written immediately. But it would be very imprudent to attempt travelling for I do not know how many days, & then it can only be by very short journeys. L[ily]'s being ill at the same time is an additional misfortune. But why should I not come. I am ready to come any day & stay any time—& I do not see that you being there is inconvenable—you are *really* on a visit, & it is nobody's concern to whom. You will judge best of everything & either you or L. will let me know.—but all my wish is to be with you & to be doing my little little to help. The blessing & comfort it was & is to me to have been with you on that former occasion no words will ever express.

In another letter on the following day, addressed to Edinburgh where Mrs. Mill seems to have moved either just before or after she fell ill, her return is further discussed, but on the evening of the next, Mill, evidently on the receipt of worse news, rushes north to join her.

Mill, who in the preceding year had become head of the Examiner's Department at India House and was thus in charge of all the political relations of the Company during this year of the Indian Mutiny, must have been exceedingly busy and during the spring his wife has to go alone to Brighton to recuperate. Even their annual holiday is delayed until September. There are a few letters[9] written while they separated for four days in order that Mill should get some walking in the Lake District while Mrs. Mill and her daughter not very successfully tried their luck on the Lancashire coast.

H. M. to J. S. M., Blackpool, 16 September 1857:[10] Dearest love/We got on well to Fleetwood (luggage & all) but it is a strange place, or rather a place *meant to be* but not built. It is like a beginning of Hearn Bay—roads planned but no houses —only a great staring Inn called Euston Hotel adding to the deserted look of the place—no lodgings fit to go to—so this morning we have driven over here (nine miles) & I write while we wait a few minutes which will account for a hurried note. This place is as they call it a little Brighton—a poor copy thereof except in the crowds of people so that it reminds me of your account of Southend. It is therefore not tempting at all, & as Lily has a great inclination to go to Lemington I decide to do so & to go on to-day. I shall order your letter to be sent on from Fleetwood but hope you will write to Post Office, Lemington as soon as you get this, that I may soon know where to direct to you dear.

I am so pleased at its being such a lovely day for Helvellyn that it makes me quite in spirits. my heart is with you all the time so do dearest enjoy the climbing and take good care not to slip.

I will write again tomorrow Adieu now

in haste ever yrs

H. M.

J. S. M. to H. M.: Salutation, Ambleside,/September 13 [1857]/Dearest—I have been very fortunate in having a most beautiful day for Hellvellyn. I ascended it from Patterdale having gone there by an early coach from here, & I returned here in the same way in the evening, walking up the pass so you see I was not tired. The view, though there were a few clouds, was splendid. It was a disappointment as to plants, as on those sunny heights everything was still more gone by than in the valleys—of all the rare plants which grow there I could only distinguish two, and those were only in leaf. But the day before I was unexpectedly successful in plants between Windermere & this place. I made a circuit & saw Mr. Crossfield's cottages which I will describe to you when I have the happiness of being with you again; they are not what we want; besides other objections they are in a real village or rather hamlet. I have planned a very nice round for today, and shall go to Broughton tomorrow down the Duddon, and to Lancaster, & I hope to Settle on Tuesday. I talked yesterday with people from Fleetwood & others from Blackpool & I am afraid they are but ugly places—I so hope you have not inflicted purgatory on yourself to give me this walk—I feel however that it will do me great good. Today the sky is gloomy—but not very threatening. Yesterday everything looked its very best. I shall write again as soon as I receive yours.

adieu my own wife from your

J. S. M.

For the second part of his walking tour Mill chose Settle in Yorkshire as his base and the remaining three letters are dated from there.

J. S. M. to H. M., Settle, 16 September 1857: This place is a prettier country town than any in the lakes & the country about looks very pretty though the mountains have not the fine forms & beautiful arrangements of the Lakes. Please darling continue to write here, as I find it is the best centre for all I want to see—within a day's walk of everything. I have time to explore Craven between this & Sunday & I shall certainly go to Manchester on Monday & to darling on Tuesday. I saw the last Times yesterday at Lancaster. The Indian news seems to me more bad than good, but not, I think, of any bad omen. I saw in a Liverpool paper an announcement from a French paper of the death of Comte. It seems as if there would be no thinkers left in the world.

J. S. M. to H. M.: Settle/Sat^y morng [September 19, 1857]/I have just got your darling letter you angel which would make me set off directly to rejoin you if I did not know that you would much rather I did not on account of the good this excursion does me. I too was feeling very sad all yesterday but for an opposite reason (partly) to yours, namely perfect beauty. It was the first *splendid* day since I have been here, & I was all day wandering over the edge of

the hills having such a sun & sky as made the views both
near & distant perfectly beautiful & I think that always
makes one melancholy, at least when one is alone, which to
me means not with you. I am now going to climb Ingle-
borough & see the caves, at least the principle of them, for
there are multitudes all about here. I fancied Leamington
would be pleasant because it has a civilized air, though very
ugly—the frequented parts of the N. of E. are generally
hideous as to the *human* part of them, but this Settle is a
nice quiet, really pretty, very little country place, not touri-
fied, the people of the place are civil & the few strangers one
sees in the coffee room are really gentlemanly. I shall enquire
at the Post Office at Manchester my own love. I will certainly
look particularly at the pictures my darling liked.

adieu till Tuesday evening, and blessings from her own

J. S. M.

During the winter 1857/8 the pressure of work caused by developments in India kept the Mills in London although the state of their
health would have made it advisable that they winter abroad.[11] In July
1858 we can follow Mill once more on one of his walking tours while
Mrs. Mill remained at Blackheath Park. He spent a week of strenuous
walking in the Peak District of Derbyshire, but neither any of his
four letters to his wife nor her two letters to him[12] are of any special
interest. One letter by each may serve as specimens.

H. M. to J. S. M., Blackheath, 12 July 1858: Monday
Even^g/I was quite in spirits all yesterday because you had
such a nice day for the journey dearest. This morning I got
your account of your day[13] which shows that all went well.
It is pleasant to hear that Matlock turned out better than we
expected. To-day has been very hot, tho' without bright sun
& looks this evening as tho' there would be rain in the night,
& already one has begun to wish for more rain the air is so
close & sultry. Among the hills no doubt you will not find
it too hot. I *am* so pleased it is fine. As the people at the Inn
are disagreeable you must leave it—I hope you have already,

for it would much lessen the good walking may do if you are uncomfortable in the house. The Times has not yet come, but I have the Telegraph—I need not tell you things in it which will be in the Times, as you will see that—but it has a very long account of Bulwers wife[14] being seized & sent to a madhouse, which seems a *most* nefarious affair. It ought to lead to Bulwer being turned out of the ministry—I hope it will, such an incarnation of vanity & dishonesty as the man is—he could not face the ridicule of his wife talking against him on the hustings. But it is a disgrace to the law that *any body* can be made prisoner & carried off on the certificate of two medical men!

If the expedition proves pleasanter than you expected, & seems to be doing you good, I do hope you will stay into the next week. It will be excessively painful to me if you come back sooner than you need, on account of what I said—or on any account. Adieu dearest if this sh^d get lost it certainly will be no prize to the finder!

J. S. M. to H. M., 15 July 1858: Bakewell/Thursday ev^g./ My darling! I received her most precious letter yesterday morning and the pleasure it gave me was almost worth the absence. As to prolonging my stay, what she so kindly & sweetly writes would induce me to do it, if it were not that this excursion has not quite fulfilled our expectations or rather hopes in the matter of health. I have found no deficiency of strength, but have never been without a dry furred tongue, & never many hours without other decided sensations of indigestion, & this in spite of the greatest care, & observance of your advice in every particular. An excursion of this sort is excellent to strengthen me against indigestion, but it does not perhaps tend so much to cure it when it exists. Perhaps the regularity of home may do better. I dare say however I shall be better for this *afterwards* as has so often been the case. As I shall therefore see her on Sunday morning & she will not get this till Saturday, I will keep all description for a nice talk & will only say that, contrary to my expectation, the place which seems most suitable for us to make any stay at is *Buxton* which I walked to yesterday, returning on the top of the omnibus. On consideration, I thought that Dovetale had not the étoffe of a place for more than a day, so I was driven there in a phaeton this morning from here—the place was not a disappointment but was soon seen & I have just come in from an eleven miles walk since I came back. Tomorrow morning I shall go to Castleton & shall have the greater part of tomorrow & the greater part of Saturday to spend there as I shall go from thence to Sheffield, no great distance, & return by a night train from there, arriving in town about five on Sunday morning when I will rest a little & breakfast & then come home to my darling. The weather has been excellent—the last two afternoons there has been a little rain not enough to do any harm, & tonight there has been a little since dusk, with some lightening. I found no plants on Tuesday or today, but yesterday was a splendid day for them, as I found five, of which Jacob's ladder was one.

Adieu with a thousand loves from your

J. S. M.

In the autumn of 1858 Mill was at last able to relinquish his post at East India House, which, since his appointment as Examiner a little more than two years before, had claimed more of his time than in earlier years. He took advantage of the transfer of the East India Company's functions to the Government to retire at the age of fifty-two instead of at sixty as he should otherwise have been entitled, and his thirty-five years of service were rewarded with a liberal pension of £1,500—more than his salary had been until the last promotion, when it had been raised to £2,000. Although officially his connexion with the Company came to an end only at Christmas, his wife's and his own state of health urgently required that they should spend the winter outside England. They left Blackheath Park for the South of France on 11 October. Helen Taylor had been staying with them on a visit from Aberdeen, probably in order to appear on that same evening in a minor part, in a first performance of Wilkie Collins' 'The Red Vial' in the Olympic (or perhaps only to see Mrs. Stirling act in it), and Mrs. Mill's letters to her begin with a comment on the *Times*'s review of the play which still reached her at Folkestone. After another night in Boulogne Mill and his wife reached Paris on the 14th to stay there for two days. The plan was to go in easy stages to Montpellier, later to move on to Hyères, where Mrs. Mill had so well recovered four years before, and to pass the following spring in Italy. But already at Dijon Mrs. Mill's health proved unequal to the strain of the railway journey and another two days' stop became necessary. Mill himself clearly was not the best person to look after the invalid in the circumstances.

H. M. to Helen Taylor, Dijon, 18 October 1858:[15] The fact is we always get the last seats in the railway carriage, as I cannot run on quick, & if he goes on he never succeeds, I always find him running up and down & looking lost in astonishment, so I have given up trying to get any seats but those that are left.

When on the following day they arrived in Lyons, Mrs. Mill had a bad cold which rapidly developed into severe congestion of the lungs with a high fever and great general weakness. On the 21st Mill has for the first time to write to Helen Taylor in her place, but at her wish still insisting that 'there was nothing to be uneasy about'. Two days later she herself could report in a pencilled note that she had got up and after a week's stay they were able to leave Lyons on the 26th 'in great hope that I shall by degrees get over the attack'. But even the two hours' journey to Valence and the somewhat longer journey to Avignon on the next day proved too much for her strength. Although on arrival there she still hoped that 'it is all over and I shall have more cheerful letters to write', and to continue at once to Montpellier, this was not to be and this letter of 27 October was to be her last. On the following day Mill desperately wrote to the doctor in Nice who had saved her life four years before.

J. S. M. to Dr. Gurney at Nice:[16] Avignon, Oct. 28, 1858/ Dear Dr. Gurney/My wife is lying at the Hotel de l'Europe here so very ill that neither she nor I have any hope but in you to save her. It is a quite sudden attack which came on at

Lyons, of incessant coughing which prevents sleeping, and by the exhaustion it produces has brought her to death's door. I implore you to come immediately. I need hardly say that any expense whatever will not count for a feather in the balance.

I am, dear Dr. Gurney

very truly yours

J. S. Mill

A day or two later Mill sent a hurried pencilled report to Helen Taylor, then back in Aberdeen, which is in part very difficult to read.

J. S. M. to Helen Taylor, 29 or 30 October 1858:[17] Dear Lily Mama had had a tremendous attack of bronchitis with congestion & fever much worse that at Lyons. We have done everything possible & today for the first time she is a little better. The cough has been unceasing & most painful preventing her lying down day or night or getting any sleep besides that the intense nervous irritation caused by the congestion the fever & the fatigue made her almost out of her mind. We have had the best physician here but his prescriptions are too weak. She has taken a number of her own. On Thursday she did not think she (?) shd recover. She thought you would see by her letters from Lyons how ill she was but she did not like to alarm you. Today she is certainly better. The cough is less frequent & the head for the first time more calm. We took every precaution on the road. She was carried by the porters in a chair to the railway at Lyons & we had a coupè to ourselves from Valence here but she says the whole (?) incidents of such a journey are totally unfitted for her. The excessive hardship of every part, the inability to have anything fit for a delicate stomach to eat, the tremendous noise everywhere, the coarse manner of the women, the intense fatigue of waiting in the railway rooms for at least half an hour & then the immense distance to go both to & from them. This inn is thought one of the best in France & we appear to have the best rooms yet bedrooms & sitting room are of red tiles with thin carpet over, which she endeav-

oured to obviate the first day by using a footstool but in vain
—but [??] far more than all the evident fatal effect upon her
of the air of the S[outh] of F[rance]. She dragged herself up
to write to you a few words on Wedy, that you might not be
anxious, hoping it would prove as she said, but she felt ill as
she wrote & got gradually worse till at night she was very
ill.   She does not wish you to come to her because she
thinks she has taken the turn to get better & therefore it
wd be a very great pity to break your good arrangements
which are a great pleasure to her to hear of. You shall know
continually how she is going on. We have got all your letters
from Monp[ellier] today here & continue to write here for it
will probably be weeks before we leave this place. All notice
of your letters must be at a future time.

She is anxious that you shd not think of coming to her.
She would (?) be extremely annoyed if you did and now she
says adieu dear girl in haste.

J. S. M.

Probably even before this letter reached her a cable[18] informed
Helen Taylor on 1 November that her mother was worse, and though
she left Aberdeen on the following day neither she nor Dr. Gurney
reached Avignon in time. Mrs. Mill died in the Hôtel de l'Europe on
3 November.

An extract from the letter to W. T. Thornton in which Mill gave
to friends in England the first intimation of the event was published
many years ago by A. Bain.

J. S. M. to W. T. Thornton, Avignon, November 1858:[19]
The hopes with which I commenced this journey have been
fatally frustrated. My Wife, the companion of all my feelings, the prompter of all my best thoughts, the guide of all
my actions, is gone! She was taken ill at this place with a
violent attack of bronchitis and pulmonary congestion. The
medical men here could do nothing for her, and before the
physician at Nice, who had saved her life once before, could
arrive, all was over.

263

It is doubtful if I shall ever be fit for anything, public or private, again. The spring of my life is broken. But I shall best fulfil her wishes by not giving up the attempt to do something useful. I am sure of your sympathy, but if you knew what she was, you would feel how little any sympathy can do.

J. S. M. to the Mair of Avignon, 3 November 1858:[20] Monsieur le Maire,/Par vos fonctions officielles, vous avez eu connaissance du malheureux evénément qui a créé pour ma famille avec la ville que vous administrez un lien indissoluble. Nous croyons ne pouvoir rendre un meilleur hommage à celle que nous avons perdu qu'en faisant autant que possible les choses que, vivante, elle eût voulu faire; et comme elle n'aurait pas pu venir s'établir à Avignon sans que les malherreux de cette ville en eussent profité, nous souhaitons que, dans la triste circonstance où nous nous trouvons, ils aient encore à la remercier de quelque chose. Veuillez, donc, monsieur le maire, accepter au profit de la Caisse des pauvres le don de mille francs, somme proportionnée à nos facultés plutot qu'à nos désires, et que nous vous prions de vouloir bien inscrire au nom de ma bien-aimée épouse, Mme Henriette Mill, née Hardy, décédée à Avignon le 3 Novembre 1858.

Agreez............J. Stuart Mill.

J. S. M. to Arthur Hardy, Blackheath, 5 December 1858:[21] My dear Sir/ Before receiving this you will already have heard the terrible & most unexpected blow which has fallen upon us. I have not felt equal to writing to you before & now when I do, language is so utterly incapable of expressing such a loss, or what that loss is to us, that it is sickening to attempt it. But you will desire to know some of the sad details. We left England on the 12th of October, intending to pass the winter at Hyères, where she had wintered before or at some other place in the south of France. For the first time we were able to do as we pleased as I had just retired from the I.H. & we were looking forward to a happy half year or year in a mild climate. She was apparently in her usual health, perhaps even better than usual, & as fit for travelling as when she set out on other much longer journeys by which her health had not suffered but benefitted. She continued pretty well up to Lyons, but when there she had a sharp feverish attack, which yielded to the usual remedies but left a good deal of cough behind it. We staid there a week, at the end of which she felt sufficiently recovered to go slowly onward, but the day after we arrived at Avignon she was again taken very ill—she was better the next day, but the improvement was not progressive and a great shortness of breathing came on. She had the best medical man the place afforded but as usual with French physicians their remedies were not sufficiently powerful & after a few days becoming alarmed, though we never suspected immediate danger, I wrote to Dr. Gurney of Nice who attended her in a dangerous illness there in 1853, asking him to come over to see her. He came instantly but found all at an end! The very day before her last we thought her illness had taken a favourable turn. From the symptoms Dr. Gurney thinks the cause of death was excessive & [?] congestion of the lungs. She is buried in the cemetery of the town of Avignon & with her all our earthly happiness. We have henceforth no interest in life but to fulfil her wishes in all we can, & to return continually to her Grave. We have bought a small house & garden near the cemetery, where we shall go early in the spring & intend to pass much of our time there until our turn comes for being buried along with her. Algernon would have written to you if I had not, but I wished to write myself [??] He & Helen are pretty well, though Helen at one time broke down & had an attack of illness, but fortunately it proved short. It is useless to write more. Believe me yrs very truly

Even before Mill returned to England two or three weeks after his wife's death, he had bought the small house within sight of the cemetery in the suburb of Saint-Veran of Avignon where his wife had been buried and in which he was to spend the greater part of the rest of his life. He then at once devoted himself to the publication of the work to which they had given most of their energies during the preceding years, which was to have received its final revision during the stay on the Continent and now was to appear as it had been left on her death: *On Liberty* was published in February 1859 with the moving dedication 'to the beloved and deplored memory of her who was the inspirer, and in part the author, of all that is best in my writings'. At the same time Mill made arrangements for the republication of a collection of some of his review articles and remained in London until April to see the first two volumes of *Dissertations and Discussions* through the press. The pamphlet *Thoughts on Parliamentary Reform*, written some years earlier, and a long review article on related subjects also were brought out at about the same time, and two other major articles, probably written after he had gone with Helen Taylor to Avignon for their first long stay, appeared later in the same year. Evidently Mill tried to bury himself in intensive work.

At Avignon a monument of the finest Carrara marble was erected at great expense over the grave of his wife, bearing the inscription[22] given on opposite page.

With this our account might well close. It cannot be the task of this study to inquire how far Mrs. Mill's ideas continued to guide her husband's work after her death. I believe that a careful study of his later development would show that in some degree he withdrew a little from the more advanced positions which he had taken under her influence and returned to views closer to those he had held in his youth. But this is an impression for which it would be impossible to give here the evidence. There is, however, one other circumstance which is of some significance for our appreciation of Mill's appraisal of his wife and which, since it is not clearly seen in the more widely read editions of the *Autobiography*, should be briefly mentioned here. After Mrs. Mill's death her daughter Helen Taylor became Mill's constant companion and devoted assistant. It had been known that he came to hold his stepdaughter in very high esteem and that he had devoted to her praise some passages in the *Autobiography* which, on Alexander Bain's urgent advice, Helen Taylor had omitted in the version published immediately after Mill's death.[23] How great Mill's admiration for her had grown[24] became apparent however only when the suppressed pass-

TO THE BELOVED MEMORY

OF

HARRIET MILL

THE DEARLY BELOVED AND DEEPLY REGRETTED

WIFE OF JOHN STUART MILL

HER GREAT AND LOVING HEART

HER NOBLE SOUL

HER CLEAR POWERFUL ORIGINAL AND

COMPREHENSIVE INTELLECT

MADE HER THE GUIDE AND SUPPORT

THE INSTRUCTOR IN WISDOM

AND THE EXAMPLE IN GOODNESS

AS SHE WAS THE SOLE EARTHLY DELIGHT

OF THOSE WHO HAD THE HAPPINESS TO BELONG TO HER

AS EARNEST FOR THE PUBLIC GOOD

AS SHE WAS GENEROUS AND DEVOTED

TO ALL WHO SURROUNDED HER

HER INFLUENCE HAS BEEN FELT

IN MANY OF THE GREATEST

IMPROVEMENTS OF THE AGE

AND WILL BE IN THOSE STILL TO COME

WERE THERE BUT A FEW HEARTS AND INTELLECTS

LIKE HERS

THIS EARTH WOULD ALREADY BECOME

THE HOPED-FOR HEAVEN

SHE DIED

TO THE IRREPARABLE LOSS OF THOSE WHO SURVIVE HER

AT AVIGNON

NOV. 3 1858

ages were restored from the manuscript in a recent complete edition of the *Autobiography*.[25] The most characteristic of these passages in which Helen Taylor is placed on the same pedestal with his wife will form a fitting conclusion.

'Though the inspirer of my best thoughts was no longer with me, I was not alone: she had left a daughter, my stepdaughter, Miss Helen Taylor, the inheritor of much of her wisdom, and of all her nobleness of character, whose ever growing and ripening talents from that day to this have been devoted to the same great purposes, and have already made better and more widely known than was that of her mother, though far less so than I predict, that if she lives it is destined to become. Of the value of her direct co-operation with me, something will be said hereafter, of what I owe in the way of instruction to her great powers of original thought and soundness of practical judgement, it would be vain to give an adequate idea. Surely no one ever before was so fortunate, as, after such a loss as mine, to draw another prize in the lottery of life—another companion, stimulator, adviser, and instructor of the rarest quality. Whoever, either now or hereafter, may think of me and of the work I have done, must never forget that it is the product not of one intellect and conscience but of three, the least considerable of whom, and above all the least original, is the one whose name is attached to it.'

APPENDICES

Appendix I

POEMS
BY HARRIET TAYLOR

I

Written at Daybreak[1]

HUSHED are all sounds, the sons of toil and pain,
The poor and wealthy are all one again;
Sleep closes o'er the high and lowly head,
And makes the living fellows with the dead.
The clouds of night roll sullenly away,
Humbly obedient to th'approach of day;
The fragrant flowers unfold their scented heads,
The birds with gladness leave their leafy beds—
But unperceived at first the orb of day,
Sending alone a faint and trembling ray;
The glowing east, streaming with floods of gold
The fleeing clouds a thousand hues unfold.
At last he comes majestically slow
Pouring bright radiance on the world below,
And springing upwards from th' embrace of night
Gilding the heavn's with beams of orient light—
O beauteous hour to minds of feeling giv'n
Filling the heart with thoughts and hopes of heav'n.
Lofty and noble purposes arise
And give the soul communion with the skies;
To Nature's God our highest hopes ascend

271

The bounding heart paints joys which cannot end—
Oh, if to mortals it could e'er be given,
To chuse the path the spirit takes to Heav'n
Guided by him, from whom my doating heart
Not opening heav'n itself could tempt to part,
Mind would ascend, on such a morn as this
On wings of glorious light to realms of bliss
And he whose love illumes this world of care
Should dwell with me in all the transports there.

To the Summer Wind[2]

WHENCE comst thou, sweet wind?
Didst take thy phantom form
'Mid the depth of forest trees?
 Or spring, new born,
 Of the fragrant morn,
'Mong the far-off Indian seas?

Where speedest thou, sweet wind?
Thou little heedest, I trow—
Dost thou sigh for some glancing star?
 Or cool brow
 Of the dying now,
As they pass to their home afar?

What mission is thine, O wind?
Say for what thou yearnest—
That, like the wayward mind,
 Earth thou spurnest,
 Heaven-ward turnest,
And rest canst nowhere find!

III

Nature[3]

MANIFOLD cords, invisible or seen
Present or past, or only hoped for, bind
All to our mother earth.—No step-dame she,
Coz'ning with forced fondness, but a fount,
Rightly pursued, of never-failing love.—
True, that too oft' we lose ourselves 'mong thorns
That tear and wound. But why impatient haste
From the smooth path our fairest mother drew?
'Tis man, not nature, works the general ill,
By folly piled on folly, till the heap
Hides every natural feeling, save alone
Grey Discontent, upraised to ominous height,
And keeping drowsy watch o'er buried wishes.

Appendix II

AN EARLY ESSAY
BY HARRIET TAYLOR[4]

ORE than two hundred years ago, Cecil said 'Tenderness & sympathy are not enough cultivated by any of us; no one is kind enough, gentle enough, forbearing and forgiving enough'. In this two centuries in how many ways have we advanced and improved, yet could the speaker of those words now 'revisit the glimpses of the moon', he would find us but at the point he left us on the ground of toleration: his lovely lament is to the full as applicable now, as it was in the days of the hard-visaged and cold-blooded Puritans. Our faults of uncharitableness have rather changed their objects than their degree. The root of all intolerance, the spirit of conformity, remains; and not until that is destroyed, will envy hatred and all uncharitableness, with their attendant hypocrisies, be destroyed too. Whether it would be religious conformity, Political conformity, moral conformity or Social conformity, no matter which the species, the spirit is the same: all kinds agree in this one point, of hostility to individual character, and individual character if it exists at all, can rarely declare itself openly while there is, on all topics of importance a standard of conformity raised by the indolent minded many and guarded by a [?] of opinion which, though composed individually of the weakest twigs, yet makes up collectively a mass which is not to be resisted with impunity.

What is called the opinion of Society is a phantom power, yet as is often the case with phantoms, of more force over the minds of the unthinking than all the flesh and blood arguments which can be brought to bear against it. It is a combination of the many weak, against the few strong; an association of the mentally listless to punish any manifestation of mental independance. The remedy is, to make all strong enough to stand alone; and whoever has once known the pleasure of self-dependance, will be in no danger of relapsing into subserviency. Let people once suspect that their leader *is* a phantom, the next step will be, to cease to be led, altogether and each mind guide itself by the light of as much knowledge as it can acquire for itself by means of unbiased experience.

We have always been an aristocracy-ridden people, which may account for the fact of our being so peculiarly a propriety-ridden people. The aim of our life seems to be, not our own happiness, nor the happiness of others unless it happens to come in as an accident of our great endeavour to attain some standard of right or duty erected by some or other of the sets into which society is divided like a net—to catch gudgeons.

Who are the people who talk most about doing their duty? always those who for their life could give no intelligible theory of duty? What are called people of principle, are often the most unprincipled people in the world, if by principle is intended the only useful meaning of the word, accordance of the individual's conduct with the individual's self-formed opinion. Grant this to be the definition of principle, then eccentricity should be prima facie evidence for the existence of principle. So far from this being the case, 'it is odd' therefore it is wrong is the feeling of society; while they whom it distinguishes par excellence as people of principle, are almost invariably the slaves of some dicta or other. They have been taught to think, and accustomed to think, so and so right—others think so and so right—therefore it must be right. This is the logic of the world's good sort of people; and if, as is often the case their right should prove indisputably wrong, they can but plead those good intentions which make a most slippery and uneven pavement.

To all such we would say, think for yourself, and act for yourself, but whether you have strength to do either the one or the other, attempt not to impede, much less to resent the genuine expression of the others.

Were the spirit of toleration abroad, the name of toleration would be unknown. The name implies the existence of its opposites. Toleration can not even rank with those strangely named qualities a 'negative virtue'; while we can be conscious that we tolerate there must remain some vestige of *intolerance*—not being virtuous it is possible also not to be vicious: not so in this—not to be charitable is to be uncharitable. To tolerate is to abstain from unjust interference, a quality which will surely one day not need a place in any catalogue of virtues. Now, alas, its spirit is not even comprehended by many, 'The quality of mercy is strained', and by the education for its opposite which most of us receive becomes if ever it be attained, a praiseworthy faculty, instead of an unconscious and almost intuitive state.

'Evil-speaking, lying and slandering' as the catechism formulary has it, is accounted a bad thing by every one. Yet how many do not hesitate about the evil-speaking as long as they avoid the lying and slandering —making what they call Truth a mantle to cover a multitude of injuries. 'Truth must not be spoken at all times' is the vulgar maxim. We would have the Truth, and if possible all the Truth, certainly nothing but the Truth said and acted universally. But we would never lose sight of the important fact that what is truth to one mind is often not truth to another. That no human being ever did or ever will comprehend the whole mind of any other human being. It would perhaps not be possible to find two minds accustomed to think for themselves whose thoughts on any identical subject should take in their expression the same form of words. Who shall say that the very same order of ideas is conveyed to another mind, by those words which to him perfectly represent his thought? It is probable that innumerable shades of variety, modify in each instance, the conception of every expression of thought; for which variety the imperfections of language offer no measure, and the differences of organization no proof. To an honest mind what a lesson of tolerance is included in this knowledge. To such not a living heart and brain but is like the planet 'whose worth's unknown although his height *be* taken, and feeling that one touch of nature makes the whole world kin' finds something that is admirable in all, and something to interest and respect in each. In this view we comprehend that

> *All thoughts, all creeds, all dreams are true,*
> *All visions wild and strange—*

to those who believe them, for after all we must come to that fine saying of the poet-philosopher,

> *Man is the measure of all Truth*
> *Unto himself*

of the same signification is that thought, as moral as profound, which has been often in different ways expressed, yet which the universal practice of the world disproves its comprehension of, 'Toute la moralité de nos actions est dans le jugement que nous en portons nous-meme'—'dangerous' may exclaim the blind followers of that sort of conscience, which is the very opposite of consciousness; would but people give up that sort of conscience which depends on conforming they would find the judgement of an enlightened consciousness proved by its results the voice of God:

> *Our acts our angels are, or good or ill,*
> *Our fatal shadows that walk by us still*

and to make them pleasant companions we must get rid, not only of error, but of the moral sources from which it springs. As the study of the mind of others is the only way in which effectually to improve our own, the endeavour to approximate as nearly as possible towards a complete knowledge of, and sympathy with another mind, is the spring and the food of all fineness of heart and mind. There seems to be this great distinction between physical and moral science: that while the degree of perfection which the first has attained is marked by the progressive completeness and exactness of its rules, that of the latter is in the state most favourable to, and most showing healthfulness as it advances beyond all classification except on the widest and most universal principles. The science of morals should rather be called an art: to do something towards its improvement is in the power of every one, for every one may at least show truly their own page in the volume of human history, and be willing to allow that no two pages of it are alike.

Were everyone to seek only the beauty and the good which might be found in every object, and to pass by defect lightly where it could not but be evident—if evil would not cease to exist, it would surely be greatly mitigated, for half the power of outward ill may be destroyed by inward strength, and half the beauty of outward objects is shown by the light within. The admiring state of mind is like a refracting surface which while it receives the rays of light, and is illuminated by them gives back an added splendour; the critical state is the impassive medium which cannot help [   ]⁵ the sun's beams, but can neither transmit nor increase them. It is indeed much easier to discern the errors and blemishes of things than their good, for the same reason that we observe more quickly privation than enjoyment. Suffering is the exception to the extensive rule of good, and so stands out distinctly and vividly. It should be remembered by the critically-minded, that the habit of noting deficiencies before we observe beauties, does really for themselves lessen the amount of the latter.

Whoever notes a fault in the right spirit will surely find some beauty too. He who appreciates the one is the fittest judge of the other also. The capability of even serious error, proves the capacity for proportionate good. For if anything may be called a principle of nature this seems to be one, that force of any kind has an intuitive tendency towards good.

We believe that a child of good physical organization who were never to hear of evil, would not know from its own nature that evil existed in the mental or moral world. We would place before the minds of children no examples but of good and beautiful, and our strongest effort should be, to prevent individual emulation. The spirit of Emulation in childhood and of competition in manhood are the fruitful sources of selfishness and misery. They are a part of the conformity plan, making each persons idea of goodness and happiness a thing of comparison with some received mode of being good and happy. But this is not the Creed of Society, for Society abhors individual character. It asks the sacrifice of body heart and mind. This is the summary of its cardinal virtues: would that such virtues were as nearly extinct as the dignitaries who are their namesakes.

At this present time the subject of social morals is in a state of most lamentable neglect. It is a subject so deeply interesting to all, yet so beset by prejudice, that the mere approach to it is difficult, if not dangerous. Yet there are 'thunders heard afar' by quick senses, and we firmly believe that many years will not pass before the clearest intellects of the time will expound, and the multitude have wisdom to receive reverently the exposition of the great moral paradoxes with which Society is hemmed in on all sides. Meanwhile they do something who in ever so small a circle or in ever so humble a guise, have courage to declare the evil they see.

APPENDIX III. FAMILY TREES

1. MILL

James Mill
6.4.1773–23.6.1836   m. 5.6.1836   Harriet Burrow
d. 15.6.1854

John Stuart	Wilhelmina Forbes	Clara Esther	Harriet Isabella	James Bentham	Jane Stuart	Henry (Derry)	Mary Elizabeth	George Grote
20.5.1806 –7.5.1873*	1808–1861	1810–1886	1812–1897	1814–1862	1816?–1883	1820– 4.4.1840	1822– 15.1.1913	c. 1825– 15.7.1853
m. 21.4.1851 at Melcombe Regis Weymouth	m.	m. 28.4.1860 at Brighton			m. 28.9.1847 at Kensington		m. 23.8.1847 at Abergavenny	
Harriet Taylor, née Hardy (q.v. under Hardy below)	Dr. King	John Stephen Digweed			Marcus Paul Feraboschi		Charles Frederick Colman	

280

* The date of John Stuart Mill's death is almost invariably given as 8 May 1873. Professor Emile Thouverez in his brochure *Stuart Mill* (Paris, Bloud & Cie, 4th edition, 1908, p. 23) reproduces the official entry in the Registres de l'Etat civil d'Avignon from which it appears that Mill died at 7 o'clock in the morning of 7 May 1873.

2. HARDY

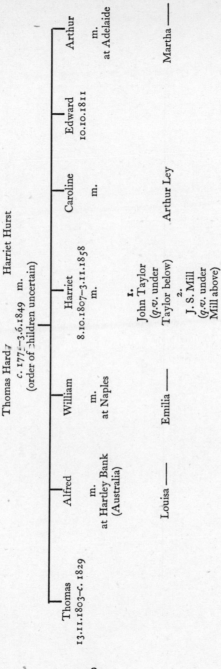

Thomas Hardy
c. 1771–3.6.1849 m. Harriet Hurst
(order of children uncertain)

Thomas
13.11.1803–c. 1829

Alfred
m.
at Hartley Bank
(Australia)

William
m.
at Naples

Harriet
8.10.1807–3.11.1858
m.

1.
John Taylor
(*q.v.* under
Taylor below)

2.
J. S. Mill
(*q.v.* under
Mill above)

Caroline
m.

Edward
10.10.1811

Arthur
m.
at Adelaide

Louisa ——

Emilia ——

Arthur Ley

Martha ——

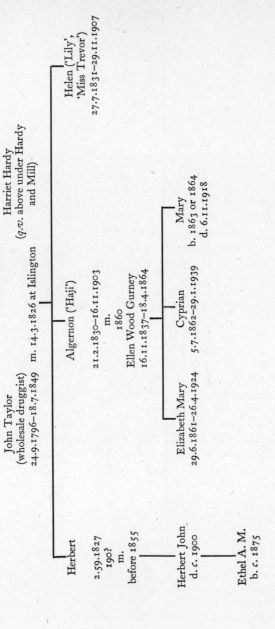

3. TAYLOR

John Taylor
(wholesale druggist)
24.9.1796–18.7.1849   m. 14.3.1826 at Islington   **Harriet Hardy**
(*q.v.* above under Hardy
and Mill)

Herbert

2.5 9.1827
190?
m.
before 1855

Herbert John
d. *c.* 1900

Ethel A. M.
b. *c.* 1875

Algernon ('Haji')

21.2.1830–16.11.1903
m.
1860
Ellen Wood Gurney
16.11.1837–18.4.1864

Elizabeth Mary
29.6.1861–26.4.1924

Cyprian
5.7.1862–29.1.1939

Mary
b. 1863 or 1864
d. 6.11.1918

**Helen ('Lily',
'Miss Trevor')**
27.7.1831–29.11.1907

Notes

INTRODUCTION

[1] *Autobiography*, pp. 149 and 174.

[2] *Autobiography*, pp. 158–9.

[3] *D.D.*, vol. II, p. 411.

[4] On receipt of the news of Mrs. Mill's death Fox wrote to Mrs. P. A. Taylor (16 November 1858): 'Mrs. Mill gone! so lovely once! so superb ever!' and on the next day he wrote to his daughter: 'Mrs. Mill died on the 3rd at Avignon. She would not have objected to being buried there, in the ground which Petrarch has given a wide-world fame; and of which it might (if she remains) be said, "A greater than Laura is here"' (Richard Garnett, *The Life of W. J. Fox* (1910), p. 99).

[5] E. C. Stanton, S. B. Anthony and J. A. Gage, *History of Woman Suffrage* (New York, 1889), vol. I, p. 219–20

[6] Knut Hagberg, *Personalities and Powers* (London, 1930), p. 196.

[7] See the Diary kept by Mary Taylor from 20 February 1904 to 4 July 1906 in MTColl. LVIII/B and Jules Veran, 'Le Souvenir de Stuart Mill à Avignon', *Revue des Deux Mondes*, September 1937.

[8] See the letter of H. S. R. Elliot to Lord Courtney, dated 8 May 1910, in MTColl. III/69.

[9] See the letter by Messrs. A. P. Watt & Son to Mary Taylor, dated 30 January 1918, in MTColl. XXIX/315, in which it is estimated that the proposed volume would run to 272 printed pages. This probably included the extensive correspondence between Mrs. Mill and Helen Taylor now among the MTColl. but not reproduced in the present volume. That typed copies of most of these letters must have existed appears from word 'typed' on many of the envelopes in which they had been kept.

CHAPTER I. HARRIET TAYLOR AND HER CIRCLE

[1] In the *Autobiography* (p. 156) Mill himself gives 1830 as the year when they became acquainted and adds that he was then in his twenty-fifth and she in her twenty-third year, which, taken literally, would fix the date between May and October of that year. That it was 1830 (and not 1831 as Bain says)

is confirmed by a letter of Mrs. Mill of 14 February 1854, quoted on p. 196.

[2] *Letters* (ed. Elliot), vol. I, p. xi. For further information and the Hardy, Taylor and Mill families see the genealogical tables in Appendix III.

[3] *Autobiography*, p. 156.

[4] Thomas Carlyle, *Reminiscences* (ed. Norton), vol. I, p. 110.

[5] MTColl. XXIX/328.

[6] MTColl. XXVIII/143, 144.

[7] Quoted by Richard Garnett, *The Life of W. J. Fox* (London, 1910), p. 98, from the manuscript recollections of Mrs. E. F. Bridell Fox, the original of which does not seem to have been preserved. The reference to her children idolizing Mrs. Taylor also suggests a later date than 1831 when the youngest would only just have been born and the two boys have been very small.

[8] MTColl., Box III/79, reprinted below in chapter III. Compare also a similar passage, *ibid.*, 77. There is also, *ibid.*, Box III/113, a draft of part of a review of *The Life of William Caxton* by W. Stevenson which appeared in 1833 as no. 31 of 'The Library of Useful Knowledge'. This draft is partly in her and partly in John Taylor's hand.

[9] *Autobiography*, p. 157. That this passage refers to Eliza Flower is confirmed by a pencil note of Helen Taylor on the original manuscript of the *Autobiography*, reproduced in the Columbia University Press edition of 1926, p. 130.

[10] MTColl. XXXII/10–39.

[11] Richard Garnett, *The Life of W. J. Fox* (1910), p. 66. It seems that unfortunately all the papers of W. J. Fox, collected for his biography by his daughter Mrs. Bridell Fox and including a biographical sketch by her, have been destroyed during the last war excepting only the collection of letters by Mill to Fox which were acquired by Lord Keynes and are now in the Library of King's College, Cambridge, and an autobiographical sketch by Fox himself which is now in Conway Hall, London.

[12] Mill reviewed the *Producing Man's Companion* both in the *Monthly Repository* (vol. VII, April 1833) and in *Tait's Edinburgh Magazine* (June 1833).

[13] First published in the *Monthly Repository* (July 1837).

[14] See Francis E. Mineka, *The Dissidence of Dissent, the Monthly Repository, 1806–38* (Chapel Hill, University of North Carolina Press, 1944).

[15] Moncure D. Conway, *Centenary History of the South Place Society* (London, Williams & Norgate, 1894), p. 89.

[16] J. A. Froude, *Thomas Carlyle, The First Forty Years* (1882 edition), vol. II, p. 190.

[17] C. G. Duffy, *Conversations with Carlyle* (London, 1892), p. 167. A

somewhat earlier description of Mill given in the *Autobiography of Henry Taylor, 1800–75* (London, 1885), vol. I, p. 79, referring to the years 1824–7: 'He was pure-hearted—I was going to say conscientious—but at that time he seemed so naturally and necessarily good, and so inflexible, that one hardly thought of him as having occasion for a conscience, or as a man with whom any question could arise for reference to that tribunal. But his absorption in abstract operations of the intellect, his latent ardours, and his absolute simplicity of heart, were hardly, perhaps, compatible with knowledge of men and women, and with wisdom in living his life. His manners were plain, neither graceful nor awkward; his features refined and regular; the eyes small relatively to the scale of the face, the jaw large, the nose straight and finely shaped, the lips thin and compressed, and the forehead and head capacious; and both face and body seemed to represent outwardly the inflexibility of the inner man. He shook hands with you from the shoulder. Though for the most part painfully grave, he was as sensible as anybody for Charles Austin's or Charles Villier's sallies of wit, and his strong and well-built body would heave for a few moments with half uttered laughter. He took his share in conversation, and talked ably and well of course but with such a scrupulous solicitude to think exactly what he should and say exactly what he thought, that he spoke with an appearance of effort and as if with an impediment of the mind.'

[18] Caroline Fox, *Memories of Old Friends* (now enlarged edition in one volume, 1883), p. 110. John Sterling in an unpublished letter to Mill of 1840 now in the Library of King's College, Cambridge, refers to this portrait as a 'medaillon'.

[19] C. M. Cox, *The Early Mental Traits of Three Hundred Geniuses* (*Genetic Studies of Genius*, ed. L. M. Terman, vol. II, Stanford University Press, 1926).

[20] *Autobiography*, p. 26.

[21] *Life and Letters of John Arthur Roebuck: with Chapters of Autobiography* (ed. R. E. Leader, London, 1897), p. 28. Cf. Mill's own statement to Caroline Fox: 'I never was a boy, never played at cricket' (*Memories of Old Friends*, p. 107).

[22] A. W. Levi, 'The "Mental Crisis" of John Stuart Mill', *The Psychoanalytical Review*, vol. XXXII (New York, 1945). Cf. p. 98: 'The real cause (of the mental crisis) was those repressed death wishes against his father, the vague and unarticulated guilt which he had in consequence, and the latent, though still present dread that never now should he be free of his father's domination.'

[23] *Ibid.*, pp. 92–3. Judging from this passage, which is almost the only one that is available, this early draft of the *Autobiography* is likely to be of very considerable importance in connexion with the subject of this book. Repeated

applications to the Executors of the late Professor Hollander for permission to examine the manuscript have, however, been unsuccesful.

[24] H. Solly, *These Eighty Years* (1893), vol. I, p. 147.

[25] H. Solly in *The Workman's Magazine* (1873), p. 385.

[26] Manuscript notes by A. S. West of a conversation with the Rev. J. Crompton in the Library of King's College, Cambridge.

[27] Mill, in a letter to be quoted later, indeed refers to George as being twenty years his junior, but that may not have to be taken quite literally. The exact dates of the births of most of the children of James Mill are unknown, as they never seem to have been baptized and in consequence, in the then state of affairs, their births never to have been registered.

[28] A comment of one of his sisters on this has been preserved in a letter now in the Library of King's College, Cambridge.

'*Harriet I. Mill to the Rev. J. Crompton, 26 October 1873:* My poor mother's married life must have been a frightfully hard one, from first to last: I hope and think that the eighteen following years, always excepting the desertion of her eldest son, were years of satisfaction and enjoyment. Here was an instance of two persons, a husband and wife, living as far apart under the same roof, as the north pole from the south; from no "fault" of my poor mother certainly; but how was a woman with a growing family and very small means (as in the early years of the marriage) to be anything but a German Hausfrau? how could she "intellectually" become a companion for such a mind as my father? *His* great want was "temper", though I quite believe circumstances had made it what it was in our childhood, both because of the warm affection of his early friends, and because in the latter years of his life he became much softened and treated the younger children differently. What would be *thought* now if the fate of *our* childhood were known? You will perhaps be surprised to hear that that mention of teaching a younger sister Latin is the sole allusion to any member of the family, except my father: that sister must have been the eldest, Willie (Mrs. King). *I* have no recollection of John's ever teaching me Latin—the only thing my father professed to teach us, expecting us, however, to know everything else and abusing us for our ignorance if we did not! I have no distinct recollection of John prior to his return from France in 1821, when we were at Marlow for the summer and he at once wrote out and pinned on the walls the way in which the hours of the day were to be passed by the four of us,—my two elder sisters, myself and James. Any regular teaching we had was from him, and he carried some of us very far in mathematics and algebra. Indeed I have been told that he said I could have taken the Senior Wrangler's degree at Cambridge.'

[29] *Autobiography*, p. 205.

[30] *Letters* (ed. Elliot), vol. I, p. 2.

[31] Compare the entry in J. L. Mallet's diary under the date of 2 March

1832 in *Political Economy Club, Centenary Volume* (London, 1921), p. 231, and Henry Crabb Robinson's Diary (Typescript in Dr. Williams' Library, vol. XIV) under the date of 27 March 1832.

CHAPTER II. ACQUAINTANCE AND EARLY CRISES

[1] This account was given orally by Carlyle to Charles Eliot Norton in 1873 after the receipt of the news of Mill's death and is recorded verbatim in *Letters of Charles Eliot Norton* (London, Constable & Co., 1913), vol. I, p. 496–7: 'A vera noble soul was John Mill, quite sure, beautiful to think of. I never could find out what more than ordinary there was in the woman he cared so much for; but there was absolute sincerity in his devotion to her. She was the daughter of a flourishing London Unitarian tradesman, and her husband was the son of another, and the two families made the match. Taylor was a verra respectable man, but his wife found him dull; she had dark, black, hard eyes, and an inquisitive nature, and was ponderin' on many questions that worried her, and could get no answers to them, and that Unitarian clergyman you've heard of, William Fox by name, told her at last that there was a young philosopher of very remarkable quality, whom he thought just the man to deal with her case. And so Mill with great difficulty was brought to see her, and that man, who up to that time, had never looked a female creature, not even a cow, in the face, found himself opposite those great dark eyes, that were flashing unutterable things, while he was discoursing the utterable concernin' all sorts o' high topics.' A similar conversation with Carlyle is recorded by C. G. Duffy, *Conversations with Carlyle* (1892), p. 167.

[2] A. Bain, *J. S. Mill*, p. 164, and R. E. Leader, *Life and Letters of J. A. Roebuck* (London, 1897), p. 38. John Arthur Roebuck (1801–79), barrister and leading radical politician, had become a close friend of Mill on his arrival from Canada in 1824. George John Graham (1801–88) probably had become acquainted with Mill about the same time but in 1830 had only just returned from five years' service as Military Secretary of Bombay. He became Registrar-General of Births and Deaths in 1838.

[3] A. Bain, *J. S. Mill*, p. 164, and Gordon S. Haight, *George Eliot and John Chapman* (New Haven, Yale University Press, 1940), p. 213.

[4] *Autobiography*, p. 156.

[5] MTColl. XXVII/32. The date is taken from the postmark on what appears to be the continuation of this letter, *ibid.*, XXVII/37.

[6] That by that time Mill was already well known to Eliza Flower may be concluded from his first but not last friendly puff he gave some of her hymns in the *Examiner* of next month. 'Musical Illustrations of the Waverley Novels ...' by Eliza Flower, in the *Examiner*, 3 July 1831, pp. 420–1. Similar notes

by Mill on songs by Miss Flower appeared in the *Examiner* for 8 April 1832 and 17 February 1833. See MacMinn, *Bibliography*, pp. 17, 20 and 25.

[7] F. E. Mineka, *The Dissidence of Dissent* (Chapel Hill, 1944), p. 405.

[8] MTColl. L/3.

[9] MTColl. XXIX/257.

[10] The following invitation which has also been preserved (MTColl. II/300) somewhat confirms the impression that these documents belong to January 1831, when Monsieur Bontemps is known to have been in London: 'Mr. and Mrs. Taylor request the pleasure of Mr. Mill's company at dinner on Tuesday next at 5 o'clock when they expect to see Mr. Fox and some friends of M. Desainteville/Finsbury Square/Jan. 28th.'

[11] See Mill's Diary of this walking tour in Mount Holyoke College, South Hadley, Mass.

[12] MTColl. IX/16.

[13] Yale University Library, postmarked 1 September 1832.

[14] Jules Bastide, French publicist (1800–79), had been condemned to death because of the part he had taken in the street disturbances which had taken place in Paris on 5 June 1832, on the occasion of the funeral of General Lamarque. He returned to Paris in 1834. Hippolyte Dussard, French economist (1798–1876). Mill had almost certainly made the acquaintance of the two men on his visit to Paris two years earlier.

[15] Major Revell was apparently one of the officers of the 'National Political Union' founded in October 1831 to assist in the agitation for the Reform Bill.

[16] Page torn.

[17] MTColl. XXVII/4. This note can be approximately dated from the fact that Mill left for Cornwall (where he spent the second part of his vacation) on Thursday, 20 September, and that according to the *Gentlemen's Magazine* for September 1832, (p. 283) 'Francis Edward Crawley esq. of Dorset Place' died on 5 September, aged twenty-nine. This was probably the same Crawley who in July 1828 with Horace Grant and Edwin Chadwick had accompanied Mill on his walking tour in Berkshire, Buckinghamshire and Surrey (see the Diary of this walking tour in Yale University Library; and the Diary of tour to Cornwall in MTColl.).

[18] The identification of the articles in the *Monthly Repository* are taken from the manuscript key in the set of this journal which originally belonged to a member of the Fox family and is now preserved in the Library of Conway Hall, London. It seems that both the identification in Richard Garnett's *Life of W. J. Fox* and in the copy of the *Monthly Repository* in the British Museum, which has served F. E. Mineka's study *The Dissidence of Dissent* (Chapel Hill, the University of North Carolina Press, 1944), also derive from this source. Apart from a brief review of a book on Australia (Robert Dawson, *The Present State of Australia*, whose author was probably a relative of

Mrs. Taylor's), which appeared already in the issue for January 1831 (vol. V, pp. 58–9), and the contributions mentioned in the text and fully listed by Mineka, that key also ascribes to Mrs. John Taylor, but with a '?', two articles signed 'Theta' in vol. VIII (1834), namely one on 'Female Education and Occupation' (pp. 489–98) and one 'On Tithes' (pp. 525–9). These attributions seem very doubtful, however, and the note on tithes at least is almost certainly by Mill, even though in a letter to Fox of February 1834 (King's College, Cambridge) he wrote, with reference to an earlier note on the same subject, 'You will have received today from her, the note on Tithe'.

[19] *Monthly Repository* (second series), vol. VI, 1832, p. 354.

[20] *Ibid.*, p. 402.

[21] 'Some Memorial of John Hampden, his Party and his Times. By Lord Nugent', *ibid.*, pp. 443–9; 'Mirabeau's Letters during his Residence in England', *ibid.*, pp. 605–8, and 'The Mysticism of Plato or Sincerity rested upon Reality', *ibid.*, pp. 645–6.

[22] Erroneously ascribed by Mrs. Taylor to Sarah Austin.

[23] *Ibid.*, p. 762.

[24] *Ibid.*, p. 827.

[25] See the letter of J. S. M. to W. J. Fox, of 3 April 1832, in the Library of King's College, Cambridge, and reprinted in R. Garnett's *Life of W. J. Fox*, p. 100.

[26] *Monthly Repository* (second series), vol. VI, 1832, pp. 649–59, reprinted in *Four Dialogues of Plato*. Translation and Notes by John Stuart Mill, edited by Ruth Borchardt (London, Watts & Co, 1946), pp. 28–40.

[27] *Monthly Repository* (second series), vol. VII, 1833, pp. 262–70, reprinted in *D.D.*, vol. I, p. 63, and in *Early Essays by John Stuart Mill*, edited by J. W. M. Gibbs (London, George Bell & Sons, 1897), pp. 201–20.

[28] Thomas Carlyle, after meeting Mill for the second time on 12 September 1831, had described him as 'a fine clear enthusiast, who will one day come to something, yet nothing poetical, I think: his fancy is not rich' (J. A. Froude, *Thomas Carlyle, The First Forty Years*, vol. II, p. 200). J. A. Roebuck similarly wrote of Mill that 'in reality he never had poetical emotions and the lessons of his early childhood had chilled his heart and deadened his spirit to all the magnificent influences of poetry' (R. E. Leader, *Life and Letters of J. A. Roebuck*, p. 38).

[29] *Autobiography*, p. 126.

[30] The following unpublished passage from the early draft of the *Autobiography* in the library of the late Professor Jacob Hollander is produced from notes taken some years ago by Mr. A. W. Levi when the manuscript was still accessible. I am especially indebted to Mr. Levi for putting these notes at my disposal.

[31] T. Gomperz, *John Stuart Mill: Ein Nachruf* (Vienna, 1889), p. 44.

[32] W. Minto in *John Stuart Mill; Notices of his Life and Work* (London, 1873), p. 33.

[33] See the letter by J. S. M. to W. J. Fox of 19 May 1833 in the Library of King's College, Cambridge.

[34] See the letter of J. S. M. to W. J. Fox of June 1833 in the same collection.

[35] The copy of *Pauline* containing Mill's notes came later into the possession of John Forster and with his library reached the Victoria and Albert Museum, London, where it is now preserved in the Forster and Dyce Collection (pressmark 48.D.46).

[36] J. S. M. to W. J. Fox, 10 October 1833, in the Library of King's College, Cambridge.

[37] W. H. Griffin and H. C. M. Minchin, *The Life of Robert Browning* (1938), p. 59.

[38] 'Two Kinds of Poetry' in *Monthly Repository* for November 1833, reprinted *D.D.*, vol. I, p. 77, and in *Early Essays by John Stuart Mill*, ed. J. W. M. Gibbs (1897), pp. 221–6.

[39] 'Tennyson's Poems' in the *London Review* (July 1835), reprinted in *Early Essays*, pp. 239–67.

[40] King's College, Cambridge.

[41] King's College, Cambridge, undated, probably June 1833.

[42] MTColl. II/324, watermarked '1831'. Where dated letters by Mrs. Taylor are on paper with a dated watermark, the years usually agree or are at least not more than a year apart, and though this letter is not likely to be of 1831 it may well be of 1832.

[43] MTColl. II/316. The second sheet is torn off, and the conclusion given after the dots follows on the margin after a few words concluding a sentence from the missing part.

[44] *Letters* (ed. Elliot), I, p. 61.

[45] *Ibid.*, pp. 62–3

[46] MTColl. L/4.

[47] There is in MTColl. II/321 also an undated fragment of a note by Mrs. Taylor expressing a similar idea and probably of about the same time: 'I on the contrary never did either "write or speak or look as I felt at the instant" to you. I have always suffered an instinctive dread that mine might be a foreign language to you. But the future must amend this, as well as many other things.'

[48] King's College, Cambridge.

[49] Page torn.

[50] Yale University Library. The English postmark is dated 7 November 1833.

[51] Page torn.

[52] Yale University Library.

[53] Yale University Library. The beginning of the letter, dealing with other matters, is not reproduced.

[54] Mrs. Taylor's brother.

[55] Dated 26 November 1833 and partly published in Richard Garnett, *The Life of W. J. Fox*, p. 151.

[56] J. S. M. to Thomas Carlyle, 25 November 1833. *Letters* (ed. Elliot), vol. I, pp. 71–80.

[57] H. Gomperz, *Theodor Gomperz, Briefe und Aufzeichnungen*, vol. I (Vienna, 1936), p. 233.

[58] For some time during the 1830's she appears to have taken a house in Kingston-on-Thames, before about 1839 she moved to Walton-on-Thames, where she lived during most of the next ten years.

CHAPTER III. ON MARRIAGE AND DIVORCE

[1] *Autobiography*, pp. 206–7, footnote.

[2] MTColl. XLI/1.

[3] *Chastity*, sexual intercourse *with* affection. *Prostitution*, sexual intercourse *without* affection. (J. S. M.'s footnote).

[4] MTColl., Box III/79, on paper watermarked '1832'. An earlier draft on part of the same on paper watermarked '1831', *ibid.*, Box III/17.

CHAPTER IV. FRIENDS AND GOSSIP

[1] R. E. Leader, *Life and Letters of J. A. Roebuck* (London, 1897), p. 38. The party at the Bullers may well have been the soirée given on 15 June 1835, mentioned in *Letters and Memorials of J. W. Carlyle* (ed. J. A. Froude, 1893), vol. I, p. 21. It cannot have been before 1835, since it was only at the beginning of that year that the Bullers came to live in London. There exists a letter by Roebuck to Helen Taylor dated 23 August 1873 (MTColl. VIII/28) which confirms Roebuck's printed account of his alienation from Mill as not due, as Mill suggests in the *Autobiography* (p. 127), to mere differences of their views on the respective merits of Byron and Wordsworth.

[2] J. A. Froude, *Thomas Carlyle, The First Forty Years*, vol. II, p. 430.

[3] J. A. Froude, *ibid.*, vol. II, p. 441.

[4] Manuscript letter in the National Library of Scotland, incompletely published in *Letters of Thomas Carlyle* (ed. C. E. Norton, 1888), vol. II, p. 200.

[5] J. A. Froude, *Thomas Carlyle, The First Forty Years*, vol. II, p. 448, and *Letters of Thomas Carlyle 1826–1836* (ed. Norton), vol. II, p. 207. See also

Carlyle's entry in his *Journal* on 12 August 1834 (the day of the dinner) quoted in *Reminiscences* (ed. Norton), vol. I, p. 114, note.

[6] There had been preliminary discussions about the creation of a new Radical Review, which in the following year led to the establishment of the *London* (later *London and Westminster*) *Review*.

[7] J. A. Froude, *Thomas Carlyle, The First Forty Years*, vol. II, p. 466.

[8] Manuscript letter in National Library of Scotland, incompletely published in *Letters of Thomas Carlyle 1826–1836* (ed. Norton), vol. II, p. 240.

[9] 'Glar', mud or any moist sticky substance.

[10] *New Letters and Memorials of Jane Welsh Carlyle* (ed. A. Carlyle, 1903), vol. I, p. 49, also J. A. Froude, *Carlyle's Life In London* (new edition), vol. I, p. 24.

[11] *Letters of Thomas Carlyle 1826–1836*, vol. II, p. 283–4. On 16 February, the day before the party, Mrs. Carlyle had written to Dr. John Carlyle: 'We are going tomorrow to Mrs. [Taylor's] whom I should like that you knew, and could tell me whether to fall desperately in love with or no' (J. A. Froude, *Carlyle's Life in London* (new edition), vol. I, p. 26).

[12] 'Hotches'=fidgets.

[13] C. G. Duffy, *Conversations with Carlyle* (1892), p. 169. The contemporary account of the episode given by Carlyle in his *Journal* (*Reminiscences*, ed. Norton, vol. I, p. 106) makes no mention of this.

[14] See particularly Carlyle's account in *Letters of Charles Eliot Norton* (ed. S. Norton and M. A. de Wolfe Howe, London, 1913), vol. I, p. 496, and Alfred H. Guernsay, *Thomas Carlyle* (London, 1879), pp. 86–7.

[15] *Letters of T. C. to J. S. M.*, p. 109, letter dated 9 March 1835.

[16] National Library of Scotland, published in *Letters* (ed. Elliot), vol. I, p. 10. See also the letter by Mill's sister Harriet written to Carlyle shortly after Mill's death (*Letters of T. C. to J. S. M.*) in which she states that 'as far as my recollection goes, the misfortune arose from my brother's own inadvertence in having given your papers among waste paper for kitchen use', p. 107.

[17] See Carlyle's letter to Mill of 30 October 1835, promising to call at Kent Terrace, in *Letters of T. C. to J. S. M.*, p. 119.

[18] Thomas Carlyle, *Reminiscences* (ed. Norton), vol. I, p. 104.

[19] *Letters and Memorials of Jane Welsh Carlyle* (ed. Froude), vol. I, p. 57.

[20] J. A. Froude, *Thomas Carlyle, A History of his Life in London* (1884), vol. I, p. 74. James Mill had died on 23 June, Carlyle's visit took place on 16–18 July, and Mill left for France on 30 July.

[21] 'Scrae', Dumfriesshire dialect for 'an old shoe'.

[22] *New Letters and Memorials of Jane Welsh Carlyle* (ed. Alexander Carlyle, London, 1903), vol. I, p. 60.

[23] *Letters of T. C. to J. S. M.*, pp. 197–8.

[24] *Letters of T. C. to J. S. M.*, p. 136. Horace Grant (1800–59), Mill's junior colleague in the Examiner's office at India House, 1826–45.

[25] National Library of Scotland, incompletely published in *New Letters of Thomas Carlyle* (ed. Alexander Carlyle, 1904), vol. I, p. 53, and part of the missing passage by J. A. Froude, *Thomas Carlyle, A History of his Life in London*, vol. I, p. 108, tacked on to a letter of different date.

[26] See *New Letters of Thomas Carlyle* (ed. Alexander Carlyle, 1904), vol. I, pp. 116 and 133 (letters dated 9 March and 18 July 1838), and in *Life in London*, vol. I, pp. 142–3 (letter dated 27 July 1838).

[27] See Thomas Carlyle, *Life of John Sterling* (1851), in *Works*, p. 221.

[28] *Letters of T. C. to J. S. M.*, p. 165.

[29] *Ibid.*, pp. 225–6. Cf. also Sterling's reply, dated 30 September 1839, given by A. K. Tuell, *John Sterling* (New York, 1941), p. 70: 'Yesterday's post brought a pleasant letter from Mill along with yours. But he says no word of that miserable matter you hint at. I think it is a good sign of a man that he feels strongly that kind of temptation, but a far better one that he both feels it and conquers it, which I trust that Mill has done and will do.'

[30] See the letters in MTColl. XXVIII/149–51, to her husband, the first of 27 July 1839, announcing her return, apparently from Brighton, to Wilton Place, the others of October addressed to her husband at that address.

[31] *Letters of T. C. to J. S. M.*, p. 174.

[32] MTColl. XXVII/2.

[33] *Letters to T. C. to J. S. M.*, p. 179, letter of J. S. M. to T. Carlyle of 24 February 1841, and of T. Carlyle to Mrs. Taylor of 7 March 1841.

[34] The visit took place on 18 and 19 July 1841. See Helen Taylor's Diary in MTColl. XLV and *Letters of C. E. Norton* (ed. G. Norton and M. A. de Wolfe Howe, London, 1913), vol. I, p. 498.

[35] This copy of *Past and Present* is now with the remnants of Mill's library in Somerville College, Oxford.—According to Carlyle's account Mill's 'great attachment' to him 'lasted about ten years, and then suddenly ended, I never knew how' (*Letters and Memorials of Jane Welsh Carlyle*, ed. J. A. Froude, vol. I, p. 2).

[36] *Letters of C. E. Norton*, vol. I, p. 499.

[37] In 1848, however, Mill sent to Carlyle a presentation copy of the *Political Economy* (F. Espinasse, *Literary Recollections* (London, 1893), p. 218).

[38] C. G. Duffy, *Conversations with Carlyle* (1892), p. 169.

[39] *Letters of Charles Eliot Norton*, vol. I, pp. 499–500. The name in square brackets is omitted in the printed version and has been kindly supplied by the Librarian of the Houghton Library, Harvard University, where C. E. Norton's papers and his diary are now preserved.

[40] Janet Ross, *Three Generations of English Women* (new revised and enlarged edition, 1893), p. 432.

⁴¹ See below, p. 129.
⁴² Janet Ross, *The Fourth Generation* (London, 1912), p. 73–4.

CHAPTER V. THE YEARS OF FRIENDSHIP

¹ MTColl. L/5. The date is given only on typed envelope of later date, probably by Mary Taylor.
² King's College, Cambridge.
³ King's College, Cambridge.
⁴ Yale University Library.
⁵ MTColl. XXVIII/235, on paper watermarked '1833'.
⁶ MTColl. II/323.
⁷ MTColl. L/7, on two sheets watermarked '1835'.
⁸ MTColl. L/6, watermarked '1835'.
⁹ Continuation missing. Another note of Harriet Taylor's of uncertain date but probably of the same period in MTColl. II/317 may be given at least.

'*H. T. to J. S. M.* Yes dear I will meet you, somewhere between this and Southend—the hour will depend on what your note says to-morrow (that is supposing the chaise is to be had of which there is very little doubt.)

'bless you dearest! I did not write yesterday. I wish I had for you seem to have expected it. I have been quite well & quite happy since that delicious evening & I may perhaps see the to-day, but if not I shall not be disappointed —as for *sad* I feel since that evening as tho' I shall never be that again.

'I am very well in all respects, but more especially in spirits.

'bless thee—to-morrow will be delightful & I am looking to it as a very great treat.

'so dear—if you do not meet me on [?] road from Southend you will know I could not have the chaise.

'Friday.'

¹⁰ King's College, Cambridge.
¹¹ A. Bain, *J. S. Mill*, p. 43.
¹² A. Bain, *J. S. Mill*, p. 163.
¹³ Thomas Falconer (1805–82).
¹⁴ *New Letters of Thomas Carlyle* (ed. A. Carlyle, 1904), vol. I, p. 2.
¹⁵ MTColl. XLVII/3.
¹⁶ Herbert Taylor, who was only a year or two George Mill's junior. This acquaintance led to a lasting friendship between George Mill and the two Taylor boys.
¹⁷ A. Bain, *John Stuart Mill*, p. 44.
¹⁸ *Ibid.*
¹⁹ See the letter of Henry and John Stuart Mill to their mother and sisters, postmarked Paris, 4 November 1836, MTColl. XLVII/4.
²⁰ A. Bain, *ibid.*, p. 44.

[21] Jane Welsh Carlyle to John Sterling, January–February 1842, in *Letters and Memorials of Jane Welsh Carlyle* (ed. J. A. Froude, 1893), vol. I, p. 138.

[22] T. Carlyle, *Reminiscences* (ed. Norton), vol. I, p. 110.

[23] MTColl. XXVIII/135.

[24] Angelo Usiglio, a refugee from Modena and intimate friend of Mazzini.

[25] The first issue of the *London and Westminster Review* brought out by John Robertson (*c.* 1810–75) had been that for July 1837. An article on Italian Literature since 1830, signed 'A. U.', appeared in the issue for October of that year, an article on Paolo Sarpi, signed 'J. M.', in April 1838 and an article on 'Prince Napoleon Bonaparte', signed 'J. M.', in December 1838. In Mill's identification of the articles in the copy given to Caroline Fox and reproduced in the 1883 edition of her *Memories of Old Friends* (pp. 102–4, note) all three articles are ascribed to Mazzini, but here Mill's memory must have been at fault, since there is also a reference to the article by Usiglio in one of the letters written by Mill to John Robertson referred to below. See also Mazzini's letter to his mother of 15 September 1837 in *Epistolario di Guisuppe Mazzini* (Imola, 1912), vol. II, p. 85

[26] *Morning Chronicle*, 22 September 1837, which refers to the expulsion from Greece of a refugee Emile Usiglio, who had arrived in Athens as an emissary of Mazzini to form a branch of 'Young Europe'.

[27] See the letters by Mill to John Robertson written from that tour in G. D. M. Towers, 'John Stuart Mill and the *London and Westminster Review*', *Atlantic Monthly*, vol. LXIX, 1892.

[28] MTColl. XXVIII/238, watermarked '1837'.

[29] MTColl. XXVIII/234, watermarked '1838'.

[30] A. Bain, *John Stuart Mill*, p. 44, quotes a letter of Henry Mill of 17 January 1839, who writes: 'As to John's health, none of us believe that it is anything very serious; our means of judging are his looks when he was here, and also what we have heard from Dr. Arnott. We are told, however, that his sending him away is because his pains in the chest, which are the symptoms, make it seem that a winter in Italy just now will afford him sensible and permanent benefit for the whole of his life.'

[31] E. G. Wakefield to W. Molesworth, 27 November 1838: 'Our noble friend Mill is ordered to Malta. His lungs are not organically diseased but will if he remains here. He thought till the other day that his disease was mortal, but yet he fagged away at the Durham case as if he had expected to live for ever' (A. J. Harrop, *The Amazing Career of Edward Gibbon Wakefield* (London, 1928), p. 109).

In his *Autobiography* (p. 211) Mill calls his illness of 1854–5 the 'first attack of the family disease', and his letters of that period show that he himself then thought it was a first attack. But he certainly must have been aware at the earlier date that he was threatened by it. Caroline Fox (*Memories of Old*

Friends (new and revised edition, 1883), pp. 97–8) records an interesting conversation with Mill when he was in Falmouth in the spring of 1840 attending his brother Henry, who was dying of consumption: 'On consumption, and why it was so connected with what is beautiful and interesting in nature. The disease itself brings the mind as well as the constitution into a state of prematurity, and this reciprocally preys on the body. After an expressive pause, John Mill quietly said "I expect to die of consumption".'

[32] Letter by John Taylor to Messrs. G. H. Gower of Leghorn, 19 December 1838, MTColl. XXIX/271.

[33] Mrs. Taylor's itinerary can be reconstructed in great detail from her passport in MTColl. Box III.

[34] Carlyle was also told by Mrs. Buller that Mill was going to Malta and promptly passed this on to John Sterling (T. Carlyle to John Sterling, 7 December 1838, in *Letters of T. C. to J. S. M.*, p. 217).

[35] MTColl. XLVII/6.

[36] A letter to John Robertson (*c.* 1810–75), editor of the *London and Westminster Review* on the affairs of the Review, printed in G. D. M. Towers, 'John Stuart Mill and the *London and Westminster Review*', *Atlantic Monthly*, vol. LXIX, 1892.

[37] MTColl. XXVIII/146.

[38] MTColl. XXVIII/147.

[39] A. Bain, *J. S. Mill*, p. 45.

[40] A. Bain, *J. S. Mill*, p. 45.

[41] MTColl. Box II.

[42] MTColl. XLVII/7.

[43] A. Bain, *J. S. Mill*, p. 164.

[44] King's College, Cambridge.

[45] MTColl. XXVIII/152. The letter is dated in a later hand 'April 28, 1840', presumably from a cover now lost.

[46] A reference to this accident in Mill's letter to W. E. Hickson of 4 March 1859 in the Huntington Library. It occurred probably early in May 1842, when according to Helen Taylor's diary Mr. and Mrs. Taylor were thrown out of a carriage. Mrs. Taylor was certainly very ill during the following months.

[47] See Mary Taylor in *Letters* (ed. Elliot), vol. I, p. XLIII.

[48] MTColl. XLV.

[49] On 6 June 1844 Mill wrote in an unpublished letter to J. M. Kemble that he was 'going out of town for some weeks', and on 14 August to the same that he had 'just returned'.

[50] *Lettres inedites de John Stuart Mill à Auguste Comte*, (ed. L. Levy-Bruhl, Paris, 1899), p. 296.

[51] Bain, *J. S. Mill*, p. 74. Bain's notes on the correspondence, dated 1844, are in MTColl. XLVII/8.

[52] MTColl. II/327, continued on second sheet in Box III/103.

[53] Probably Mill's letter of 30 October 1843, in which he extensively sums up his position on the Women question, or his letter of 8 December 1843, with which he breaks off that discussion.

[54] MTColl. XXVIII/233. The letter is marked in pencil in another hand '1845?', but this is probably too late, since it suggests that Mrs. Taylor's boys were still children while in 1845 'Herby' would have been eighteen. It may well be about 1840 or even earlier.

[55] Mrs. Taylor's brother.

[56] Probably the membership card of the Zoological Society, admitting to the Zoological Gardens within a few minutes' walk of the Taylors' house.

CHAPTER SIX. A JOINT PRODUCTION

[1] *Autobiography*, pp. 207–10. The whole passage is too long to quote in full, but I think it could be shown that in it Mill attributes to Mrs. Taylor's influence ideas which he demonstrably owes to the Saint-Simonians and Comte.

[2] MacMinn, *et. al., Bibliography*, pp. 59 and 69.

[3] *Autobiography*, p. 199.

[4] Autograph letter in possession of Mrs. Vera Eichelbaum, Wellington, New Zealand, quoted with her kind permission.

[5] MTColl. XXVIII/170.

[6] MTColl. XXVIII/174; Sir John Easthope, Bt., 1784–1865, was successively M.P. for St. Albans, Banbury and Leicester, and since 1834 proprietor of the *Morning Chronicle*.

[7] Probably Charles Farebrother, a member of the Vintner's Company and Alderman from 1826 until his death in 1858.

[8] MTColl. XXVIII/178.

[9] MTColl. XXVIII/179.

[10] *Political Economy and the Philosophy of Government; a series of essays selected from the Works of M. de Sismondi: with a Historical Notice of his Life and Writings* (London, 1847).

[11] MTColl. XXVIII/180.

[12] The dedication was repeated in a limited number of gift copies of the second edition of the *Political Economy* (1849), but omitted in the third, which appeared in 1853 after Harriet Taylor had become Mrs. Mill, because, as she explains in a letter to her brother Arthur Hardy, 'it would have been no longer appropriate' (MTColl. XXVII/50, dated 7 September 1856).

[13] MTColl. XXVII/40.

[14] Continuation missing.

[15] King's College, Cambridge.

[16] MTColl. L/8.

[17] According to the Parliamentary report in the *Daily News* of 24 July 1848, which presumably Mrs. Taylor had read, W. J. Fox had said in the debate in the House of Commons on the 'Suspension of the Habeas Corpus Act (Ireland)' on 22 July 'that the sooner the bill was passed into law the better. He would do all in his power to aid the government in carrying it at once'.

[18] Eire Evans Crowe (1799–1868) from 1846 to 1851 editor of the *Daily News*.

[19] *The Reasoner, A Weekly Journal, Utilitarian, Republican and Communist*, edited by G. J. Holyoake, was at that time running a series of long extracts from Mill's *Political Economy*, which it thought at the price of £1 10s. to be beyond the reach of most of its readers. The passage quoted from *The Reasoner* later in the letter has not been traced and probably occurred in a much earlier issue.

[20] In a report of their Paris correspondent on the debate of the Constituent Assembly on the Constitution in the *Daily News* of 24 July 1848 (third edition, p. 3) it was stated that 'the only event which signalized the day was the effrontery of M. Proudhon, who moved a resolution in the 4th bureau, that the fiction, as he regards it, of the acknowledgement of the existence of God, with which the preamble opens, should be erased. This proposition was of course rejected without one dissentient vote.'

[21] If the correct reading of this name is 'Trench', which is not quite certain, the reference is presumably to Richard Chenevix Trench (1807–86), Archbishop of Dublin. He does not appear to have published a work in two volumes and the comment therefore must refer to two distinct books of his.

[22] The following paragraph is on a separate sheet but seems to form a postscript to the preceding letter, although the passage quoted from Hume has not been traced in the newspapers of these days.

[23] MTColl. II/322.

[24] In a letter from their Paris correspondent in the *Daily News* of 27 July 1848, on the debate of the French Assembly on the proposed Law of the Clubs, it was said that 'much amusement was produced by the ardour with which M. Flocon assailed the clause of the measure which interdicted the presence or participation of females in the debates'.

[25] This may refer to Mill's unheaded article on French Affairs in the *Daily News* of 9 August 1848; no earlier article is traceable and no such further article on the position of women as suggested by Mrs. Taylor seems to have appeared.

[26] This may refer to the article in the *Daily News* on 9 August, referred to before. No other article is listed in MacMinn, *et al.*, *Bibliography*.

[27] Frances d'Arusmont, *née* Wright (1795–1852), a Scotswoman who had helped to start the Women's movement in America. She had been to England

in 1847 when Holyoake got into trouble for publishing, apparently without permission, a lecture of hers in the *Reasoner*.

²⁸ A. Bain, *J. S. Mill*, p. 90.

²⁹ MTColl. XXVIII/199.

³⁰ MTColl. XXVIII/203.

³¹ MTColl. XXVIII/217.

³² MTColl. XXVIII/219–327 and XXVII/109.

³³ In Yale University Library.

³⁴ André-Michel Guerry (1802–66), French statistician, author of an *Essai sur la statistique morale de la France* (Paris, 1833), which contains probably the identical maps to which Mill refers and from which the author concludes that 'les départments ou l'instruction est a moins repandus sont ceux ou il se commet le plus des crimes'. He published later a larger work: *Statistique morale de l'Angleterre comparée avec delle de La France* (Paris, 1864).

³⁵ Lieut.-Col. William Henry Sykes, F.R.S. (1790–1872), naturalist and soldier, one of the founders of the Royal Statistical Society, a Director of the East India Company since 1840 and Chairman of its Court of Directors in 1856.

³⁶ F. P. G. Guizot, *De la democratic en France* (*Janvier 1849*) (Paris, 1849).

³⁷ The first two volumes of T. B. Macaulay's *History of England*, which had appeared in December 1848

³⁸ MTColl. XLVII/11.

³⁹ Probably George Henry Lewes (1817–78).

⁴⁰ *Autobiography*, p. 198–9. Cf. also the paragraph added to the Preface of the second edition of the *Political Economy*: 'The additions and alterations in the present edition are generally of little moment; but the increased importance which the Socialist controversy has assumed since this work was written, had made it desirable to enlarge the chapter which treats of it; the more so, as the objections therein stated to the specific schemes propounded by some Socialists have been erroneously understood as a general condemnation of all that is commonly included under that name. A full appreciation of Socialism, and of the questions which it raises, can only be advantageously attempted in a separate work.'

⁴¹ Yale University Library.

⁴² The passages on pp. 247–8 of vol. I of the first edition of the *Political Economy* which were deleted run as follows: 'Those who have never known freedom from anxiety as to the means of subsistence, are apt to overrate what is gained for positive enjoyment by the mere absence of that uncertainty. The necessaries of life, when they have always been secure for the whole of life, are scarcely more a subject of consciousness or a source of happiness than the elements. [p. 248] There is little attractive in the monotonous routine, with-

out vicissitudes, but without excitement; a life spent in the enforced observance of an external rule, and performance of a prescribed task: in which labour would be devoid of its chief sweetener, the thought that every effort tells perceptibly on the labourer's own interests or those of some one with whom he identifies himself; in which no one could by his own exertions improve his conditions, or that of the objects of his private affections; in which no one's way of life, occupations, or movements, would depend on choice, but each would be the slave of all.'

The whole of this passage has been replaced in the second edition by the much more sympathetic account on pp. 254–6 which begins: 'On the Communistic scheme, supposing it to be successful, there would be an end to all anxiety concerning the means of subsistence; and this would be much gained for human happiness.'

[43] See the passage from the first edition quoted in the preceding footnote; it must have been suggested by Mrs. Taylor when the first edition was written.

[44] Nothing in the chapter as it stands in the second edition seems to correspond to this sentence, but it may well have been an earlier draft of the last paragraph which begins (p. 265): 'We are as yet too ignorant either of what individual agency in its best form, or socialism in its best form, can accomplish, to be qualified to decide which of the two will be the ultimate form of society.' This replaces the paragraph in the first edition (p. 254) which relegates the 'proper sphere for collective action' to 'the things which cannot be done by individual agency' and which argues that 'where individual agency is at all suitable, it is almost always the most suitable'.

[45] First edition, p. 250: 'I believe that the conditions of the operatives in a well-regulated manufactory, with a great reduction in the hours of labour and a considerable variety of the kinds of it, is very much like what the conditions of all would be in a Socialist Community. I believe the majority would not exert themselves for anything beyond this, and that unless they did, nobody else would; and that on this basis human life would settle itself in one invariable round.' In spite of what Mill said above, the second sentence of this was omitted entirely in the second edition (p. 257), while the word 'Owenite' was substituted for 'Socialist' in the first sentence.

[46] W. E. Hickson, then editor of the *Westminster Review*, where the article on 'Lord Brougham and the French Revolution' appeared.

[47] Yale University Library.

[48] *Principles of Political Economy* (second edition), vol. I, pp. 102–6.

[49] A 'political and socialist journal' started in Paris the year before to advocate the rights of all women.

[50] Probably a first attempt at what two years later became the article on 'The Enfranchisement of Women'.

[51] Major-General Sir Archibald Galloway (1780?–1850) and John

Shepherd, in 1849 Chairman and Deputy Chairman of the East India Company respectively.

[52] The rest of the last line, about five or six words, has been cut away.

[53] MTColl. XXVIII/225.

[54] MTColl. XXVII/109.

[55] Mill's review of volumes V and VI of George Grote's *History of Greece* appeared in the *Spectator* for 3 and 10 March 1849 (vol. XII, pp. 202–3 and 227–8).

[56] Yale University Library.

[57] W. J. Fox, *Lectures Addressed Chiefly to the Working Classes*, vol. IV (London, 1849), p. xix–xx. The paragraphs quoted there from the *Political Economy* are taken from vol. II, pp. 525 and 526 of the first edition.

[58] Ralph Waldo Emerson's lecture on England, delivered before the Boston Mercantile Library Association on 27 December 1848, was reported at considerable length in *The Times* of 14 March 1849. According to this report, 'he spoke of the steady balance of the qualities of their nature as their great characteristic, and the secret of their success. Everything in England betokens life. . . . The English surpass all others in general culture—none are so harmoniously developed. They are quick to perceive any meanness in an individual. And it is reasonable that they should have all those fastidious views which wealth and power are wont to generate.'

[59] James Anthony Froude, *The Nemesis of Faith*, 1849. The brother mentioned was Richard Hurrell Froude.

[60] *The Spectator* of 10 March 1849, which contained the second part of Mill's review of G. Grote's *History of Greece*.

[61] J. A. Froude had been chosen for the post by the professors of University College, London, but as a result of the attacks of the newspapers was asked to withdraw, and withdrew.

[62] What is left of this page reads: 'the old way, & . . . has the advantage of taking . . . Toulouse, but I suspect the means of conveyance by it are much slower & more precarious, till we reach Bourges or Chateauroux where we join the railway. I think from what has been in the papers that the whole or nearly the whole of the . . .'

[63] Yale University Library. The date of the letter itself is missing with its beginning, but as the English postmark of the cover probably belonging to it seems to be 18 March, its date is probably 16 or 17 March.

[64] In his review of volumes V and VI of George Grote's *History of Greece* in the *Spectator* for 3 and 10 March 1849, in the conclusion of which he had said (p. 228): 'If there was any means by which Grecian independence and liberty could have been made a permanent thing it would have been by the prolongation for some generations more of the organization of the larger half of Greece under the supremacy of Athens; a supremacy imposed, indeed, and

upheld by force—but the mildest, the most civilizing, and, in its permanent influence on the destinies of human kind, the most brilliant and valuable, of all the usurped powers known to history.'

65 Henry Fleming (d. 1876), Assistant Secretary of the Poor Law Board from its creation in 1849 and Secretary for many years from 1860. Since he had been introduced there by Charles Buller, who was the first Chairman of the Poor Law Board, it would seem probable that Mill knew him through the Buller circle.

66 Yale University Library.

67 See above, p. 128.

68 Mrs. Charles Buller, the mother of Mill's friend Charles Buller, had died on 13 March 1849, within ten months of the death of her husband (17 May 1848) and her eldest son Charles (29 September 1848).

69 The incomplete sentence left of the first page appears to deal merely with the weather of the preceding days.

70 *Political Economy* (first edition), vol. I, p. 441: 'Is it not to this hour the favourite recommendation for any parochial office bestowed by popular election, to have a large family and to be unable to maintain them? Do not the candidates placard their intemperance on walls, and publish it through the town in circulars?' In the second edition, p. 457, the change mentioned in the text is made and the following footnote added which presumably contains the two sentences contributed by Mrs. Taylor: 'Little improvement can be expected in morality until the producing large families is regarded with the same feelings as overfondness for wine or any other physical excess. But while the aristocracy and clergy are foremost to set the example of incontinence, what can be expected from the poor?'

71 Mill's proposal, developed in the series of articles in the *Morning Chronicle* in the winter of 1846/7, advocating the creation of peasant properties on the waste lands in Ireland.

72 Probably V. P. Considerant, *Le Socialism devant le vieux monde, ou, le vivant devant les morts* (Paris, 1848).

73 The following paragraph begins on a new sheet of a different shape from that on which the preceding part of the letter is written and it is merely probable that it continues the same letter.

74 See above, p. 142.

75 This club was founded, as the 'Anonymous Club', by John Sterling in July 1838, a little more than six years before his death. See Sterling's letter, dated 14 July 1838, in which he informs Mill of the formation of the club, in A. K. Tuell, *John Sterling*, p. 366, and T. Carlyle, *The Life of John Sterling*, part II, chapter VI, where a list of the original members is reproduced. The newspaper attacks on the Sterling Club were started by the *Record* on 8 March 1849, and continued throughout the year.

NOTES

[76] Julius C. Hare had in 1848 published a memoir of the life of John Sterling as an introduction to the collected edition of the latter's *Essays and Tales*.

[77] John Pringle Nichol, F.R.S., 1804–59, since 1836 Professor of Astronomy at the University of Glasgow, contributor to the *London and Westminster Review* during Mill's editorship when he was in regular correspondence with Mill. No book of his on America seems to have appeared.

[78] MTColl. XXVIII/227.

[79] MTColl. XXVIII/229.

CHAPTER VII. JOHN TAYLOR'S ILLNESS AND DEATH

[1] MTColl. L/9–37. From this point onwards and through the rest of the volume only selected passages from the correspondence are reproduced.

[2] MTColl. L/16.

[3] MTColl. L/17.

[4] MTColl. L/28.

[5] MTColl. L/30.

[6] MTColl. L/18.

[7] MTColl. L/12.

[8] MTColl. L/27.

[9] MTColl. L/25.

[10] MTColl. L/28. A sheet in J. S. M.'s hand, docketed by him 'Extracts from letters of Sterling respecting me', is in MTColl. XLIX/21, but does not contain any of the passages complained of below.

[11] MTColl. L/31.

[12] MacMinn, *et al.*, *Bibliography*, p. 71. The article appeared in the *Daily News* for 14 July 1849.

[13] MTColl. L/32.

[14] MTColl. L/34.

[15] MTColl. L/36.

[16] MTColl. L/37.

CHAPTER VIII. MARRIAGE AND BREAK WITH MILL'S FAMILY

[1] MTColl. L/39. The only evidence for assigning an approximate date to this letter is the identity of the notepaper with that of the following.

[2] MTColl. L/38.

[3] The two Ohio Conventions took place at Salem on 19 and 20 April 1850 and at Acron on 28 and 29 May 1851.

⁴ William Lloyd Garrison (1805–79), Wendell Phillips (1811–84) and Frederick Douglas (1817–95).

⁵ At the time of publication the article appears generally to have been believed to be by Mill, and Charlotte Brontë refers to it as such in a letter dated as early as 20 September 1851, quoted in Mrs. Gaskell's *Life of Charlotte Brontë*, (Everyman edition, p. 344). Mill commented upon it in a letter, presumably to Mrs. Gaskell, saying: 'I am not the author of the article I may claim to be its editor: and I should be proud to be identified with every thought, every sentiment and every expression in it. The writer is a woman, of the largest and most genial sympathies, and the most forgetful of herself in her generous zeal to do honour to others, whom I have ever known' (*The Brontës: Their Lives, Friendships and Correspondence*, The Shakespeare Head Brontë, ed. T. J. Wise and J. A. Symington, Oxford, 1932, vol. III, p. 278).

⁶ Manuscript in Huntington Library. See also the further letters to Hickson dated 10 and 19 March 1851, and of 19 March 1850, in the same collection. W. E. Hickson (1803–70) had taken over the *Westminster Review* from Mill in June 1840.

⁷ *Letters* (ed. Elliot), vol. I, p. 158, giving also a facsimile reproduction.

⁸ Draft of letter to Wilhelmina King, MTColl. XLVII/15, letter to Jane Ferraboschi, Yale University Library.

⁹ See George Mill's letter to Mrs. Mill, quoted below, p. 175, and the quotation from J. S. Mill's letter given in A. Bain, *J. S. Mill*, p. 93.

¹⁰ Page torn.

¹¹ Harriet I. Mill to the Rev. J. Crompton, 26 October 1873, at King's College, Cambridge.

¹² In a letter of about the same time (in Yale University Library, dated 27 July 1851) in which Mill's old friend and former colleague at India House, Horace Grant, congratulates him somewhat belatedly on his 'marriage with an amiable woman capable of understanding and appreciating your exertions', he also reports that 'some time ago I saw Mary & her children & thought she looked well and happy. Her exertions in the ragged schools somewhat surprized me,—as she used to be rather timid: but I dare say that the apparition of a beautiful female among a set of young thieves & vagabonds accustomed only to be cuffed about by their superiors, must have been quite that of a ministering angel, & productive of great good.'

¹³ MTColl. XLVII/18. Docketed in Mill's hand: 'Mary—a reply August 14, 1851. Her rejoinder August 30.' These have not been preserved.

¹⁴ The daughter of Mill's eldest sister, Wilhemina King.

¹⁵ MTColl. XLVII/4.

¹⁶ The address of the firm David Taylor & Sons.

¹⁷ Draft in MTColl. XLVII/5, dated as above and endorsed in same hand 'copied July 16 1851'.

[18] Draft in MTColl. XLVII/20. There is also another even more violent and probably earlier draft, *ibid.*, XLVII/45.

[19] MTColl, XLVII/21.

[20] MTColl. XLVII/22.

[21] MTColl. XLVII/24.

[22] MTColl. XLVII/23.

CHAPTER IX. ILLNESS

[1] *Letters of Charles Eliot Norton* (ed. S. Norton and M. A. de Wolfe Howe, London, 1913), vol. I, p. 330.

[2] See Lord Ashburton's letter to Mill in Yale University Library:

'Bath House/May 26, 51/My dear Mill/I have promised Lady Ashburton to write to you, & I execute my promise most readily, for I should be sorry that you had reason to think, that we could overlook the occurrence in your life, which must add so much.

'We rejoice at it also on our account. We hope to gain by the change as well as yourself. We feel sure that you will live no longer for your books alone, that you will allow some human sympathies to have access to your thought.

'It is possible that you may then be forced to remember that there were once certain friends, who thought that they had a hold over you, who thought themselves as necessary to you as you are to them.

'Now these friends, no wise daunted by former ill success, are very anxious to gain over Mrs. Mill to their side, and I must say that it would be most unfair if you did not give them an early opportunity of doing so. We will therefore allow you no subterfuge of any kind, no means of escape from this your destiny.

'It is written that on some day this month, or an early of next, you will either tell us where we may call on Mrs. Mill, or you will appoint a time when you will bring Mrs. Mill to call here. Hear and obey. The fates have willed it./Yours Ashburton.'

[3] See John Chapman's Diary in Gordon S. Haight, *George Eliot and John Chapman* (New Haven, Yale University Press, 1940), p. 169–70, under the date of 24 May 1851: 'Mrs Hennell says that the lady he [Mill] has just married was a widow, her husband having been dead for a year and a half, that during the life of her former husband a "violent friendship" arose between her and him which caused him to think it desirable to go to the Continent, wither she, it is said, followed him; and now (in consequence of these circumstances she presumes) Mrs. Thornton Hunt declines to visit Mr. & Mrs. Mill.'

[4] *Political Club, Minutes and Proceedings*, vol. VI (Centenary Volume, London, Macmillan, 1921), pp. 65–8, from which it appears that Mill

opened the discussion at six of the twenty meetings of the Club held in the years 1851–3.

[5] MTColl. LI.

[6] Algernon Taylor, *Memories of a Student* (2nd edition enlarged, London, Simpkin Marshall, 1895—a first edition had been printed for private circulation only), p. 10. Algernon Taylor adds that after Mill's death 'a musical paper—the "Musical Standard" if I remember right—drew attention to his considerable if little known, musical taste and capacity'. Later in the same volume (p. 233) mention is made of the fact that Mill also played chess well.

[7] MacMinn, *et al.*, *Bibliography*, p. 76.

[8] *Remarks on Mr. Fitzroy's Bill for the more effectual Prevention of Assaults on Women and Children.* Privately printed 1853. See MacMinn, *et al.*, *Bibliography*, p. 79.

[9] Four of these letters, dated 26, 29, 31 August and September 1853, are in Yale University Library and one, undated but probably of 27 August, in MTColl. II/305. All the letters by Mill to his wife quoted in this chapter are in Yale University Library.

[10] Described earlier as 'the big physiology'.

[11] Evidently the essay on 'Nature' published posthumously in 1874 as part of the volume *Nature, the Utility of Religion, and Theism*, but in 1853 intended to form part of a volume of essays on which Mill was working and out of which ultimately *On Liberty, Utilitarianism* and perhaps some other of his later works grew.

[12] The review of volumes 9–11 of G. Grote's *History of Greece* on which Mill had spent much time during the summer in which it appeared in the *Edinburgh Review* for October.

[13] George Cornewall Lewis (1806–63), editor of the *Edinburgh Review* from 1852 to 1855.

[14] Page torn by seal.

[15] The youngest brother, George, actually had died a few months before in Madeira, by his own hand, thereby anticipating but a little the termination of the disease for which he had vainly sought a cure.

[16] Russell Ellice was then chairman of the Court of Directors and David Hill and W. T. Thornton (1813–80) officials of the East India Company, as was also Thomas Love Peacock (1785–1866), the novelist, who from 1836 to 1856 was head of the Examiner's Department, in which post Mill succeeded him.

[17] J. S. Mill's younger brother, recently returned from India.

[18] William George Prescott, George Grote's partner in the banking firm of Prescott, Grote & Co., and one of the three original members of the Utilitarian Society.

[19] *Letters* (ed. Elliot), vol. II, pp. 357–86.

20 'Parliamentary Purification' in *Edinburgh Review*, vol. XCVIII/200, pp. 566–624, presumably by William Rathbone Greg (1809–81), who in the preceding years had regularly written for this Review on similar subjects.

21 This letter to Lord Monteagle, dated 20 March 1853, and acknowledging his pamphlet on the Representation of Minorities, is printed in *Letters* (ed. Elliot), vol. I, p. 173.

22 Probably the pamphlet *Thoughts on Parliamentary Reform*, published only in 1859, but according to Bain, *J. S. Mill* (p. 103), written some years previously.

23 Among the correspondence Mill had found on his return was a request from John Chapman, then the editor of the *Westminster Review*, that Mill should review Harriet Martineau's abridged translation of Comte's *Positive Philosophy* published by John Chapman in 1853.

24 Sir James Clark, Bt., F.R.S. (1788–1870), physician in ordinary to Queen Victoria.

25 MTColl. L(i). This is a pencilled note, very faded, and some of the readings are uncertain. It is numbered 15, while Mill's letter to which it replies is his 14th.

26 The Utility of Religion became the title of the second essay contained in the posthumous volume on *Nature, the Utility of Religion, and Theism* (1874). According to Helen Taylor's Introduction to the volume it was, with the essay on *Nature*, written about this time.

27 A review of *Letters of Rachel Lady Russell* (ed. J. R. [Earl Russell], London, 1853), in the *Examiner* of 4 February 1854, pp. 68–9.

28 7, 13 and 15 February, and 6 March.

29 28 February.

30 This letter of G. O. Trevelyan, dated 8 March 1854, and two later ones, with the draft of Mill's replies, are in the 'Hutzler Collection of Economic Classics' in Johns Hopkins University.

31 See also Trevelyan's letters to Mill, dated 11 and 24 May 1854, in MTColl. I/27–8.

32 Frederick James Furnival (1825–1910).

33 J. S. M. to H. M., 4 February 1854. The letter in which he grants permission, dated 13 February, is printed in *Letters* (ed. Elliot), vol. I, p. 177.

34 J. S. M. to H. M., 14 March 1854.

35 The contemplated reprint of this chapter cannot now be traced and it is doubtful whether it ever appeared. The translations of the French passages were later used in the Popular edition of *Political Economy*, and the additions appear all in the 4th edition of 1857. The 'saving clause' inserted at Mrs. Mill's suggestion is evidently the sentence put in square brackets in the following passage as it appears on p. 350 of the 4th edition but not contained in the draft of the passage sent by Mill to his wife: 'One of the most discreditable

indications of a low moral condition given of late by the English working classes is the opposition to piece work. [When the payment per piece is not sufficiently high, that is a just ground for objection.] But dislike of piece work, except under mistaken notions, must be dislike to justice or fairness, a desire to cheat, by not giving work in proportion to the pay. Piece work is the perfection of *contract*: and contract, in all work, and in the most minute detail—the principle of so much pay for so much service carried to the utmost extremity—is the system, of all others, in the present state of society, most favourable to the worker, though most unfavourable to the non-worker who wishes to be paid for being idle.'

[36] J. S. M. to H. M., 8 April 1854.

[37] Francis Hopkins Ramadge, M.D. (1793–1867), senior physician to the infirmary for asthma and consumption and other diseases of the lung, had in 1834 published a book *Consumption Curable* which went into many editions and was translated into several foreign languages.

[38] J. S. M. to H. M., 8 April 1854.

[39] J. S. M. to H. M., 5 April 1854.

[40] The original of this letter to Mill by his mother is in the MTColl. XLVII/24. It begins: '4 Westbourne Park Villas/29 March/My dear John/I am sorry that you did not tell me whether you had got rid of your cough, I am afraid from that you have not. As to myself . . .' and continues as quoted by Mill. It is signed 'Your Affect^te Mother/H. Mill' and has the following postscript: 'James's address is/Ullaport/North Britain/The next time you write will you tell me what pension he has got?'

Of John Mill's letter to his brother James for which the mother supplied the address, a torn-off last page is in MTColl. XLVII/25, postmarked 31 March 1854. After an incomplete sentence about somebody's health it continues: 'I do not know how far you take interest in passing events. The time is very near when the new arrangements for the India Act will come into operation. For my part, except the throwing open the civil service to competition, all the changes appear to me to be for the worse. It is the most faulty piece of work these ministers have turned out—whom otherwise I prefer to any ministers England has yet had./yrs aff^y/J. S. Mill.'

[41] The eldest of Mill's sisters, who was living in Germany.

[42] These notes are in MTColl. XLVII/28, 29. One may be reproduced here:

'*Clara E. Mill to J. S. M.:* 4, Westbourne Park Villas, April 10./Dear John/In case you should not otherwise be aware of it, I think it right to tell you that my poor Mother is very seriously ill. The doctors have pronounced her complaint to be tumour of the liver, I don't think they apprehend any immediate danger, but they do not conceal the fact that at any age it would be a very serious affair, and in her case there is no doubt that her strength is decreasing. Sir James Clark saw her some 10 days ago & Mr. Quain (32 Cavendish Square) saw her on Saturday & comes twice a week at least—from either of these you can of course get any information you may wish./My Mother does not know that I am writing./C. E. Mill.'

[43] J. S. M. to H. M., St. Malo, 14 June 1854.

[44] MTColl. XLVII/32.

[45] Draft in MTColl. XLVII/31. The last paragraph first ran: 'If you sh^d have occasion to write to me do it to my house at Blackheath and my wife will forward it. My wife sends her best wishes & regrets that her health had made it impossible for her to call on you as she much wished to have done' and the last seven words replaced first by 'would otherwise have done long before this' and then by 'much wished to have done' and finally replaced by the paragraph in the text.

[46] All these letters are in Yale University Library.

[47] Later incorporated into *Utilitarianism*. Bain (*J. S. Mill*, p. 112) refers to a letter which suggested to him that *Utilitarianism* was written in 1854, but from the letters here quoted it seems more likely that the essays written then, though used in the composition of *Utilitarianism*, were not yet planned as a book under that title.

[48] Probably the *Thoughts on Parliamentary Reform*, published five years later.

[49] MTColl. XLVII/38.

CHAPTER X. ITALY AND SICILY

[1] Mrs. Mill at the time, it seems, was suffering from some other complaint in addition to her lung trouble. On 30 October 1855 she wrote to her brother Arthur in Australia (MTColl. XXVII/48): 'I have been so reduced in strength since my bad illness in 1853 when I broke a blood vessel in the lung and was not expected to recover for some months, and since that I have twice undergone a surgical operation, that I have seldom had strength to write more than a few lines at a time.'

[2] All the letters by Mill from which passages are quoted in this and the next chapter are in Yale University Library.

[3] So described in a letter to August Comte on 12 August 1842. See *Lettres Inédites de John Stuart Mill à Auguste Comte* (Paris, 1899), p. 94.

[4] Apparently a letter by the Queen to Mr. Sidney Herbert, reprinted in *The Times* of 5 January 1855: 'Windsor Castle, Dec. 6, 1854. Would you tell Mrs. Herbert that I begged she would *let me see frequently* the accounts she receives from Miss Nightingale or Mrs. Bracebridge, as *I hear* no *details of the wounded*, tho' I see so many from officers, &c., about the battle-field, and naturally the former must interest *me* more than any one.

NOTES

'Let Mrs. Herbert also know that I wish Miss Nightingale and the Ladies would tell these poor noble and sick men that NO ONE *takes* a warmer interest, or feels *more* for their sufferings, or admires their courage and heroism MORE than their Queen. Day and night she thinks of her beloved troups. So does the Prince.

'Beg Mrs. Herbert to communicate these my words to those ladies, as I know that *our* sympathy is much valued by these noble fellows.

'Victoria.'

[5] Frederic Lucas, M.P., born 1812, barrister and convert to Catholicism, and friend of Carlyle, since 1840 editor of *The Tablet*. He returned to London in May 1855 and died there in the autumn of the same year. According to his biographer 'he latterly gave much time to the study of political economy, and took a special interest in the social theories of John Stuart Mill'. In 1851 Lucas and Charles Gavan Duffy had asked Mill on behalf of the Council of the Tenant League to stand for Parliament for an Irish constituency. See *Autobiography*, p. 237, and *Letters* (ed. Elliot), vol. I, p. 159, the *Life of Frederic Lucas, M.P.* by his brother Edward Lucas, 2 vols. (London, 1886), especially vol. II, pp. 122 and 126, and C. G. Duffy, *Conversations with Carlyle*, p. 166.

[6] Probably Abraham Hayward.

[7] The younger Lady Duff Gordon would have been Lucy, the daughter of Sarah Austin.

[8] Compare Mill's account of the conception of the book *On Liberty* in the *Autobiography*, p. 212: 'I had first planned and written it as a short essay in 1854. It was in mounting the steps of the Capitol, in January, 1855, that the thought first arose of converting it into a volume.'

[9] Father Kyne, a catholic priest who had accompanied Frederick Lucas to Rome.

[10] Lord Aberdeen's Cabinet, succeeded by Lord Palmerston's first ministry, after a motion for a committee of inquiry into the mismanagement of the Crimean expedition had been passed on 29 January by 305 to 148 votes.

[11] Edward Lucas in the biography of his brother recounts that he had 'frequently heard Father Kyne, himself a man of considerable information dilate upon the conversation, discussion and casual remarks of the two men [Mill and Lucas] which he said eclipsed all that he had ever heard in the way of conversation' (*The Life of Frederic Lucas, M.P.*, by his brother Edward Lucas (London, 1886), vol. II, p. 126).

[12] See *Report from the Select Committee for the Savings of the Middle and Working Classes*, Parliamentary Papers, 1850, vol. XIX, especially Mill's answers to questions 839, 847–51, 879–80, 906 and 913.

[13] The British Consul at Palermo.

[14] Goethe, who in 1787 had in the course of his Italian journey made a tour of Sicily rather similar to Mill's, was thirty-seven at that time.

[15] George Finlay (1799–1875), historian and author of a *History of Greece*, had taken part in the Greek war of independence and been acquainted with Lord Byron.

[16] Sir Thomas Wyse (1791–1892), since 1849 British Minister to Athens and earlier Secretary of the Board of Control for India.

CHAPTER XI. GREECE

[1] J. S. M. to H. M., Corfu, 10 April 1855. All the letters by Mill reproduced in this chapter are in Yale University Library.

[2] Sir H. Ward, the Lord High Commissioner for the Ionian Islands.

[3] Sir J. Young.

[4] Joseph Hume, the Radical politician, had died on 20 February 1855.

[5] On the resignation of W. E. Gladstone as Chancellor of the Exchequer and two other ministers, Sir George Cornewall Lewis had become Chancellor and R. V. Smith President of the Board of Control.

[6] Colonel Wodehouse, Resident in Ithaca.

[7] A.D.C. to the High Commissioner.

[8] Henry Reeve (1813–95), who for fifteen years had been foreign editor of *The Times* and in 1855, when on becoming Chancellor of the Exchequer G. C. Lewis relinquished the post, succeeded him as editor of the *Edinburgh Review*, a post which he held until his death forty years later.

[9] MTColl. XXVII/46. This is a copy of the concluding part of the letter with the evidently erroneous date 'March 1855' added later.

[10] The Irish botanist whose acquaintance Mill had made at Corfu.

[11] The *sous-préfet* of Yerochori, to whom they had had an introduction.

[12] Christopher Wordsworth (Bishop of Lincoln), *Greece, pictorial, descriptive and historical, with upwards of three hundred and fifty engravings by Copley, Fielding etc.* (London, 1839). A new edition of this work had appeared in 1853.

[13] Mill did visit Greece again after Mrs. Mill's death and in 1862 spent some months with Helen Taylor there and in Constantinople.

[14] The English doctor in Florence whom he had consulted.

CHAPTER XII. LAST YEARS AND DEATH OF MRS. MILL

[1] Yale University Library.

[2] MTColl. LI/1.

[3] MTColl. LI and LII.

[4] One from York, evidently of 14 February, in MTColl. LII/125, and seven from London, probably of 16, 17, 18, 19, 24, 25 and 26 February, in Yale University Library.

[5] Yale University Library.

[6] Yale University Library.

[7] If this refers, as seems probable, to Book I, chapter VIII, § 5 of the *Political Economy*, which had been considerably revised in the previous (third) edition, no further change appears to have been made on this occasion.

[8] Yale University Library. The following undated fragment, also in Yale University Library, probably belongs to the same period. It is on a single sheet which has apparently been deliberately mutilated by the lower part having been cut away, and the text of the two sides is in consequence not consecutive nor is it possible to say which part comes first.

'*J. S. M. to H. T., February 1857(?)*: if you did but know with what joy I would leave everything & live all my life in Australia if you cannot be in health anywhere else how dreadful it would be if from considerations relating to me that were left undone till it were useless.

'O my beloved have pity on me & save that precious life which is the only life there is for me in this world—'

[Beginning of second page:] 'so needed, so longed to be with you—& always with you—as when you are ill. it is true I am pained by the sense of my own helplessness & uselessness in mechanical matters when they are so much needed. but your perfect love can do what . . .'

[9] Four letters by Mill to his wife, of 13, 16, 18 and 19 September, are in the Yale University Library. There is only the one letter by Mrs. Mill referred to in the next footnote.

[10] MTColl. XXVIII/240.

[11] H. M. to her mother, 4 December 1857, MTColl. XXVII/83.

[12] J. S. Mill's letters from Matlock 11 and 12 July, Edensor 13 July, and Bakewell 15 July 1858, are in the Yale University Library, and Mrs. Mill's letters of 12 and 13 July in MTColl. XXVIII/236 and 237.

[13] A letter posted at Matlock Sunday evening delivered at Blackheath the next morning!

[14] Sir Edward Bulwer-Lytton (later Lord Lytton) (1803–73), the novelist who shortly before had become Secretary for the Colonies in Lord Derby's second Cabinet.

[15] MTColl. LIII/(i) 1–29, for Mrs. Mill's letters from the journey to Helen Taylor with Helen Taylor's replies; also Mrs. Mill's letter to Algernon Taylor, Paris, 15 October 1858, MTColl. XXVII/119.

[16] Yale University Library. In a letter which appeared in the *Literary Guide* of 1 July 1907, Mary Taylor stated that she held a letter of Mill to Dr. Gurney offering him a fee of £1,000 for attending his wife. This would

suggest that the doctor first refused to come, which is contradicted by the correspondence. Miss Taylor, however, was in a special position to know since Dr. Gurney was her uncle—her father, Algernon Taylor, had married Dr. Gurney's sister in 1860.

[17] Yale University Library. The punctuation, mostly lacking in the original, has been interpolated.

[18] Yale University Library. Helen Taylor's reply in MTColl. LIII(i)/29.

[19] A. Bain, *J. S. Mill*, p. 102. The announcement of Mrs. Mill's death, which Mill sent to Thornton with this letter, appeared in *The Times* of 13 November 1858.

[20] Jules Veran, 'Le Souvenir de Stuart Mill à Avignon', *Revue des Deux Mondes*, 1 September 1937, p. 216.

[21] Draft in Yale University Library. Compare also the letters to George Grote of 28 November 1858, and to Pasquale Villari of 6 and 28 March 1859, in *Letters* (ed. Elliot), vol. I, pp. 213, 216 and 217.

[22] In MTColl. XLI/11 there are several successive drafts of this inscription in Mill's hand, three of which give the date of Mrs. Mill's birth wrongly as 8 October 1808 (instead of 1807), in one instance substituting this for an earlier '1806'.

[23] Alexander Bain to Helen Taylor, 13 September 1873, MTColl. IV/17. In an earlier letter (6 September 1873, MTColl. IV/15) Bain had also unsuccessfully urged Helen Taylor to omit some of the more extravagant passages of Mill's praise of his wife. Although so far as the passages referring to herself were concerned, Helen Taylor at least in part followed Bain's advice; she left instructions that the complete manuscript was 'to be published without alterations or omissions within one year after my death'. These instructions were not carried out and complete publication had to wait until the 1924 edition quoted in the note 25.

[24] The following description by an American visitor of Mill's relation to Helen Taylor towards the end of his life is of interest in this connexion:

'*C. E. Norton to Chauncey Wright, 13 September 1870:* I doubt whether Mill's interest in the cause of woman is serviceable to him as a thinker. It has a tendency to develop the sentimental part of his intelligence, which is of immense force, and has only been kept in due subjection by his respect for his own reason. This respect diminishes under the powerful influence of his daughter, Miss Taylor, who is an admirable personage doubtless, but is what, were she of the sex that she regards as inferior, would be called decidedly priggish. Her self-confidence, which embraces her confidence in Mill, is tremenduous, and Mill is overpowered by it. Her words have an oracular value for him,—something more than their just weight; and her unconscious flattery, joined with the very direct flattery of many other prominent leaders of the great female army, have a not unnatural effect on his tender, susceptible and sympathetic nature. In putting the case so strongly I perhaps define it with too great a force, but you can make the needful allowance for the over-distinctness of words' (*Letters of Charles Eliot Norton* (London, 1913), vol. I, p. 400).

[25] *Autobiography of John Stuart Mill*, published for the first time without alterations or omissions from the original manuscript in the possession of Columbia University with a preface by John Jacob Coss, New York, Columbia University Press, 1924. The passage quoted occurs on pp. 184–5.

APPENDICES

[1] MTColl., Box III/206, and other drafts of the same poem, *ibid.*, 204, 207 and 208, the last dated 1828.

[2] *Monthly Repository* (new series), vol. VI, p. 617.

[3] *Monthly Repository* (new series), vol. VI, 1832 (September).

[4] MTColl., Box III/78, on pages watermarked '1832'.

[5] A gap left in the manuscript for one word later to be filled in.

ADDENDUM

Jane Welsh Carlyle : A New Selection of Her Letters, arranged by Trudy Bliss (London, Victor Gollancz Ltd., 1950), which appeared when the present volume was in proof, not only contains a few further relevant passages from Mrs. Carlyle's correspondence (especially pp. 60, 82, and 125) but also makes it probable that the voluminous Carlyle correspondence at Edinburgh may contain still more information about Mill and Mrs. Taylor.

On Mill's writings on poetry see now also J. R. Hainds, 'J. S. Mill's *Examiner* Articles on Art', *Journal of the History of Ideas*, April 1950, vol. XI, no. 2.

Index

INDEX

INDEX

INDEX

INDEX